Autodesk Inventor 2021
Parametric design and iLogic for beginners

EXPERTBOOKS

www.expertbooks.eu

Trademarks:

All brand names and product names used in this book are trademarks, registered trademarks, or trade names of their respective holders. The author and the publisher are not associated with any product or vendor mentioned in this book.

Limit of Liability/Disclaimer of Warranty:

The publication is designed to provide tutorial information about CAD software. The author and the publisher made every effort to ensure that the contents of this book are accurate and complete. However, the author and the publisher not give anyone any representation or warranty and is not responsible for any loss or damage which is a consequence of the use of information contained in this publication.

ISBN: 9798686428263

ExpertBooks Publisher publishes manuals for users of CAD software. For more information about our publications, please visit **www.expertbooks.eu**

CONTENTS

INTRODUCTION

This manual is intended for people for whom this is the first contact with Autodesk Inventor software. However, individuals who are familiar with the program will find useful information here. No additional files for download are required to complete the design described - all files will be created from scratch in the exercises in sequence. Exercises presented in this manual have been implemented in Autodesk Inventor 2021; however, most of this manual is also compatible with previous versions of Autodesk Inventor software. The book presents three examples of the use of parameterization.

Example No 1: Designing a complete product

In the first example, you will learn how to work in Inventor, from scratch. You will create a project of a simple drill vise, on which you will learn the basic operations of modeling and creating drawing documentation. This example emphasizes the principles of project management, from a single part through designing parts in the context of the assembly, checking the basic kinematics of the product, and further creating a complete drawing documentation containing item numbers and a parts list, as well as an exploding view of the product, rendered illustration and video to be both used for marketing this product.

Then, thanks to the program parameterization and skillful file management, you will quickly create a new version of the drill vise with a complete set of drawing documentation as well as a rendered illustration and video of the new version of the product. The approach proposed in this example will facilitate the application of Inventor parameterization and file management in designing varieties of products of similar design, which use many common components and it will accelerate obtaining flawless drawing documentation of the new version of the product.

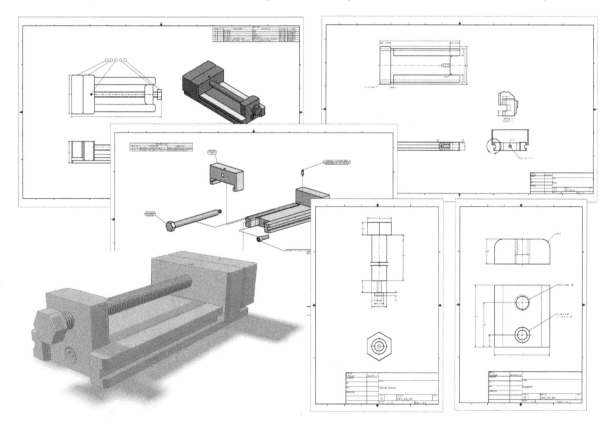

Example No 2: Component libraries

Most of the products being designed, use components purchased from external suppliers. For this reason, parametric 3D models of purchased components, which can be quickly inserted into the project instead of modeling each time from scratch, offer the greatest possible convenience for the constructor. In addition, component library files should be properly described, so that they are correctly presented in the bill of materials and also it should be placed in the library resources area, which will protect them from accidental editing.

In this example, you will create two parts purchased from suppliers: a rubber foot with fixed dimensions and a metal handle that is available in several sizes. The examples presented here will teach you how to prepare your own parametric libraries of purchased components.

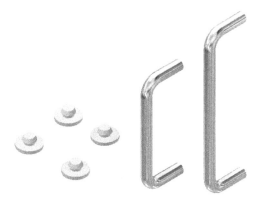

Example No 3: The parametric generator of product versions

In the third example, you will create a parametric generator for making a simple metal casing that allows you to obtain a model of any size, with or without handles and pre-prepared drawing documentation for each version of the casing. The generated version of the casing can be further modified in order to obtain the final appearance.

In this example, you will learn the basics of designing sheet metal parts, the use of parameters in parts and in the assembly, and you will learn the basics of programming using iLogic. The approach presented here will teach you how to create and use iLogic parametric version generators.

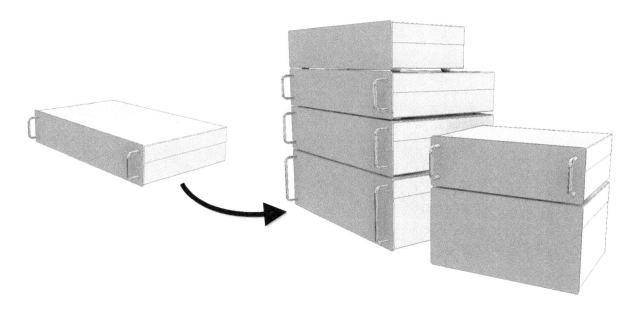

PREPARATION FOR EXERCISES

The Autodesk Inventor software is ready for operation immediately after installation and is pre-configured to create designs in line with the general guidelines of the ANSI standard, allowing you to immediately start creating 3D models and associated documentation 2D. It is good practice, however, to adopt the program's configuration to the needs in terms of compliance with the company's internal standard.

In this section, you'll make a little configuration adjustment of the Autodesk Inventor software which will cover:

- create your own main project definition file that indicates the location of the working files
- adjustment of the drawing title in the template of the drawing file for displaying data from 3D models

Autodesk Inventor software has many areas in which you can make configuration changes to even better tailor the program to your needs. See the program's help for more information.

Creating the main project file

Each device designed in Autodesk Inventor 2021 contains a set of related files. Each part, assembly, presentation and drawing created are stored in a separate file and have its own unique file extensions. The program needs to know the location of these files in order to open them for editing. It is necessary to memorize the location of the folders that stores models, presentations and drawings files in a **project file**.

The project file has its own extension ***.ipj** and is placed by default in the root folder of the projects, which becomes the working folder titled **Workspace**. The project file stores information about the access paths to different folders occupied by CAD files, library files of materials, styles library files, template files, files Content Center, etc. There are two ways to access files saved in a project:

- each planned device has its own project file
- all projected units are covered by a one shared single project file

The exercises in this manual will use the second approach - one project file suitable for all planned products. Here, we can assume, that all main folders with files of the designed devices should be placed in the main projects folder **C:\DesignOffice**.

The use of a single project file for all designs is the recommended technique work and facilitates the subsequent implementation of Autodesk Vault software.

This folder will contain project folders and resource folders.

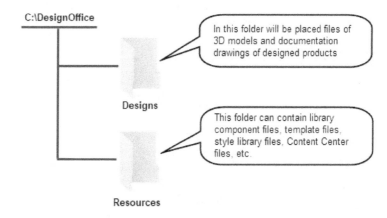

C:\DesignOffice

In this folder will be placed files of 3D models and documentation drawings of designed products

Designs

This folder can contain library component files, template files, style library files, Content Center files, etc.

Resources

*The folder structure presented above is just a suggestion. You can create a different folder structure, better suited to your needs. For example, in teamwork, the **Resources** folder can be placed in the shared area on the server.*

1. Using Windows File Explorer create the **C:\ DesignOffice** folder and the **Designs** and **Resources** subfolders on the **C:** drive of your computer, as in Fig. 1.

Fig. 1

2. Run the Autodesk Inventor 2021 software.

3. Create new project file. On the **Get Started** tab, in **Launch** panel, click the **Projects** icon shown in Fig. 2.

Fig. 2

In the **Projects** dialog box click the **New** button at the bottom. In the **Inventor project wizard** select **New Single User Project** option, shown in Fig. 3. Click **Next**.

Fig. 3

On the next page of the **Inventor project wizard** specify project file name and location, as shown in Fig. 4. You can choose a different drive to place the main folder of the project.

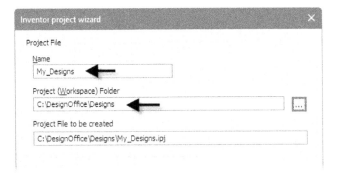

Fig. 4

Click **Finish** followed by **OK** when prompted.

The program creates a project file **My_Designs.ipj**, in folder **C:\DesignsOffice\Designs**. A new project file is placed on the list of projects in the upper part of the **Projects** window, as shown in Fig. 5. The checkmark on the left side indicates that this is an active project. Only one project can be active at any given time.

Fig. 5

Click **Done**.

Adjusting the title block in the template file of the drawing

Now you will modify the template file of drawing. You can assume, that the title block should be automatically populated with the name and part number of the 3D model, which was used to generate the first drawing view. Because it is not default behavior, thus you should make modification in title block definition in the template file.

Drawings can be saved in files with ***.dwg** or ***.idw** extension, depending on your needs.

1. Open template file **Standard.dwg** for editing. The file is located in folder **C:\Users\Public\Documents\ Autodesk\Inventor 2021\Templates\en-US**. If you prefer **IDW** template file type, open the **Standard.idw** file. Click **Yes** in the message window which informs you that opened file is not in the search path.

2. Change the definition of the title block. In the browser, right-click **ANSI-Large**, and in the menu select **Edit Definition**, like in Fig. 6a. The program displays a sketch of the title block.

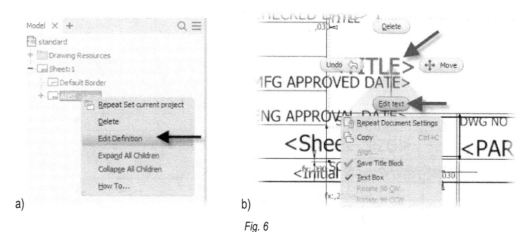

a)   b)

Fig. 6

In the sketch of title block you will change the text attributes that stores the name of the drawing and the part number.

3. Change the attribute with the name of drawing. Right-click item **<TITLE>** and select **Edit text** in the menu, like in Fig. 6b. The program displays the **Format Text** dialog box.

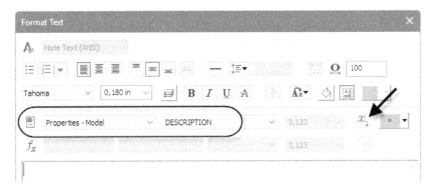

Fig. 7

In the **Format Text** dialog box, delete the **<TITLE>** attribute from a text area. Next, select **Properties – Model**, from **Types** list and select **DESCRIPTION** from **Properties** list. Click **Add Text Parameter** button, indicated by an arrow in Fig. 7. This way you have placed new a attribute like in Fig. 8.

Fig. 8

Click **OK**.

The new attribute will be introduced to the title block area containing the name of the drawing, as in Fig. 9a.

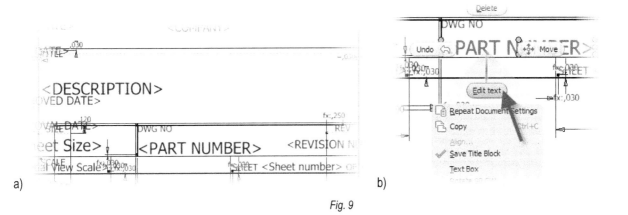

a)   b)

Fig. 9

4. Change the attribute which stores part number. The value of this attribute should be read from the iProperties model. Right-click item **<PART NUMBER>** and select **Edit text** in the menu, like in Fig. 9b. The program displays the **Format Text** dialog box.

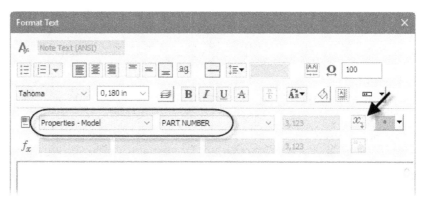

Fig. 10

In the **Format Text** dialog box, delete the existing **<PART NUMBER>** attribute from a text area. Next, select **Properties – Model**, from **Types** list and select **PART NUMBER** from **Properties** list. Click **Add Text Parameter** button, shown in Fig. 10. This way you have placed a new attribute like in Fig. 11.

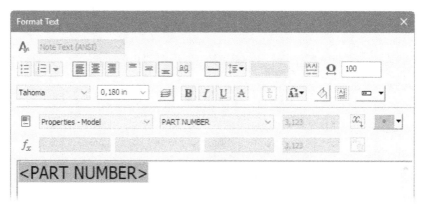

Fig. 11

Click **OK**.

The new attribute will be introduced to the area of title block containing the part number of the part or assembly.

5. Finish editing the title block. Click on **Finish Sketch** icon in the **Exit** panel. Click **Yes** in **Save Edits** dialog box.

6. Save the drawing template file and close.

Now, you can start designing in Autodesk Inventor!

EXAMPLE NO 1. DESIGNING A COMPLETE PRODUCT

The best way to get to know Autodesk Inventor is to make a design of any simple device, which will present all the main steps of creating and editing a design. The main subject of the first design will be a simple drill press vise shown in Fig. 12a. By creating a simple device, you will understand the correct way of creating the design in Autodesk Inventor 2021 and familiarize yourself with the basic commands.

In the design, you will perform complete 3D modeling of the drill press vise assembly and create an exploded view of the device. You will then create a technical drawing of assembly, technical drawings of parts and mounting drawing with the exploded view. Additionally, you will create an illustration of the device and a video demonstration of the vice.

In addition to creating 3D models and preparing drawings, Autodesk Inventor is helpful in managing related files and reducing duplication of work. After completing the first version of the vise you will create a second version with minor changes shown in Fig. 12b, along with complete drawing documentation, based on the files of the first version.

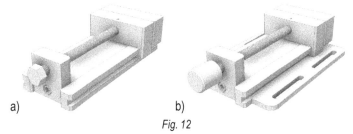

a)   b)

Fig. 12

In Fig. 13a there is shown a technical assembly drawing of the first version of the vise, and Fig. 13b shows assembly drawing of the second version.

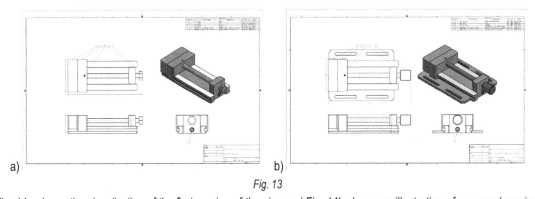

a)   b)

Fig. 13

Fig. 14a shows the visualization of the first version of the vise and Fig. 14b shows an illustration of a second version, which was created using the settings saved with the first version.

a)   b)

Fig. 14

Let's start the first design!

Exercise 1. Modeling of parts. Movable jaw of the vise

9

Exercise 1
Modeling of parts. Movable jaw of the vise

In the Autodesk Inventor software, you can create new parts in a single part environment or in assembly environment – in the context of the assembly. Parts created in the single part modeling environment have no reference to other parts of the assembly. Parts created in the context of an assembly can use the reference to geometrically reference the existing part of the assembly. In both cases, the model part is saved in its own part file with the extension ***.ipt**.

In this exercise, you will design a 3D model of a jaw of the vise in the single part environment. Fig. 15a shows a part model which will be built in this exercise – **The Jaw**. Inventor software allows you to design each part in many different ways. In this exercise, the order of operations has been chosen so as to reduce the difficulty and demonstrate another basic technique.

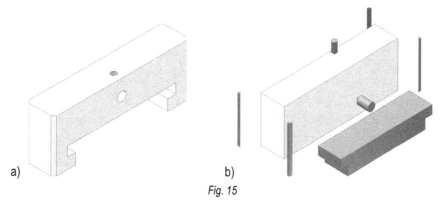

a)   b)

Fig. 15

Each part designed in Autodesk Inventor 2021 is made up of several "features" These "features" can be compared to "building blocks" from which you can build the shape of the part. Some of the features add material to a model while others remove it. The model of the jaw, which will be built in this exercise, can be built as a set of features shown in Fig. 15b. The dark gray shapes are subtracted from the light gray shape.

Besides modeling, an important part of the work in Inventor software is to correctly describe the parts. In the end, the model of the jaw will be complemented with information describing the part and the material from which the part is made. As a first, you will create a part file, based on a standard parts template.

1.   Start creating a new part. In **My Home** window click the **Part** icon, as shown in Fig. 16.

*Using the **Part** icon from the **My Home** window you will create a new part file based on the template **Standard.ipt**.*

Fig. 16

By default, when you select the template file, the program enables the parts modeling environment and waits for the decision of the user to create a new part. One method is to insert another part as a base for further modeling, and the second method is to create a flat sketch of the first feature.

Before taking further actions, let's look at the window of the user interface. Autodesk Inventor 2021 offers several modes of operation, which also causes some changes in the user interface depending on the current operating mode. Fig. 17 shows a user interface window in parts modeling mode.

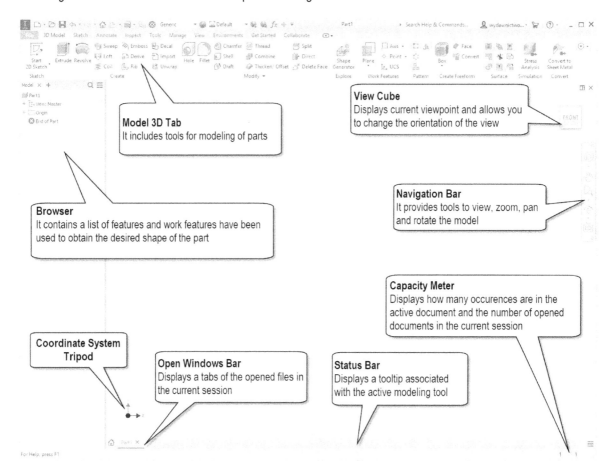

Fig. 17

In this mode, the most important set of the modeling tools is stored on the **3D Model** tab. Each applied feature, for example, **Extrude**, **Revolve**, **Hole**, etc. will be placed in the **Browser** window, creating a history of the construction of the part. In the **Origin** folder in the browser, there are located the planes, axes and the center point of the coordinate system modeled part. The **Status Bar** will display information about the active tool.

Important elements of the user interface which will be used extensively are tools for manipulating the view model: the **ViewCube** and the **Navigation Bar**. The current position of the model in 3D space helps determine the **Tripod** of coordinate axes shown in the lower left corner of the screen. Tripod XYZ axes are denoted colors: red, green and blue, which can also be represented as follows: **RGB = XYZ**. This mapping is easy to remember and, in many situations, will facilitate how the model is oriented in space.

You will start modeling the new part by creating a sketch on the selected coordinate system's plane.

2.   Create a new sketch. In the **3D Model** tab in the **Sketch** panel, click on **Start 2D Sketch** icon. The program displays a set of default planes of the coordinate system and is expected to indicate the plane to put on the new sketch.

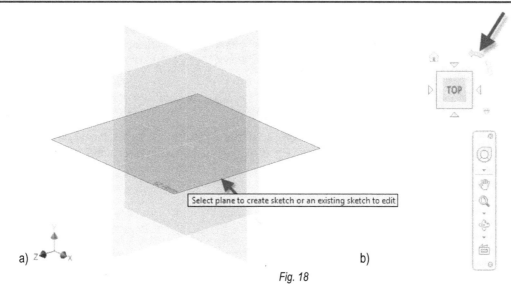

a)   b)

Fig. 18

Click **XZ Plane**, shown in Fig. 18a. By default, the program sets the view of the indicated sketching plane (option set in the **Application Options**). Be sure the **ViewCube** is set as in Fig. 18b. If necessary, turn the cube by clicking the corresponding arrows shown in Fig. 18b.

Stop for a moment to look at the user interface in sketch mode.

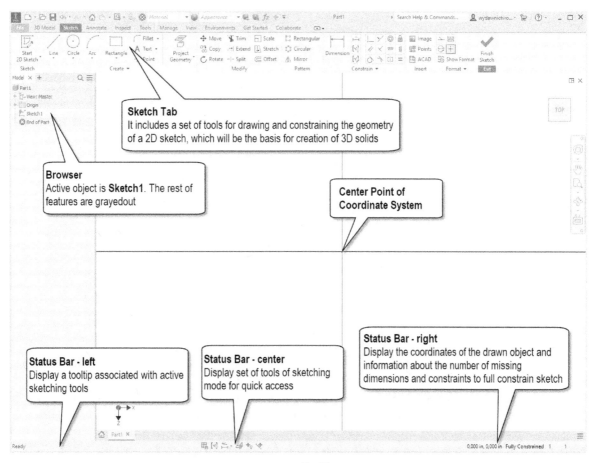

Fig. 19

In this mode, the program displays the tools for drawing a sketch, which can be found on the **Sketch** tab and the main lines of the coordinate system. In the browser, the active object is the **Sketch1** – you will create it now. The two intersecting thick lines, visible on the sketching plane, are the axes **XZ** of the coordinate system. The intersection point is the point **0,0** of the coordinate system.

You can now start drawing objects in the **Sketch1**. Since this is the first sketch in this part, it is automatically assigned to number 1, visible in a browser.

3.   Draw a rectangle with the following dimensions: **4.5-inches** x **1.35 inch**. On the **Sketch** tab, in the **Create** panel, click the **Rectangle** icon. Draw a rectangle like in Fig. 20, starting from the upper left corner of the rectangle. Do not specify the position of the lower right corner of the rectangle - this point can remain undecided. Note that the program automatically displays fields for entering the lengths of the sides.

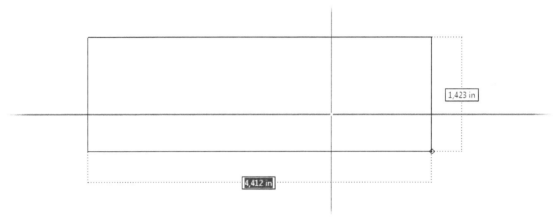

Fig. 20

The active area is highlighted and it is expected that you specify the length of the values. Enter **4.5** and press **TAB**, which updates the length of the segment and then move to the field controlling the height of the rectangle, like in Fig. 21. You can repeatedly move from field to field by pressing the **TAB** key.

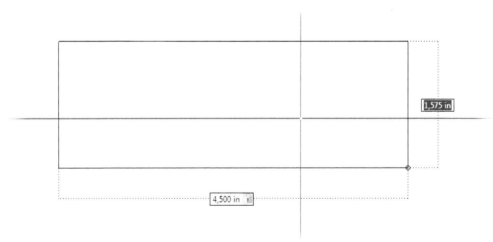

Fig. 21

Enter **1.35** and press **ENTER** key. The program approves the value and displays the dimensions of the rectangle and used constraints, like in Fig. 22. Press the **ESC** key to complete the command.

By turning the mouse wheel, you can adjust the visibility of the rectangle to the screen size.

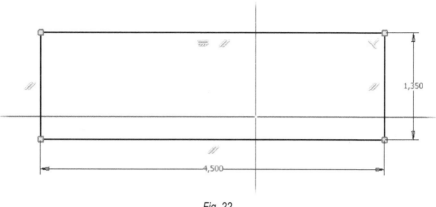

Fig. 22

 Dimensions made in the sketch can be displayed in the 2D drawing of that part. Therefore, it is worth dimensioning the sketches in that way so they can be used immediately in a final technical drawing.

The drawn rectangle is not fully constrained, what is indicated by the message **2 dimensions needed**, displayed on the right side of the status bar, like in Fig. 23. In order to fully constrain the rectangle, it is necessary to immobilize it first. It can be done by using the appropriate geometric constraints and dimensions in relation to stationary objects.

0,000 in, 0,000 in 2 dimensions needed 1   1

Fig. 23

In addition, the rectangle is offset from the center of the coordinate system. If possible, place the parts symmetrically in the middle of the coordinate system, which allows the usage of e.g. the planes of symmetry to create mirrored copies of positioning elements. At this stage, you can set the rectangle object at the origin of coordinates, by using dimensions or constraints. Let's choose the second option - geometric constraints. Using a coincident constraint, you can determine the position of the center point of the horizontal line in the middle of the coordinate system. As a result, you achieve a fully constrained sketch.

 Geometric constraints are used to control the interactions between the sketch entities, such as perpendicularity, parallelism, collinearity, concentricity, symmetry, compliance point, etc.

 4. Determine the symmetry of the rectangle's edge in relation to the coordinate system using geometric constraints. On the **Sketch** tab in the **Constrain** panel, click the **Coincident Constrain** icon. Select the midpoint of the upper line of the rectangle denoted by 1 in Fig. 24, then the center point of the coordinate system denoted by 2. A green dot will inform you that the midpoint is selected.

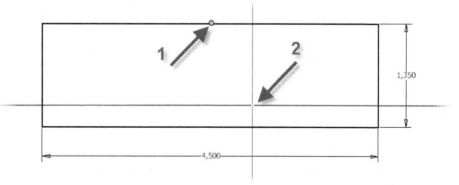

Fig. 24

The program will set the sketch as in Fig. 25 and displays the information in the status bar: **Fully Constrained**. Press **ESC** key to finish constraints.

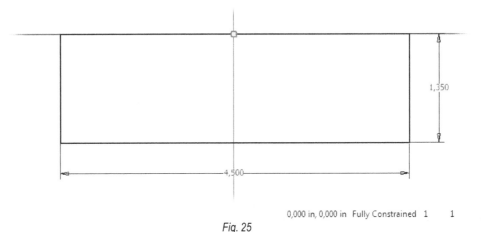

0,000 in, 0,000 in Fully Constrained 1   1

Fig. 25

The first sketch is considered to be ready. Now you need to finish the sketch and you will use it to create the first solid feature, which will be a straight draw in the **Z** direction at the height of **2.2** inches.

 5. Finish the sketch. Click **Finish Sketch** icon on **Sketch** tab. After the completion of the sketch, the software sets a sketch in isometric view and switches user interface to create solid features. Axis and the **Sketch** tab get switched off.

 *How to return to the sketch editing? Just double-click the **Sketch1** entry in the browser and the program will enter the sketch mode.*

 6. Create a solid block by extrusion. On the **3D Model** tab, in the **Create** panel, click the **Extrude** icon. The program will display an **Extrude properties** panel, in which you can set all parameters of the operation. Because there is only one closed loop in the sketch, the program will automatically display the preview of the solid feature.

In the **Distance A** field of the properties panel, enter the value of **2.2** inches, as in Fig. 26a. The program will update the preview of shape as in Fig. 26b.

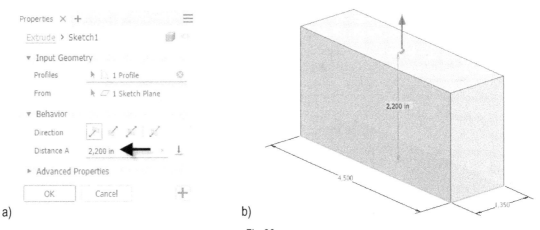

a)   b)

Fig. 26

Click **OK**. The program will create a block shown in Fig. 27a.

This is the first feature of the part. The following note will appear in the browser: **Extrusion1**, which contains **Sketch1**. This sketch was "consumed by" the shaping feature.

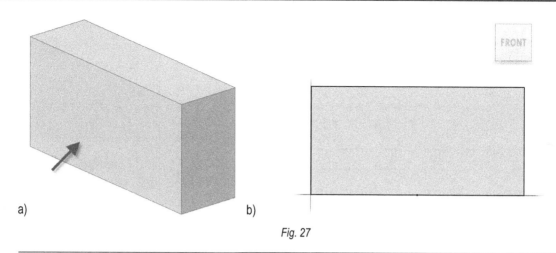

Fig. 27

---

*How to return to the editing extrude? Just double-click the entry **Extrusion1** in the browser and the program will enter the edit extrusion parameters.*

Now you will create the second feature that will form a cutout. You will place the sketch of the new feature on a flat surface of the existing solid model. But first, you will check the settings of automatic edge-projecting. You will use auto-project for modeling parts in the first project.

7. Check the setting of the auto-project option. On the **Tools** tab in the **Options** panel, click the **Application Options** icon. In the **Application Options** window go to the **Sketch** tab and make sure that the option **Autoproject edges for sketch creation and edit** is checked, like in Fig. 28. If necessary, select this option. Click **OK** to apply and close a window.

Fig. 28

8. Define a new sketch on the surface of the model. On the **3D Model** tab in the **Sketch** panel, click on **Start 2D Sketch** icon. The program will display a sketching symbol next to the cursor. Click the side face of the model denoted by an arrow in Fig. 27a. After you point to the face, the program will create a sketch plane and will set the sketch plane parallel to the screen plane, as in Fig. 27b.

You will draw the sketch shown in Fig. 29a. The order of creating sketch will be as follows: drawing the outline (with the possibility of using any dimensions), organizing the geometry of the sketch by using geometric constraints and finally complementing the sketch by additional dimensions.

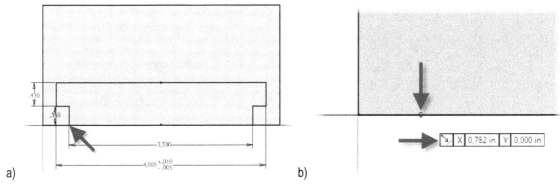

a)   b)

Fig. 29

9. Draw a sketch of the cutout. On the **Sketch** tab in the **Create** panel, click on **Line** icon. Start drawing from the bottom left of the sketch. Point at the start point of the line on the projected edge of the surface, at the place indicated by the arrow in Fig. 29a. The program indicates precise positioning of the start point of the line on the lower edge of the block by displaying the tying compliance symbol as in Fig. 29b. Draw a line straight up so that the constraint symbol shows perpendicularity or parallelism and enter the value **0.35** inch in the edit box as shown in Fig. 30.

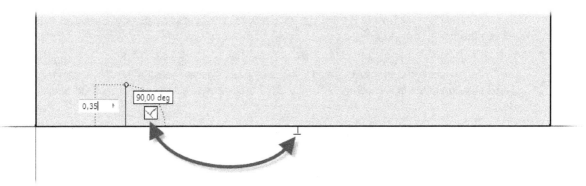

Fig. 30

Symbols of constraints of parallelism and perpendicularity appear always in pairs, indicating towards which object occurs determination of parallelism or perpendicularity. Types of symbols that appear depend on the kind of object that was under the cursor just before an indication of the start point of the line - above the perpendicular or parallel object.

Press **ENTER** key. The program will approve the first section of the line. The command is waiting for an indication of the end point of the next section, which will be launched from the end of the previous section of the line. Move the cursor left to create a horizontal line of approximately **0.4** inches (do not enter the value into the edit box). Next, move the cursor up and create a vertical line of **0.43** inch (enter a precise value into the edit box). Complete outline to obtain a shape as in Fig. 31.

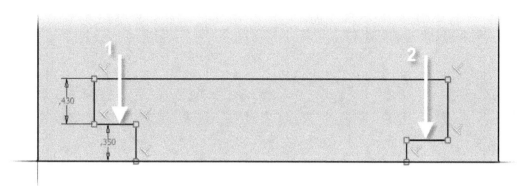

Fig. 31

*If for some reason you stopped drawing a line you can continue by calling the command **Line,** again. In order to precisely starting a new line from the end of the previous line, you should set the cursor to the endpoint that way that it was displayed a green dot. This will automatically set the coincident constraint to ends of the lines.*

Press the **ESC** key to stop drawing the line.

The next step is to determine the position of the segments of the sketch in relation to each other using geometric constraints. You will determine collinear constraint and equal length for two segments. Then you will set the sketch symmetrically in relation to the center of the model's edge.

10. Set collinearity for the segments of the sketch. On the **Sketch** tab in the **Constrain** panel, click on the **Collinear Constrain** icon. Select elements of the sketch denoted by 1 and 2 in Fig. 31. The program will modify the position of the lines.

11. Set an equal length of the segments. On the **Sketch** tab in the **Constrain** panel, click the **Equal** icon. Again, select the elements of the sketch denoted by 1 and 2 in Fig. 31. After using both constraints the sketch looks similar to the one in Fig. 32.

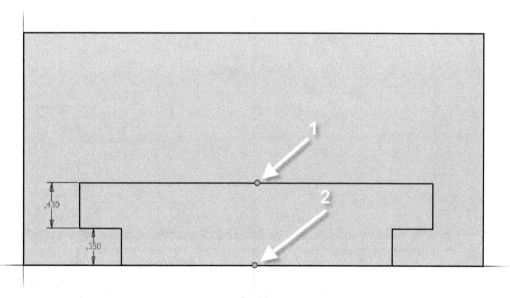

Fig. 32

12. Set the symmetry of the sketches in relation to the center of the edge of the model. On the **Sketch** tab in the **Constrain** panel, click on **Vertical Constraint** icon. Select midpoints of the lines denoted by 1 and 2 in Fig. 32.

The program displays an auxiliary vertical line. Press **ESC** key to stop adding constraints. Now the outline cutouts are symmetrical, as in Fig. 33.

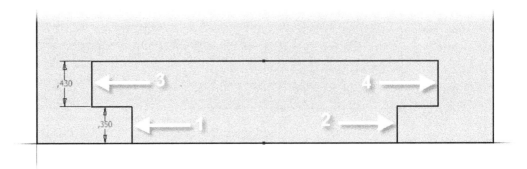

Fig. 33

The status bar displays the following message: **2 dimensions needed**. Now you will put two missing dimensions to control the width of both steps of the cutout. One of the dimensions will be supplemented by deviations of values. The dimension with deviations can be displayed on the technical drawing.

13. Apply dimensions. On the **Sketch** tab in the **Constrain** panel, click on **Dimension** icon. Select the line denoted by 1 in Fig. 33, and next select the line denoted by 2. Move the cursor below the model and confirm the position of the dimension. Enter **3.5** inch in **Edit Dimension** box.

Enter the second horizontal dimension, which will be supplemented by the upper and lower deviation of values. Select lines denoted by 3 and 4 in Fig. 33, and then move the cursor to the position below the first placed dimension and confirm the position of the dimension. Enter the **4.0** inch in the **Edit Dimension** box. To apply the values of deviations, click arrow icon located to the right of edit field and select **Tolerance** in menu, like in Fig. 34a.

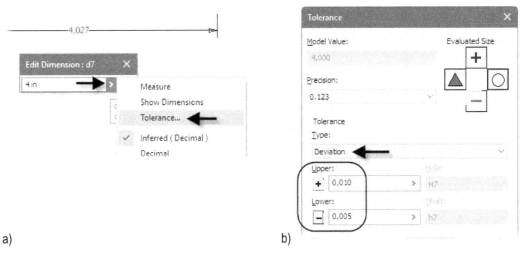

a)   b)

Fig. 34

To set the values of the deviations, in the **Tolerance** dialog box select **Deviations** from the **Type** list and enter values for the **Upper** and the **Lower** deviations, like in Fig. 34b. You can change the sign of deviation by clicking the **+** or **–** button. Click **OK**. In the **Tolerance** dialog box and next confirm the value of the dimension.

Press **ESC** key to stop dimensioning. Ready to use, a fully constrained sketch is shown in Fig. 35.

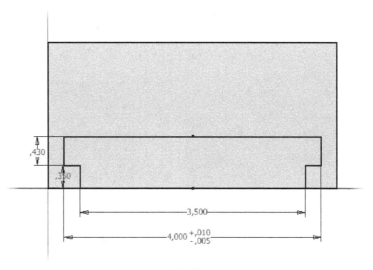

Fig. 35

How to return to dimension edit? Just double-click on the dimension and program will display edit dimension box.

The tolerance and fit values can also be given to the dimensions in the technical drawing of the part.

---

14. Finish the sketch. Click on **Finish Sketch** icon. After the completion of sketching the program sets the model in isometric view and goes into the creation of solid features. Coordinate axes and **Sketch** tab are turned off.

15. Create a cutout using the just created sketch. On the **3D Model** tab in **Create** panel, click on the **Extrude** icon. The program displays the **Extrude properties panel** and is waiting for you to choose the proper loop of the sketch, from which it will make a cutout.

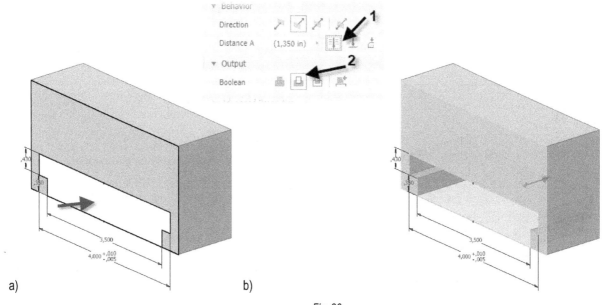

a)   b)

Fig. 36

Select the loop denoted by the arrow in Fig. 36a. The program displays the preview of a feature with parameters used in the previous extrusion. Set parameters for the through cutout by selecting the appropriate options. In the **Behavior** section select **Through All**, denoted by 1 in Fig. 36b, that automatically turns on a **Cut** operation, denoted by 2.

After setting the parameters, click **OK**. The program creates cutout shown in Fig. 37a. In the browser, you will find a second feature named **Extrusion2**.

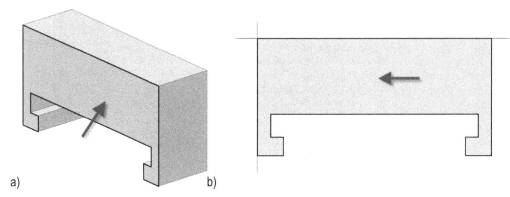

a)   b)

Fig. 37

The next step is to make a hole in which will be located one end of a clamping screw. The program offers many options for the location of the hole. Now, you will use the location of the hole from a sketch, in which you will put the center point of the hole.

16. Define a new sketch on the flat face of the model. On the **3D Model** tab in the **Sketch** panel, click on the **Start 2D Sketch** icon. Click the face denoted by an arrow in Fig. 37a. When you point on the face the program creates a sketch plane, projects the edges of the face to the new sketch and sets the sketch plane parallel to the plane of the screen, as in Fig. 37b.

17. Insert the center point of the hole. On the **3D Model** tab in the **Sketch** panel, click on **Point** icon. Insert the center point of the hole in the place indicated by the arrow in Fig. 37b (approximately) and press **ESC** to finish. The center point is shown in Fig. 38a.

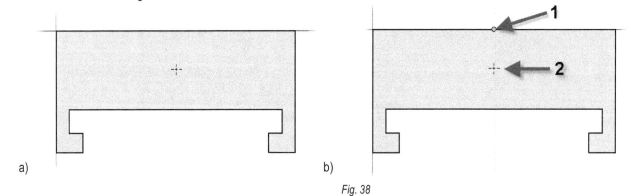

a)   b)

Fig. 38

The center point of the hole should be positioned symmetrically at a distance of **0.71** inches from the top edge of the jaw. To determine the vertical symmetry, you will apply the constraint, while the distance will be determined by the dimension.

18. Set the center point of the hole symmetrically with respect to the upper edge. On the **Sketch** tab in the **Constrain** panel, click on the **Vertical Constrain** icon. Pick the midpoint of the line denoted by 1 and then select the point denoted by 2, in Fig. 38b. The program displays an auxiliary vertical line. The midpoint of the edge is properly selected when the filled green dot is displayed. Press **ESC** key to stop adding constraints.

19. Set a center of the hole at a given distance from the edge. On the **Sketch** tab in the **Constrain** panel, click on the **Dimension** icon. Place the vertical dimension of **0.71** inches between the upper edge and the center point of the hole. Press **ESC** key to stop dimensioning. The center point of the hole, symmetrically positioned at a given distance is shown in Fig. 39a.

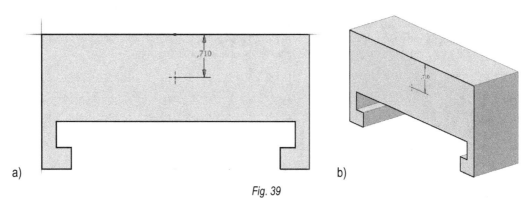

Fig. 39

20. Finish the sketch. Click on **Finish Sketch** icon to the right of the tab. The program sets an isometric view of the part as in Fig. 39b.

21. Create a hole. On the **3D Model** tab in the **Modify** panel, click on the **Hole** icon. The program recognizes the center point of the hole and displays the preview of the hole with current parameters. In the **Hole properties** panel, select the type, termination of the blind hole with diameter **7/16** inch and depth **0.65** inches, like in Fig. 40a. The program updates the preview of the hole.

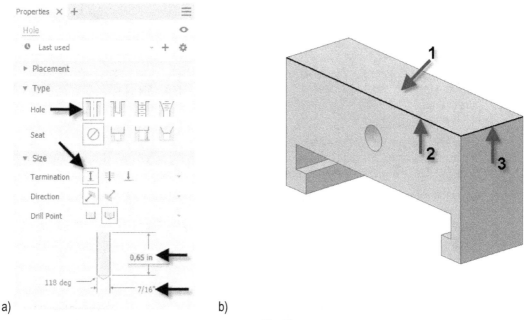

Fig. 40

Click **OK**. The program creates a hole shown in Fig. 40b. In the browser, there is a new entry: **Hole1**.

*How to modify a hole? Just double-click in the browser on the entry **Hole1** and the program automatically turns on the **Hole properties panel** in the edit mode.*

Now you can put the second hole with the diameter **0.25 inch**, fully threaded, designed for locking the screw. You will use another method of localization of the hole.

22. Create the threaded hole. Click again on the **Hole** icon in the **Modify** panel. Because now you do not have a sketch of the insertion point, the program as a default offers options for the insertion hole by indicating the plane and the reference edges to determine the distances.

Select an upper face of the jaw at the point indicated by 1 in Fig. 40b. After selecting the plane, the program is expecting an edges indication of reference - select edge denoted by 2 in Fig. 40b, and then select the edge denoted by 3. Currently, the preview of the hole is similar to the one shown in Fig. 41a.

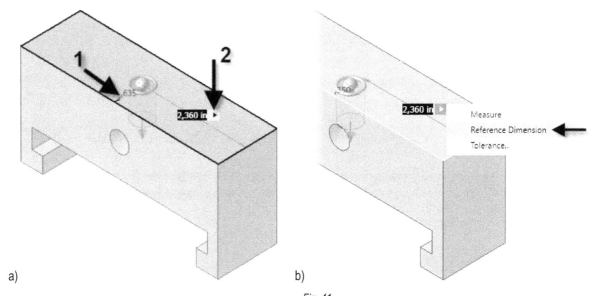

a)   b)

Fig. 41

Now, you need to precisely determine the offset distance from the specified edge. Click on the dimension indicated by 1 in Fig. 41a. In the edit field, type a value of **0.35 inch**, and then press the **TAB** key to enter the edit field of the second dimension. To set the hole in the symmetry of the long edge of the jaw you will use a dimension that controls the length of this edge.

In the edit field, you will put the value of dimension that controls the length of the edge, divided by 2. However, instead of a numerical value, you can put the variable name of the existing dimension. This way, if there is a change in length of the jaw, the hole will always remain in symmetry.

Click on the arrow to the right of the dimension edit field, denoted by 2 in Fig. 41a. From the menu, select **Reference Dimensions**, shown in Fig. 41b. Now, you will indicate the feature from which you will take a dimension. Click on the longest edge of the model - the program displays dimensions of the first feature as in Fig. 42a.

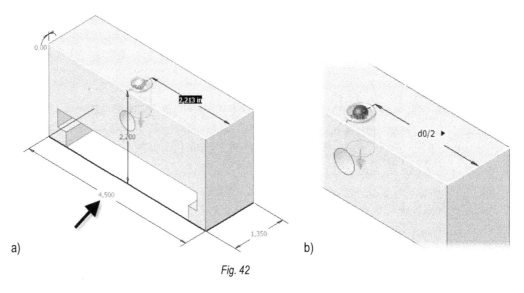

a)   b)

Fig. 42

Click on the dimension **4.500,** as indicated in Fig. 42a, which moves the variable name of the dimension (in this case, **d0**) to the dimension edit filed of the dimension reference edge of the hole. Complete contents of the fields by typing "**/2**", as in Fig. 42b.

In **Hole properties** panel, shown in Fig. 43a, select the threaded hole (1), select thread type **ANSI Unified Screw Threads** (2), select size **0.25** inch (3), set a thread on full depth (4), select termination type **Distance** (5), set a depth of hole **0.6** inches (6).

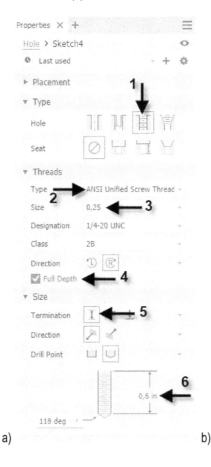
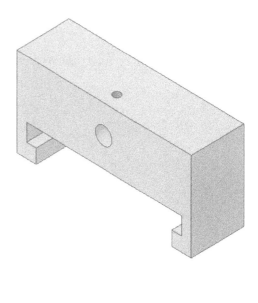

a)   b)

Fig. 43

Click **OK**. The program creates a hole shown in Fig. 43b.

You can assume that the jaw has all the necessary features. At the end of the modeling process, you can apply finishing features such as chamfers and fillets. You will create four chamfers of edges, size **0.125-inch x 45°**.

23.   Create a chamfer. On the **3D Model** tab in the **Modify** panel, click on the **Chamfer** icon. The program displays a **Chamfer** dialog box, with **Edges** button enable, which means that the program is waiting for you to select the edges for chamfering. Select four edges, indicated by arrows in Fig. 44a. By default, the program proposes chamfering in the equal distance from the edge, which gives the chamfer angle equal to 45°. Make sure that the value of chamfering is **0.125 inch**. You can smoothly adjust the value of chamfering by moving the arrow located at the last indicated edge of chamfering. Preview of chamfering is shown in Fig. 44b.

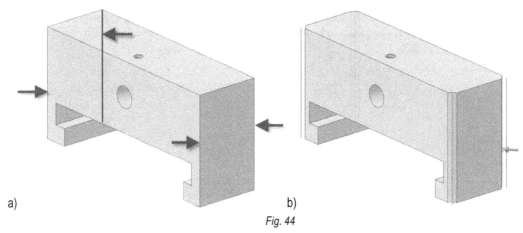

a)   b)

Fig. 44

Click **OK**., to apply chamfering. The finished model of the jaw is shown in Fig. 45a.

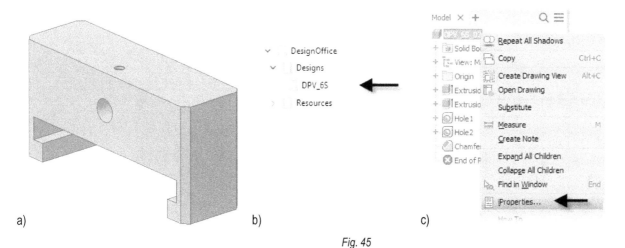

a)   b)   c)

Fig. 45

The geometry of the jaw model was created. Now, you will save the file for the first time and then you will fill the part properties and save the file again.

24. Save the part file in the folder **...\DesignOffice\Designs\DPV_6S**. In the **Save** dialog box create a missing subfolder, as in Fig. 45b. The part name is **DPV_6S_02.ipt**.

It is recommended that part file has the same name as the part number and the name of the technical drawing file of the given part, which will allow unambiguous identification of parts and the technical drawing and you will avoid duplicating of the file names. The file name can be changed at any time. If the part file is already used in the assembly or its drawing was done, to change its name, use the Design Assistant program or Autodesk Vault to properly update the names of the related files: assembly file and the drawing files.

Created model of the jaw is stored in a file named **DPV_6S_02.ipt**. In reality, there is only one information you know about that part. You would like to enter the metadata to the part file, which clearly will identify this part, such as part number, description, and the material from which the part was made. You can also enter other metadata as required. These data should appear in the BOM in an assembly file, in the list of parts in the assembly drawing and in the final technical drawing of this part.

25. Assign additional data to the part, and select material. In the browser right-click on the file's name: **DPV_6S_02** and select **iProperties** in the menu, as in Fig. 45c. In the **DPV_6S_02 iProperties**, go to the **Project** tab and enter in the appropriate fields, the data presented in Fig. 46a.

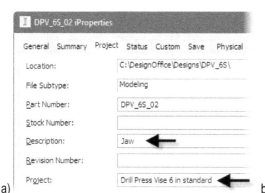
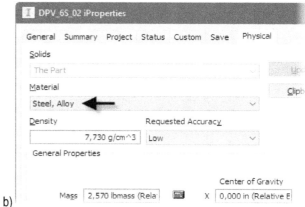

a)   b)

Fig. 46

You should pay attention to the fact that the property **Part Number** is the same as the file name. The program automatically performs this assignment at the time of the first "save of the". Now, you should still enter material data.

Select material. Go to the tab **Physical** and from **Material** drop-down list select **Steel, Alloy**. The program assigns the material and calculates the physical parameters of the parts that are visible on the **Physical** tab, as in Fig. 46b.

After selecting the material, click **OK**.

Each **Material** has assigned an **Appearance** in the material library. After closing this dialog box, the part will be presented in an appearance that has been assigned to the material **Steel, Alloy**: **Semi – Polished**. You can override the appearance by selecting a different appearance from the drop-down list, located in the quick access toolbar, shown in Fig. 47. Going back to the appearance specified in the physical properties occurs when you select **Clear Override** from the list of items.

Fig. 47

You already have the first 3D model. At the end of this exercise, you will familiarize yourself with the basic tools to manipulate the image of the 3D model in screen space. Check the following tools by yourself.

- **Image panning** – icon **Pan** in the navigation bar or holding down the **F2** key. Moving the mouse while holding down the left button starts panning image.

- **Image Zoom in/Zoom out** – icon **Zoom** in the navigation bar or pressing, holding down the **F3** key. Moving the mouse forward and backward while pressing the left button starts a zoom in/out.

- **Orbit model** – icon **Free Orbit** in the navigation bar or pressing, holding down the **F4** key. Moving the mouse while pressing the left button starts free rotation.

- Back to the previous view – **F5** key.

- Home view – **F6** key.

- Clicking the wall, edge or corner of the **ViewCube** sets the model view according to the selected element of the cube.

26. Save again the part file and close. End of exercise.

Exercise summary

You have done the first 3D model in the Autodesk Inventor software. In this exercise, you have learned the basic techniques of creating sketches and several basic features. In the next exercise, you'll see how you can easily create a technical drawing of the part in Autodesk Inventor software.

Exercise 2
The technical drawing of the part. The jaw drawing

Now you will create a drawing of the jaw part. In this exercise, you will learn basic techniques for creating 2D documentation from 3D models. Fig. 48 shows a drawing of the part, which will be built in this exercise.

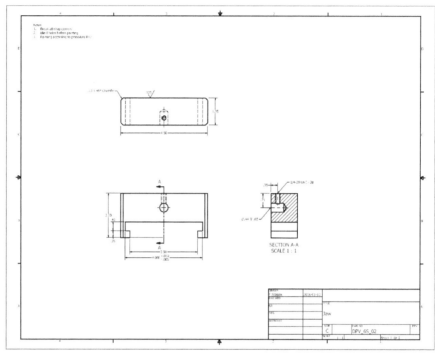

Fig. 48

The 2D drawing is stored in a separate file with the extension **IDW** or **DWG**. Just as a 3D model of the part, the 2D drawing is created based on the template file **Standard.idw** or **Standard.dwg**. In the **My Home** window in the area of **New,** you can see the current type of template file configured, based on the image icon, which explains Fig. 49.

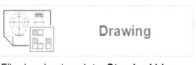
File drawing template: **Standard.idw**

File drawing template: **Standard.dwg**

Fig. 49

Different icons types of template file will also be visible in the pull-down menu which starts from the **New** icon in the quick access toolbar.

---

*The change of type of file template to create 2D drawings can be done in the **Application Options** dialog box which can be accessed by clicking the **Application Options** icon in the **Options** panel, under the **Tools** tab. In the **Drawing** tab, select the file type from the list **Default Drawing File Type**.*

---

1. Start creating a new drawing file of the jaw. Click on **Drawing** icon in **My Home** window, shown in Fig. 50, which will create a new drawing file based on **Standard.dwg** template.

Fig. 50

The program goes into the creation of 2D drawing mode and automatically displays the drawing sheet format **D**, containing the default frame and title block, as in Fig. 50. The **D** format is the default format proposed in this drawing template.

Before taking further actions, let's look at the window of the user interface in the drawing preparation mode.

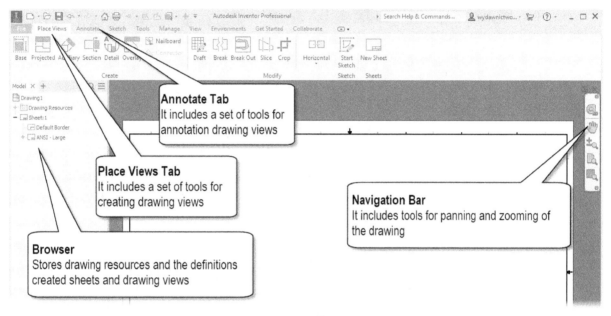

Fig. 51

The technical drawing of the jaw should be placed on the sheet format **C**. You will need to change the sheet form.

2. Change the drawing sheet. In the browser, right-click **Sheet: 1** and select **Edit Sheet**, as in Fig. 52a.

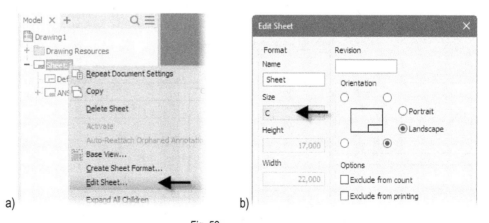

Fig. 52

In the **Edit Sheet** dialog box, on the **Size** list, select **C**, as in Fig. 52b. Click **OK**.

You will now place three drawing views – two orthogonal views and one cross-section view. As a first, you will create a base view, which represents a front view of the jaw model and then you create a view from the top. You assume that a base view should be drawn on a scale of **1:1**, and the hidden edges will be displayed in ortho view.

3. Create a front view and a top view of the jaw model. On the **Place Views** tab, in the **Create** panel, click on **Base** icon. If you close your jaw model then click **Open an existing file** button in the **Drawing View** dialog box, denoted by 1 in Fig. 53, and locate the file **DPV_6S_02.ipt** saved in the previous exercise. After selecting the file, the program places preview of a model view in the sheet. However, if the file was not closed the preview is automatically displayed.

Set the scale of the base view on the **1:1** scale by selecting from the list (2). Make sure that the style of the view displays hidden lines (3). In the **Display Options** tab enable **Thread Features** and **Tangent Edges** (4). The correct settings for the base view in the **Drawing View** dialog box are shown in Fig. 53.

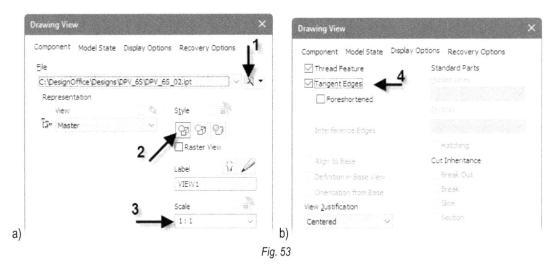

Fig. 53

The scale can also be set dynamically by pulling the green, bold corner of the envelope preview.

Make sure that **ViewCube** presents a **Front** wall in the plan view of the drawing sheet, as in Fig. 54a. Changing the cube orientation changes the drawing view plane.

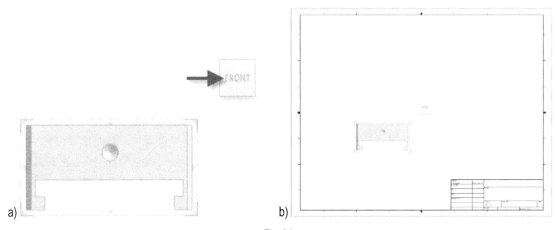

Fig. 54

Move the **Drawing View** dialog box out of the drawing area, then set the outline of the base view as in Fig. 54b, by "grabbing" the center of the view area and moving to the new location. By default, this command offers the ability to place multiple orthogonal and isometric views in one invocation of the command.

The program now expects to indicate the position of a new orthogonal or isometric view.

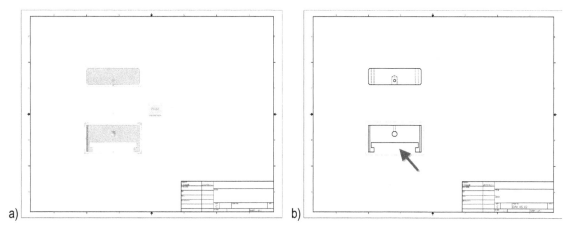

Fig. 55

Show location of the view containing a view from the top, above the base view, as in Fig. 55a. The program will create an outline showing the location of the view and is expecting you to indicate the position of the next view.

Finish creating drawing views. Click the right mouse button and select **OK**. The program generates two drawing views shown in Fig. 55b.

It is worth to note that the drawing title block was automatically filled with the name and part number.

4. Next view is a sectional view which will pass through the holes. In the **Place Views** tab, in the **Create** panel, click the **Section** icon. The program is expecting to indicate the view in which it places the section line. Click the view indicated by an arrow in Fig. 55b.

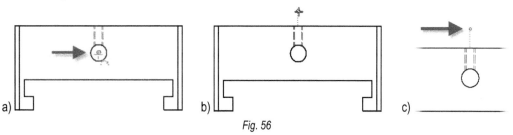

Fig. 56

Now, set the section line in order to accurately pass through the holes. Hover over the center of the circle hole – do not click. When you see a green dot, as in Fig. 56a, move the cursor vertically above the edge of the line so that a dotted line is displayed in the symmetry of the hole, as in Fig. 56b. Click at the position of the arrow like in Fig. 56c.

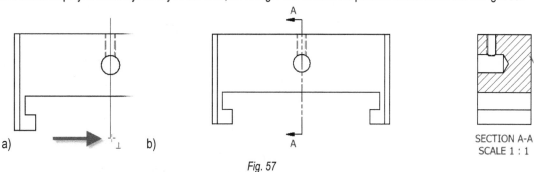

Fig. 57

Locate the end of the section line. Pull the line down and click on the point of the arrow like in Fig. 57a.

The section line will consist of only one section. Now, right-click and select **Continue**. The program will display a **Section View** dialog box, where you can determine the options of the section view. Leave the default settings without making any changes.

Move the outline of section view to the position on the right side of the base view and click. The program will generate a cross-sectional view as in Fig. 57b.

You have generated the necessary drawing views. Now you add centerlines, dimensions, mechanical symbols and remarks to the drawing views. Firstly – centerlines.

The program provides tools for manual or automated application of centerlines. Here you will use the automatic option.

5. Add center lines to the base view. Click the right mouse button in base view and select **Automated Centerlines** from the menu, like in Fig. 58a. The program displays an **Automated Centerlines** dialog box.

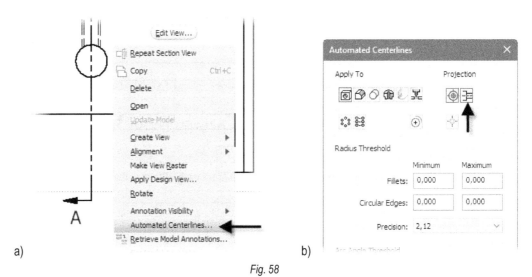

Fig. 58

In the **Projection** section enable **Objects In View, Axis Parallel**, indicated by an arrow in Fig. 58b. Click **OK**. The program inserts centerlines in base view, as in Fig. 59a.

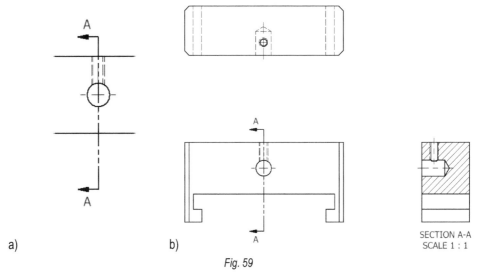

Fig. 59

6. Repeat the operation to insert centerlines for other views. Remember to include the option **Objects In View, Axis Parallel**, for each view. A set of centerlines is shown in Fig. 59b.

You can extend the centerline by pulling the handle, which appears when you select the line. Tools to manually create centerlines are located in the Symbols panel, on the Annotate tab.

Now you can add dimensions to the views. The program offers the option of acquiring the dimensions from the sketches and a tool for manual dimensioning. Sketches created in the model of the jaw are dimensioned in such a way that the dimensions in sketches can be applying in the final drawing immediately. Now you use the option to automatically acquire dimensions of the sketches.

7. Add dimensions to the view. Click the right mouse button in the area of the base view and select **Retrieve Model Annotations** as shown in Fig. 60a. The program will display **Retrieve Model Annotations** dialog box, with the **Sketch and Feature Dimensions** tab active. By default, on the drawing view there are all dimensions displayed, which are parallel to the viewport plane. We do not need all the dimensions in this view.

Be sure that **Select Features** option is set and click **Select Dimension Source** button, like in Fig. 60b. This option allows you to select the features from which you want to acquire dimensions to the current view.

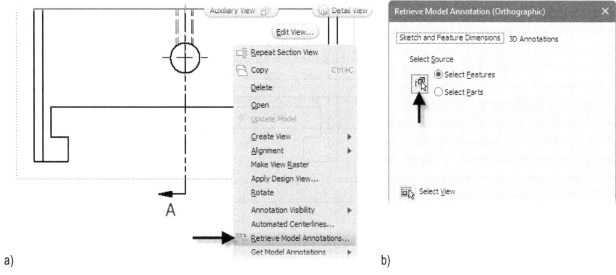

a)   b)

Fig. 60

In this view, you put dimensions of the cut and the height of the jaw. Click edge denoted by 1 in Fig. 61a, and then the edge denoted by 2. The program displays dimensions of the features, like in Fig. 61b.

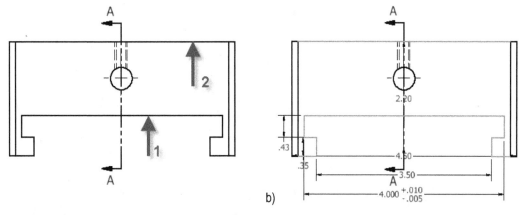

a)   b)

Fig. 61

You can now choose the dimensions that should be visible permanently in this view. In the **Retrieve Model Annotation** dialog box, click **Select Dimension Source** button again to turn off selecting of a feature, and pick all dimensions except for horizontal dimension of **4.50**, and then click **Apply**. The program will keep the chosen dimensions in grayed out mode, like in Fig. 62a and enable the **Select View** button for indication of the next view to acquire dimensions.

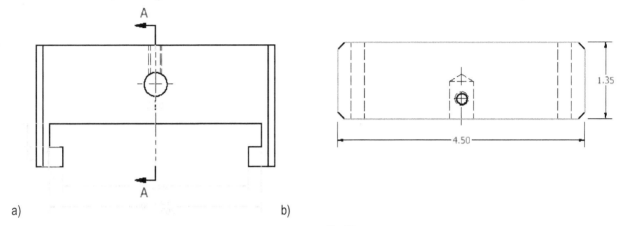

a)   b)

Fig. 62

Click on the view from the top, which is located above the base view, then click **Select Dimension Source** button and select the edge of the long side. The program will display the main dimensions of the model as in Fig. 62b.

In the **Retrieve Model Annotation** dialog box, click **Select Dimension Source** again to turn off selecting of a feature, pick both displayed dimensions and then click **Apply**. The program will keep the chosen dimensions in the grayed out mode like on Fig. 63a, and enable the **Select View** button for indication of the next view for acquiring dimensions.

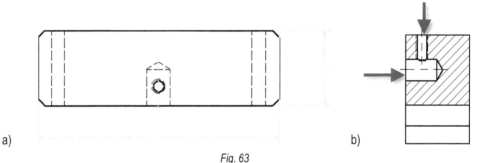

a)   b)

Fig. 63

Click section view, then click **Select Dimension Source** button and select edges of the holes indicated by the arrows in Fig. 63b. The program displays the dimensions of the holes, as in Fig. 64a.

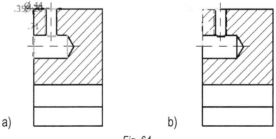

a)   b)

Fig. 64

Choose only dimensions locating holes. In the **Retrieve Model Annotation** dialog box, click **Select Dimension Source** button again to turn off selecting of a feature then select dimensions with a value of **0.71** and **0.35**, and click **Apply**. The program will keep the chosen dimensions in the grayed out mode like in Fig. 64b.

Click **Cancel** to exit the command. On the screen, you will see a set of dimensions shown in Fig. 65.

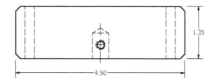

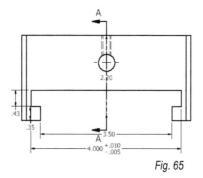

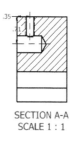

SECTION A-A
SCALE 1 : 1

Fig. 65

---

*In this case, there is no need to manually insert dimensions. However, if there is the need to manually insert dimensions you can use for this purpose a **Dimension** tool, located in the panel **Dimension**, on the **Annotate** tab. The dimensions inserted manually will be automatically updated when you change the size of the part.*

---

8. Arrange dimensions. On the **Annotate** tab in the **Dimension** panel, click the **Arrange** icon. Drag the selection box around all three views to select all dimensions. Then right-click, and in the menu select **OK**. The program will arrange the placement of dimensions using the settings stored in the dimension style definition.

In the default dimension style, usually, it will be necessary to manually move apart overlapping dimensions and change the position of the anchors. To move dimension just click on the dimension and move to a new position. To change the position of the anchor point simply selects the displayed handle and move to another vertex on the same level. Finally, rearranged dimensioning is shown in Fig. 66.

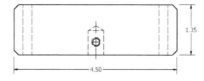

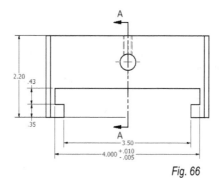

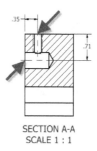

SECTION A-A
SCALE 1 : 1

Fig. 66

Now you will be annotating the holes. The program offers a special tool to place the hole annotation on the reference line. Hole annotation is formed on the basis of the template which describes the type of hole defined in the library of styles and standards. In this model, you have two holes: one threaded and one plain blind.

9. Add a hole annotation. On the **Annotate** tab, in the **Feature Notes** panel, click on **Hole and Thread** icon. Select the holes in cross section at the positions indicated by arrows in Fig. 66. Place the annotations like in Fig. 67a. Press **ESC** key to stop annotating.

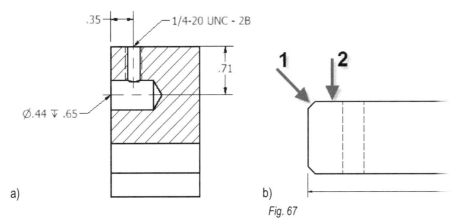

Fig. 67

In the end, you place a dimension of the chamfer using a special tool.

10. Add a dimension of the chamfer. On the **Annotate** tab in the **Feature Notes** panel, click on the **Chamfer** icon. Select the edge of the jaw in top view to place chamfer annotation, denoted by 1 in Fig. 67b. As a reference edge select the edge denoted by 2. Place a chamfer annotation as in Fig. 67a. Press **ESC** key to exit.

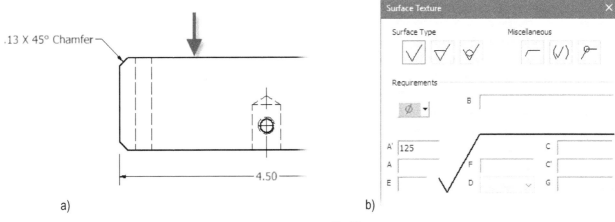

Fig. 68

The Autodesk Inventor 2021 software offers a comprehensive set of mechanical symbols that are required in the technical drawings. As an example, you could put the symbol of surface texture on the front face of the jaw.

11. Add a surface texture symbol. On the **Annotate** tab in the **Symbols** panel, click on the **Surface** icon. Select edge indicated by an arrow in Fig. 68a and press **ENTER** key. In the **Surface Texture** dialog box, enter a roughness value of **125** in the **A'** field, like in Fig. 68b. Click **OK**. Press **ESC** key to exit. The added a surface texture symbol is represented as shown in Fig. 69.

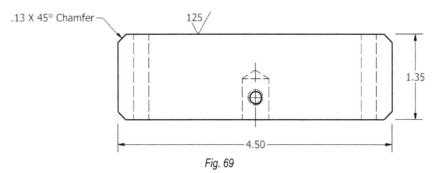

Fig. 69

The technical drawings of parts usually are complemented by a technical note. The Autodesk Inventor can use the **Text** tool to include notes about some technical detail. The list of notes can be numbered automatically.

12. Add a technical note. On the **Annotate** tab in the **Text** pane, click on **Text** icon. Select the location of the notes in the upper left corner of the sheet frame. In the **Format text** dialog box, keep the default text settings and enter three comments as shown in Fig. 70. Select all three rows and apply numbering option to the list of notes, indicated by the arrow. Click **OK** to finish.

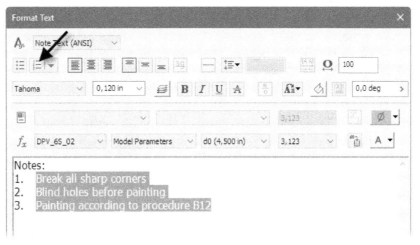

Fig. 70

The text of the technical notes will be presented as in Fig. 71. Press **ESC** key to finish.

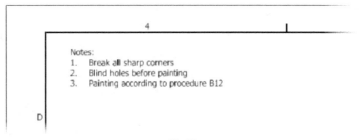

Fig. 71

You can assume that the technical drawing of the jaw is ready.

13. Save the file in folder **...\DesignOffice\Designs\DPV_6S**. By default, the program will suggest a name for the drawing file which will be the same name as the name of the part model file, which was used to create the first drawing view: **DPV_6S_02**. Extension of drawing file is **DWG**. Close drawing file.

End of exercise.

Exercise summary

You learned to model simple parts and making technical drawings of the parts. Now turn to the next degree of initiation - work in the assembly. In the next exercise, you will define an assembly file and create a new part in the assembly file: The Body. In addition, during the work, you will try to launch commands in a new way - using the right-click menu and the gesture function.

Exercise 3
Part modeling in the assembly file. Corps of the vise

In the exercise *Modeling of parts. Movable jaw*, on page 9, you created a model of the part in the single part environment, which allowed you to become familiar with the basic tools and the ways of modeling single parts. However, in the daily practice, the technique of mechanical devices design is based on the work in the assembly level - new parts are created directly in the assembly. Thanks to this approach you can improve the cooperation and matching of components.

In this exercise, you will create a new file of the main unit of a vise, and then in the assembly file, you will create the first component – the **Body** of the vise. In further exercises, you will insert the jaw and create other parts. In Fig. 72 a body of the vise is shown (which you will build in this exercise).

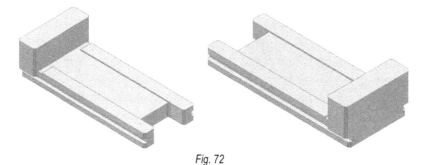

Fig. 72

In addition, in this exercise, you will initiate already-known tools in a different way than in the first exercise. You will use the right button menu and functions of gestures. Of course, all commands ran in a new way are also available in panels on tabs, but mastering an alternative way of launching the tools will allow you to choose a better way of operating in software.

1. Create an assembly file of the drill press vise. In the **My Home** window, click the **Assembly** button shown in Fig. 73. The program will create an assembly file based on **Standard.iam** template.

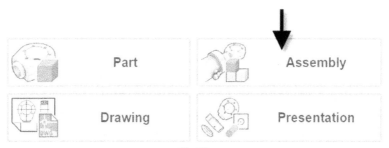

Fig. 73

The content of the screen in the assembly modeling mode is shown in Fig. 74.

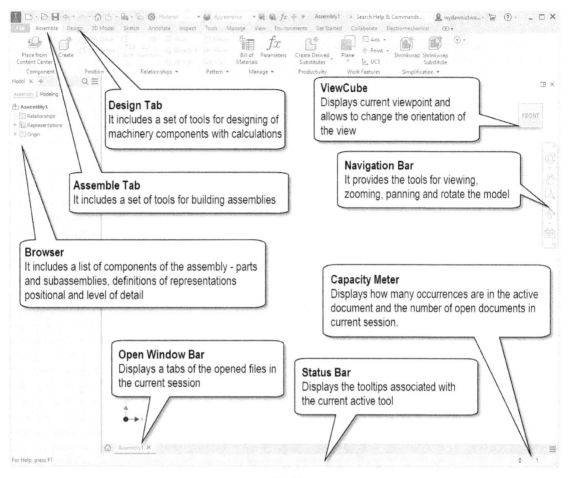

Design Tab
It includes a set of tools for designing of machinery components with calculations

ViewCube
Displays current viewpoint and allows to change the orientation of the view

Assemble Tab
It includes a set of tools for building assemblies

Navigation Bar
It provides the tools for viewing, zooming, panning and rotate the model

Browser
It includes a list of components of the assembly - parts and subassemblies, definitions of representations positional and level of detail

Capacity Meter
Displays how many occurrences are in the active document and the number of open documents in current session.

Open Window Bar
Displays a tabs of the opened files in the current session

Status Bar
Displays the tooltips associated with the current active tool

Fig. 74

The new assembly file is currently empty. You can insert existing components (parts or assemblies) or start modeling the new ones. Now, you will choose the second option - you will start modeling a new component, which will be the corps of the vise. This is the main component of our device, which will be also a reference to other created or inserted components.

2. Create a new part in the assembly file. On the **Assemble** tab in the **Component** panel, click on **Create** icon. In the **Create In-Place Component** dialog box, enter the name of a new part: **DPV_6S_01**. Make sure that the template for creating a new part is the **Standard.ipt** and define the localization of the new part's file in subfolder **DPV_6S**. The correct settings in this dialog box are shown in Fig. 75a.

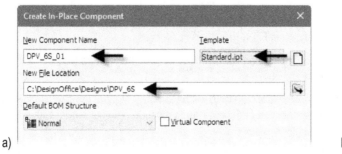
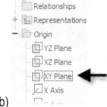

a)   b)

Fig. 75

Click **OK**.

The program is expecting you to indicate the plane of the new part, on which (by default) you will put a new part. You are expected to place the corps on the XY plane of the main assembly. Expand the **Origin** folder in the browser and click the **XY Plane**, indicated in Fig. 75b.

The program will create a new entry for new the part in the browser, as in Fig. 76a and is waiting for the user's decision. The contents of the screen are now the same as in single part modeling mode. Now, you can perform two operations: insert geometry from an external file as a base for further work or start creating a new part beginning with a sketch. You will start modeling of a new part from a sketch.

a)   b)

Fig. 76

 3. Create a new sketch. On the **3D Model** tab in the **Sketch** panel, click on **Start 2D Sketch** icon. The program displays a set of default planes of the coordinate system and is expected to indicate the plane to put on the new sketch.

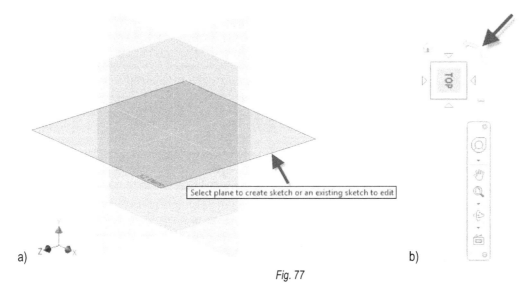

a)   b)

Fig. 77

Click **XZ Plane**, shown in Fig. 77a. By default, the program sets the view of the indicated sketching plane (option set in the **Application Options**). Make sure the **ViewCube** is set as in Fig. 77b. If necessary, turn the cube by clicking on the corresponding arrows shown in Fig. 77b.

The program will start the sketch mode (which you came across creating a model of a jaw). In the browser, all other items are grayed out, as in Fig. 76b.

Main plate (with dimensions of 9.95 x 4.00 inch) will be the first shape of the body. In this exercise, some commands will be run from the right menu button and the gestures menu to get you familiar with a new, faster way of launching commands.

 4. Draw a rectangle of the main body plate. Click the right mouse button and select the menu item **Two Point Rectangle**, as in Fig. 78a. Remember that in the right-click menu, the **Two Point Rectangle** command is "at 1.30 o'clock ". Use the following dimensions to draw the rectangle: **9.95 x 4.00 inch,** as in Fig. 78b.

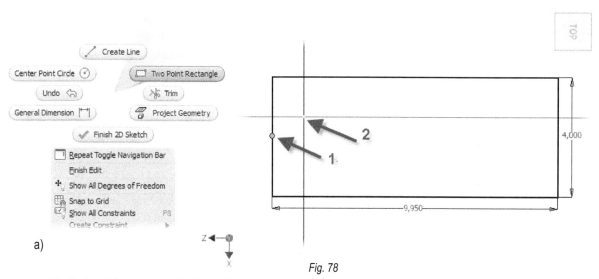

a)

Fig. 78

The body will be a symmetrical part. You set the center of the left shorter side of the rectangle at the center point of the coordinate system what will simplify facilitating the subsequent operations using the symmetry of the model.

6. Mate the midpoint of the side of the rectangle with a center point of the coordinate system. On the **Sketch** tab in the **Constrain** panel, click on **Coincident Constraint** icon. Select to constrain the midpoint of the short side of the rectangle, denoted by 1 in Fig. 78b, and then select the center point of the coordinate system, denoted by 2. Press **ESC** key to finish. Your sketch is ready.

7. Finish the sketch. Right-click and select **Finish 2D Sketch**. Remember that the finish sketch command is "**at 6.00 o'clock**". The program sets a sketch in isometric view.

8. Create a main plate of the body using extrusion. Right-click and select **Extrude**, as in Fig. 79a. Remember that the command for extrusion is located "**at 1.30 o'clock**".

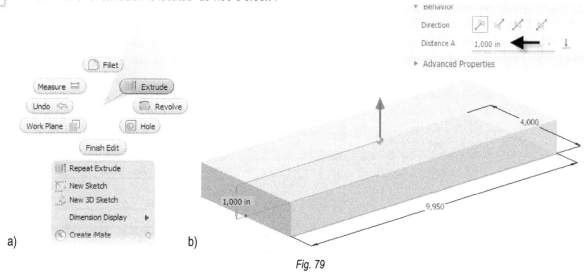

a)   b)

Fig. 79

Determine the height of extrusion per **1** inch in the positive direction of the Z axis, as in Fig. 79b. Click **OK**. to confirm.

The program has placed (in the browser) the first feature of the new part – **Extrusion1**.

Now, you will create a retaining wall of the corps, using the extrude command, but with the option to draw asymmetric. First, you need to create a sketch of the retaining wall.

9. Create a sketch of the retaining wall. Right-click on the top face of the plate, denoted by an arrow in Fig. 80a and select **New Sketch** in the menu, like in Fig. 80b. Remember that command for starting a new sketch is located "**at 6.00 o'clock**".

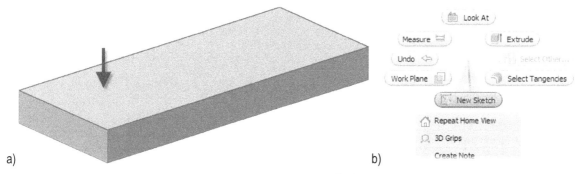

a)   b)

Fig. 80

The program will set a model in the view of the sketching plane. The sketch of retaining wall is a rectangle sized: **4.50 x 1.35 inch**. This time, run the command of drawing a rectangle using the function of gestures.

10. Run the command to draw a rectangle. Press and hold the right mouse button on the mouse and pull in the direction of "**at 1.30 o'clock**". Release the button. For a moment, the program displays the name of the command that is located in this place, as in Fig. 81a, and then runs the command **Two Point Rectangle**. Draw a rectangle using the following dimensions: **4.50 x 1.35 inch**, as in Fig. 81b.

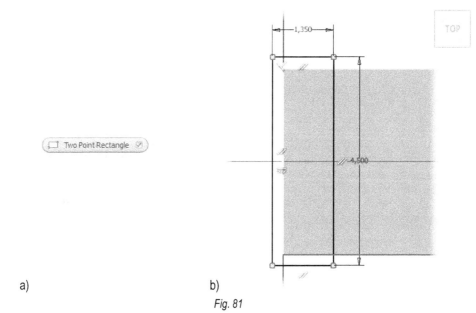

a)   b)

Fig. 81

11. Using the coincident constraint set the long side of the rectangle at the origin of coordinates as in Fig. 82a.

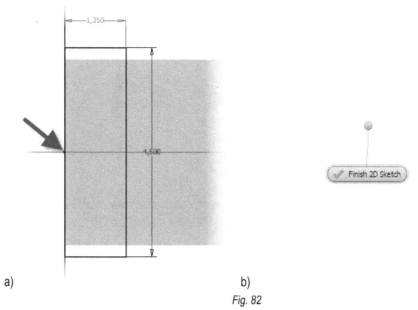

a) b)

Fig. 82

  12. Finish your sketch. Press and hold the right button of your mouse and pull towards: "**at 6 o'clock**". Release the button. For a moment, the program displays the name of the command that is located in this place, as in Fig. 82b. Then, it finishes the sketch and sets the model in isometric view.

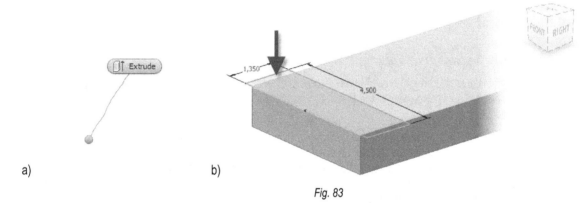

a) b)

Fig. 83

You will create a retaining wall by asymmetric extrusion in relation to the sketch plane.

  13. Create your retaining wall. Press and hold the right button of your mouse and pull towards: "**at 1.30 o'clock**". Release the button. For a moment, the program displays the name of the command that is located in this place, as in Fig. 83a, and then will run the command **Extrude**.

Sketch can be divided into several closed loops, which can be used to perform the operation. For this reason, the program does not select any loops but expects it to be identified by the user. Select the rectangle indicated in Fig. 83b.

In the **Extrude properties panel** select behavior option **Asymmetric**, as in Fig. 84a.

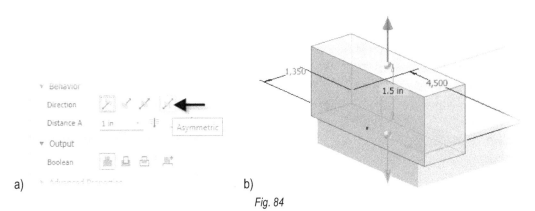

b)

Fig. 84

The program presents a preview of the extrusion in opposite directions, with different values of extrusions. In the filed **Distance A** enter a value **1.5 inch**, and in the filed **Distance B** enter the value **0.35 inch**, as in Fig. 85a.

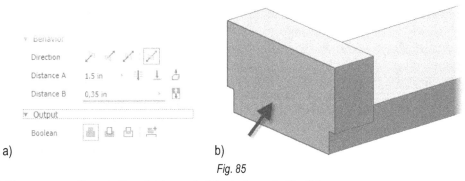

a)   b)

Fig. 85

Click **OK**. The program will create the retaining wall of the body, as in Fig. 85b.

Other items to create are grooves in which the jaw of the vise will be moving. You will create one groove, and the other will be created as a mirror copy of the first one. You will start by drawing the sketch of the groove on the lower, shorter wall of a plate of the corps.

14. Create a new sketch. Hover the cursor over the body's face indicated in Fig. 85b, on which you will place the sketch of the groove. Press and hold the right mouse button of your mouse and pull towards: "**at 6 o'clock**". Release the button. The program displays for a moment the name of the command that is located in this place, as in Fig. 86a then launches the sketch mode and sets the face parallel to the screen plane. If necessary, rotate the view, so that the sketching will be more comfortable.

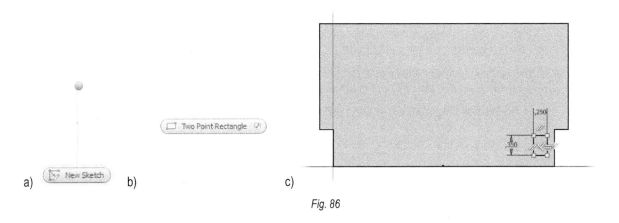

a)   b)   c)

Fig. 86

15. Draw a rectangle. Press and hold the right mouse button of your mouse and pull it towards: "**at 1.30 o'clock**". Release the button. The program displays for a moment the name of the command that is located in this place, as in Fig. 86b, and then runs the command **Two Point Rectangle**. Draw a rectangle using following dimensions: **0,25 x 0,35 inch**, as in Fig. 86c. Press **ESC** key to finish.

Your rectangle will now be aligned with the edge of the model using collinear constraints.

16. Set the two sides of rectangle collinear to the edges of a model. On the **Sketch** tab in the **Constrain** panel, click **Collinear Constrain** icon. Select the edge of the face and a left side of the rectangle denoted – respectively - 1 and 2 in Fig. 87a. After applying this constrain your rectangle is moved to the position as in Fig. 87b.

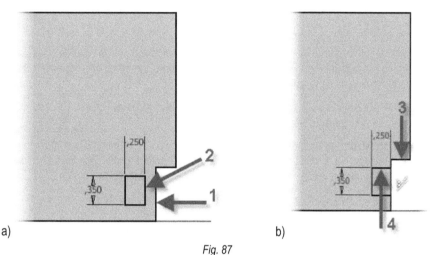

a)   b)

Fig. 87

Next, select the edge of the face and upper side of the rectangle denoted – respectively – 3 and 4 in Fig. 87b. After applying this constraint rectangle is moved to the position as in Fig. 88a. The sketch is **Fully Constrained** – see on the status bar. Press **ESC** key to finish.

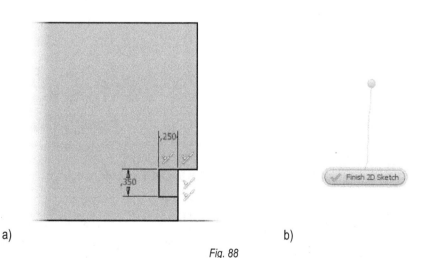

a)   b)

Fig. 88

17. Finish the sketch. Press and hold the right mouse button of your mouse and pull towards: "**at 6 o'clock**". Release the button. For a moment, the program displays the name of a command that is located in this place, as in Fig. 88b then finishes the sketch and sets the model in isometric view.

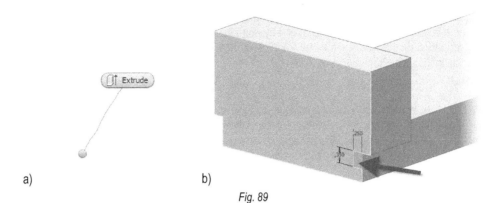

Fig. 89

18. Create a groove by extrusion. Press and hold the right mouse button on your mouse and pull towards: "**at 1.30 o'clock**". Release the button. For a moment, the program displays the name of a command that is located in this place, as in Fig. 89a then runs command **Extrude**.

In the existing sketch, you can distinguish several closed loops, which can be used to perform the feature. Select the center of your rectangle indicated by the arrow in Fig. 89b.

The program displays a preview of the result of extrusion using parameters from the previous operation. Set the parameters of the extrusion to create a throughout cut, selecting the appropriate options in **Extrude** properties panel select **Through All** which automatically turn on the option **Cut**, like in Fig. 90a.

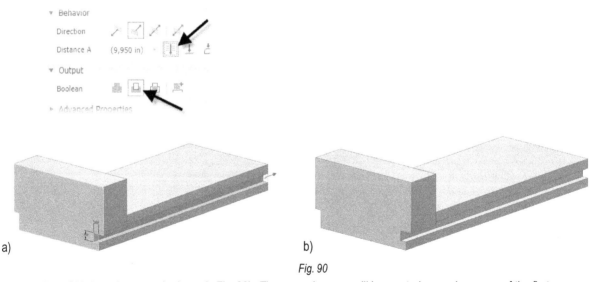

Fig. 90

Click **OK**. A ready groove is shown in Fig. 90b. The second groove will be created as a mirror copy of the first groove.

Mirrored feature reflects the changes that occur in the base feature, which means that the modifications of the first groove will be transferred to the groove formed as a mirrored feature. But it is an only one-way relationship. While editing the feature, which is a mirrored feature, the changes are not transferred to the base feature. To create a mirror, feature a plane of symmetry is required, which may be a flat wall of the model or a work plane.

19. Create a mirrored copy of the existing groove. On the **3D Model** tab in the **Pattern** panel, click on the **Mirror** icon. The program displays the **Mirror** dialog box with the **Features** button enabled by default, awaiting to determine the features contributing to the mirroring. Select a groove on the model or in the browser, by selecting **Extrusion3**.

After selecting features to create a mirrored copy, click the **Mirror Plane** button. Expand the **Origin** folder in the browser and select the **YZ Plane**, like in Fig. 91a. The program displays a preview of results, like in Fig. 91b.

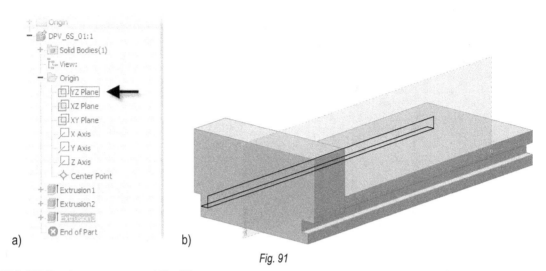

a)   b)

Fig. 91

Click **OK**. Ready grooves present Fig. 92.

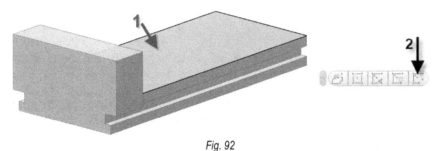

Fig. 92

Now you will create the notch in the upper part of the main plate of the body, which creates a guide rails for moving jaw. At this point, you will also use the **Extrude** tool for removing material. Therefore, you will need to create a sketch and perform an extrusion using a cut option. In addition, you will use another way of running a command to create a sketch.

20. Create a sketch for the guide rails. Click upper face of the plate, denoted by 1 in Fig. 92, and then click on **Create Sketch** icon in the mini toolbar, denoted by 2. Set the view of a model like in Fig. 93a.

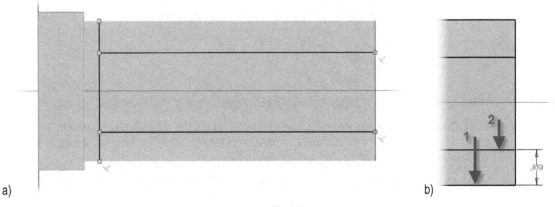

a)   b)

Fig. 93

21. Draw the lines shown in Fig. 93a. Pay attention to the lines as they need to be drawn parallel or perpendicular to the projected model edges and the starting points of lines starts on the projected edges of the model's faces.

22. Dimension the sketch. Press and hold the right mouse button of your mouse and pull towards: "**at 7.30 o'clock**". Release the button. For a moment, the program displays the name of the command that is located in this place. Place your dimension with a value of **0.85** inches between the first pair of lines indicated by the arrows in Fig. 93b.

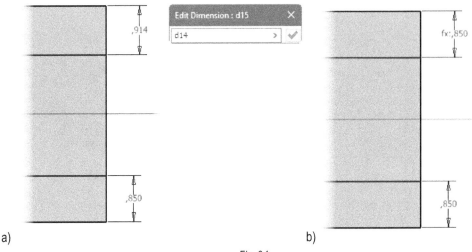

Fig. 94

The interval of the second pair of lines, located above the horizontal axis, should have the same value as the spacing of the first pair of lines. Insert dimension between the second pair of lines, as in Fig. 94a. Instead of typing **0.85** inches manually, click on an existing dimension of **0.850**, which will move the parameter name of the dimension to the dimension edit box, as in Fig. 92a (numbering of the parameters may be different than in the manual). Confirm new parameter in the **Edit dimension** edit box. From this moment, the second dimension is parametrically linked to the first dimension and is denoted by **fx:** as in Fig. 94b.

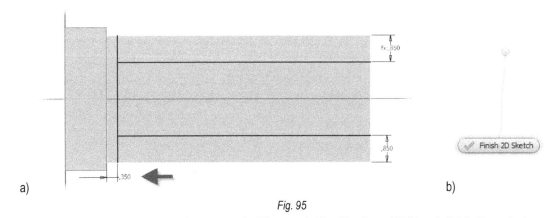

Fig. 95

Place dimension of value **0.35** inch between vertical lines, as in Fig. 95a. Press **ESC** key to finish dimensioning.

23. Finish the sketch. Press and hold the right mouse button of your mouse and pull towards: "**at 6 o'clock**". Release the button. For a moment, the program displays the name of the command that is located in this place, as in Fig. 95b then finishes the sketch and sets the model in isometric view.

24. Using the **ViewCube** set the model in the view like in Fig. 96a. To do this, click on the suitable corner of the cube.

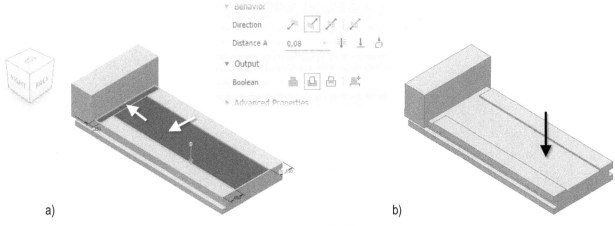

a)   b)

Fig. 96

25. Using the extrusion feature create a cutout that forms two rails and the channel. Press and hold the right mouse button of your mouse and pull towards: "**at 1.30 o'clock**". Release the button. For a moment, the program displays the name of the command that is located in this place, then runs command: **Extrude**. To carry out the cutting, select two loops simultaneously, as in Fig. 96a. Determine the depth of the cut to **0.08 inch**. Correct settings in extrusion properties panel are shown in Fig. 96a, whereas, a completed feature is shown in Fig. 96b.

26. Create a notch in which the screw support will be placed. Set sketch plane at the bottom of deepening denoted by an arrow in Fig. 96b. Draw a connecting line with the projected edges of the deepening. Determine the distance of the line from the edge to **1.25 inch**, as in Fig. 97a. Your ready notch is shown in Fig. 97b.

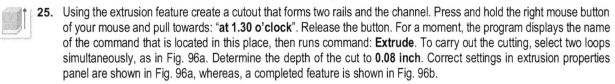

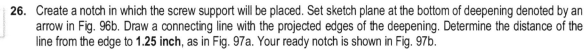

a)   b)

Fig. 97

27. Create a fillet radius of the two edges of a notch. On the **3D Model** tab, in the **Modify** panel, click on **Fillet** icon. Select edges indicated by the arrows in Fig. 98a. In the edit field of the upper mini toolbar, enter a value of fillet radius of **0.125** inches, like in Fig. 98b. The program shows you the preview of the fillet edges and the arrow on the last selected edge, which can be used to manually change the radius of the fillet, like in Fig. 98c.

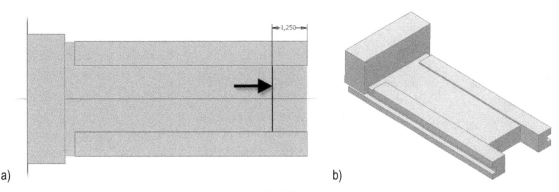

a)   b)   c)

Fig. 98

Click **OK** to confirm the feature. The last feature of the model that needs to be done is chamfer.

28. Create a chamfer of the almost all vertical edges of the body (using **0.125** inches). Illustration Fig. 99 shows the finished chamfers in two views.

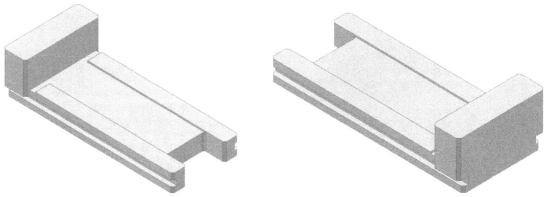

Fig. 99

The geometry of the part is essentially complete. Some changes might be introduced as the project develops. The final step, ending modeling part is to describe the parts by supplementing with iProperties. Before that, as in the case of the jaw model, you will write down the part file, as the program will automatically fill in the **Part Number** property.

29. Save the file (of the part). You are in the part edit mode, which means that the saving applies only to the part file.

30. Assign additional data to the part, and select material. In the browser, right-click on file: **DPV_6S_01:1** and select i**Properties** from a menu. In **DPV_6S_01 iProperties** dialog box, go to the **Project** tab and enter, in the appropriate fields, data presented in Fig. 100a.

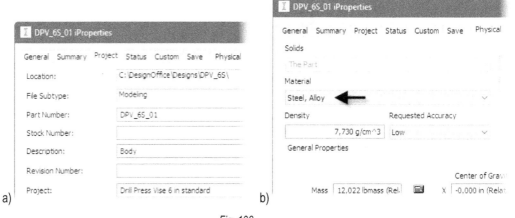

Fig. 100

Select your material. Go to the tab **Physical** and from **Material** drop-down list select **Steel, Alloy**. The program assigns the material and calculates the physical parameters of the parts that are visible on the **Physical** tab, as in Fig. 100b.

After selecting the material, click **OK**.

31. Again, save the file part. You are still in the editing part mode, which means that the saving applies only to the file part.

When you are working in the assembly file, in the part edit mode, you can see that other components are grayed out in the browser, as in Fig. 101a, which means that the active level of editing is, in this case, the **DPV_6S_01** component. To return to the assembly level you need to finish editing the body of the vise. This way, it will be possible to save an assembly file on your disk.

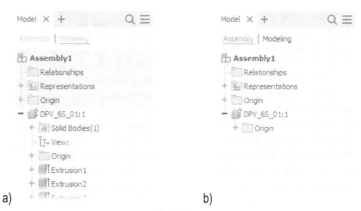

a)   b)

Fig. 101

32. Go to the main level of assembly. Right-click and select **Finish Edit** in the menu. Alternatively, press and hold the right button on the mouse and pull towards: "**at 6.00 o'clock**". Release the button. Another way to go back to previous editing level may be clicking **Return** icon in the **Return** panel on the **3D Model** tab.

In the browser, the transition to the level of the main assembly collapses edited component and turns off the graying of other components, as in Fig. 101b. As a result, you can easily see at what level you are editing.

33. Save assembly file in folder **...\DesignOffice\Designs\DPV_6S**. Filename: **DPV_6S_00.iam**.

34. Assign additional data to the assembly file. In the browser right-click on file **DPV_6S_00.iam** and select **iProperties** form menu. In the **DPV_6S_00 iProperties** dialog box, go to the **Project** tab and enter in the appropriate areas, data presented in Fig. 102.

Fig. 102

The **Part Number** field was filled as a result of the saving file. Therefore, it is important to save the assembly file with the correct name before filling data with iProperties. Click **OK**.

35. Save the final assembly file taking into account the input. Do not close the assembly model. End of exercise.

Exercise summary

You have learned how to start a new assembly file and how to create new parts in the assembly environment. You were introduced to a few new tools related to the modeling of parts and checked the various ways to run commands. In the next exercise, you will put a jaw into the assembly model of the vise (created earlier) and you will set its location using assembly constraints. Then, you will make some adjustments to the parts to fit each other better.

Exercise 4
Inserting and positioning parts in the assembly

In the previous exercise, you have created a file of the main assembly for the designed device and one of its parts - the body/corp. In the design of drill press vise, the body is the main structural component, which will be a reference for other components. In this exercise, you will put the movable jaw and you will determine its location. If necessary, you will correct the alignment of the parts in assembly. In Fig. 103a, an inserted jaw is shown.

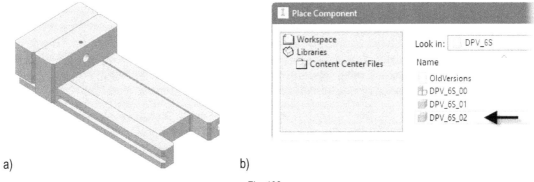

a)   b)

Fig. 103

 1. Insert the Jaw. On the **Assemble** tab in the **Component** panel, click on **Place** icon. In the **Place Component** dialog box, go to **DPV_6S** folder and select **DPV_6S_02** file, like in Fig. 103b, and click the **Open** button.

Place the jaw near the corps in empty space. By default, the program proposes inserting next occurrences of the same component. Press **ESC** key to finish. In Fig. 104a, an exemplary location of the jaw is shown. The inserted jaw can be freely rotated and moved – it can move freely in all degrees.

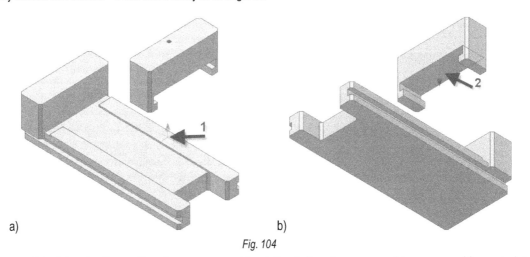

a)   b)

Fig. 104

To accurately determine the position of one component in relation to the other, you need to use assembly constraints. Each assembly constraints applied locks with one or more degrees of moving freely. Usually, to completely constrain the component, you should apply three constraints. In our model, you will apply constraints between the flat faces and work planes. You will begin with positioning the jaw on the rails of the body.

2. Locate the jaw. On the **Assembly** tab in the **Relationships** panel, click on **Constraint** icon. The program will display **Place Constraint** dialog box, where the default constraint is set to **Mate**, used mostly to constraint different types of combinations of planes, axes, edges, and points. The program is now waiting for you to select two objects to apply.

*The **Mate** constraint offers two solutions: **Mate** and **Flush**. A **Mate** solution you will apply when the directional arrows point the opposite directions. A **Flush** solution you will apply when the directional arrows point the same direction*

You will constrain two planes. As a first plane, select the guide rail plane, denoted by 1 in Fig. 104a. Next, rotate the model, and as a second plane select the bottom face of the jaw, denoted by 2 in Fig. 104b. The program will show a preview of the applied constraint with the default offset value of **0** inches.

Click **Apply**. The result of using this constraint may be as in Fig. 105a. The **Place Constraint** dialog box is still open.

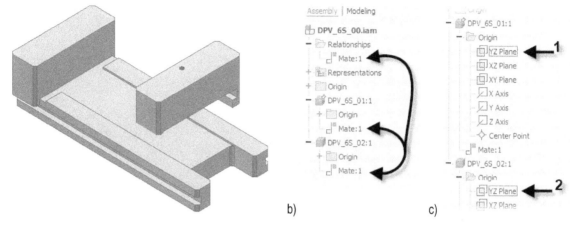

a)   b)   c)

Fig. 105

After approval, the browser will contain the symbol and the name of the constraint, e.g. **Mate:1**, in both constrained components, as shown in Fig. 105b. Additionally, the program collects applied constraints in **Relationships** folder.

The second constraint needs to be applied between the symmetry planes of the two parts: the body and the jaw. You will also check the influence of that type of solution used for the **Mate** constraint.

The program is again waiting for you to select the first plane to apply the constraint. Expand the **Origin** folder in the component **DPV_6S_01: 1** and click **YZ Plane**, denoted by 1 in Fig. 105c. To select the second plane, expand the **Origin** folder in the component **DPV_6S_02: 1** and click **YZ Plane**, denoted by 2. The default solution of **Mate** constraint is **Mate**, and the preview of the applied constraint should be as in Fig. 106a. It is important that the jaw's face and the retaining wall's face opposite of each other. This way, a hole on the back face of the jaw will be placed correctly.

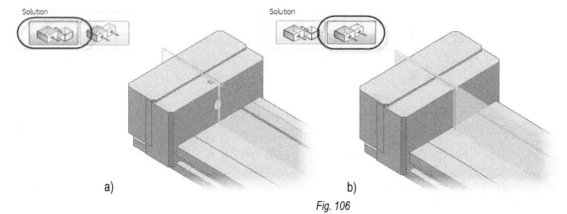

a)   b)

Fig. 106

Choosing the solution **Flush**, as in Fig. 106b will result in rotating of the face with a hole an about 180 deg, which is an incorrect position of the jaw – you need to return to the **Mate** solution.

Click **OK**. to confirm the constraint and for now, to close the **Place Constraint** dialog box.

*How to edit the assembly constraints? Just right-click in the browser on the name of constraint and click **Edit** in the menu. The program displays the **Edit Constraint** dialog box, which is similar to the **Place Constraint** dialog.*

How to quickly change the offset distance between constrained planes? Just double-click on the name of constraint in the browser and enter a new value in the editing dimension dialog box.

3. Move the jaw. Click on the jaw and hold the button on your mouse, then move it, what will move the jaw along the rail of the body. Note, that the jaw has only one degree of freedom: movement.

4. Set the model view as in Fig. 107a.

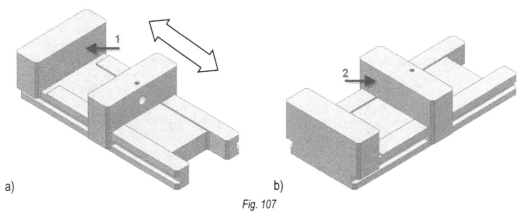

a)   b)

Fig. 107

5. Create the constraint which will control the offset of the jaw from the retaining wall. On the **Assemble** tab in the **Relationships** panel, click on the **Constrain** icon. The program displays **Place Constraint** dialog box and waits for you to select two planes to constrain.

As a first plane select face of the retaining wall, denoted by 1 in Fig. 107a. As a second plane select front face of the jaw, denoted by 2 in Fig. 107b. The program mates both planes, as in Fig. 108a. Click **OK** to confirm and stop applying constraints.

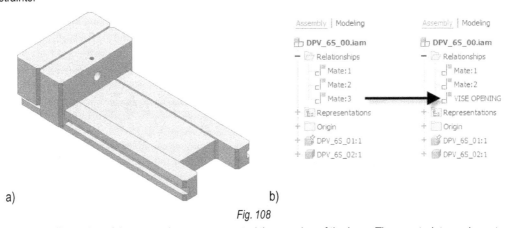

a)   b)

Fig. 108

By editing the offset value of the constraint, you can control the opening of the jaws. The constraints are important for the analysis of the kinematics of the assembly. Therefore, it is worth to add a tag in the browser, e.g. by changing its name, which will later on make it easier to find the constraint (for editing the parameter controlling the kinematics of the assembly).

6. Change the name of the constraint which controls an opening of the jaws. Click twice, individually with a little pause, in the position **Mate:3** to enter the edit name mode (or click and press the **F2** key). Type new name: **VISE OPENING**, as in Fig. 108b, and press **ENTER**.

You can assume that the jaw has been placed properly. Now, make sure that both parts are properly matched and make some adjustments, if necessary. You can see that the height of the retaining wall is greater than the height of the jaw, as shown in Fig. 109a.

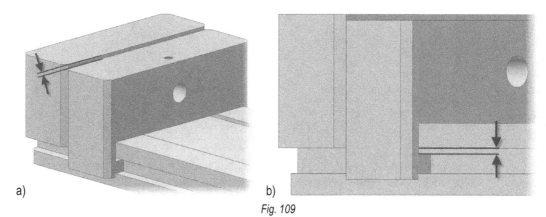

a)   b)

Fig. 109

In addition, you can notice, that the hooks of the jaw are not fit into grooves in the body, as shown in Fig. 109b. It is necessary to correct the fit. But before making any corrections you will make a measurement to ensure the implemented corrections.

 7. Measure the difference in height between the top face of the jaw and top face of the retaining wall. On the **Inspect** tab in the **Measure** panel, click the **Measure** icon. The program displays the **Measure** panel and is expected to indicate the objects to be measured. Select the top face of jaw and the top face of the wall, denoted by – respectively – 1 and 2 in Fig. 110a.

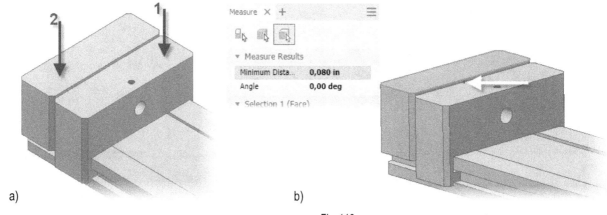

a)   b)

Fig. 110

The program displays a vector showing the distance and displays the measured value in the **Measure Distance** window, as shown in Fig. 110b. Close the distance measurement dialog. Now, you can be sure that the retaining wall is higher by **0.08** inch than the jaw. In a similar way, you will measure the gap between the hook of the jaw and the face of the groove.

Press **ESC**.

 8. Measure the height difference between the face of the hook of the jaw and the face of the groove. On the **Inspect** tab in the **Measure** panel, click on **Measure** icon. The program displays the **Measure** panel and is expected to indicate the object that needs to be measured. Select a top face of the hook denoted by 1 in Fig. 111a, then turn the model and select face of the groove denoted by 2 in Fig. 111b.

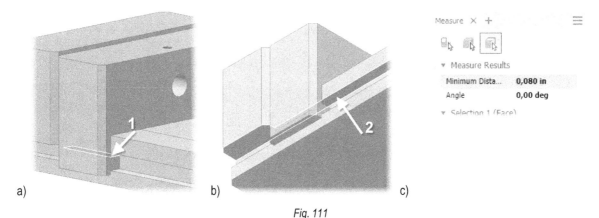

a)   b)   c)

Fig. 111

The program measured the distance equal to **0.08** inch, as shown in Fig. 111c. It seems like the undercut in the jaw is too high. It turns out, that the correction of the undercut in the jaw of 0.08 inch will solve both problems of matching. Now, close the distance measurement dialog.

To adjust the size of the undercut in the jaw, enter edit mode, find a feature which creates the undercut and change the dimension which controls the height of the cut. You can easily carry out this modification in the assembly file, which will be shown now.

9.   Enter the edit mode of the jaw. Double-click on the model of the jaw on the graphics screen or double-click **DPV_6S_02:1** in the browser. The program makes inactive components grayed out on the model and in the browser and provides you with a list of features forming the jaw, in the browser, as in Fig. 112a.

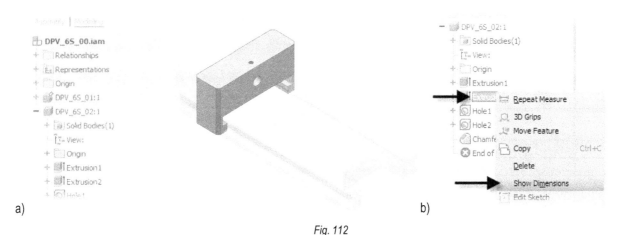

a)   b)

Fig. 112

10.   Drag the cursor over the features in the browser. Note, that when you move the cursor, the program distinguishes the feature of the 3D model, making it easier to find the feature responsible for the given shape.

11.   Change the height of the cut-out in the jaw. In the browser, right-click the position **Extrusion2** and select **Show Dimension**, as in Fig. 112b. The program will display the dimensions of the feature, as in Fig. 113a. Click twice on the size: **0.430** inches, marked with an arrow. In the edit box, enter the value: **0.350** inches and confirm.

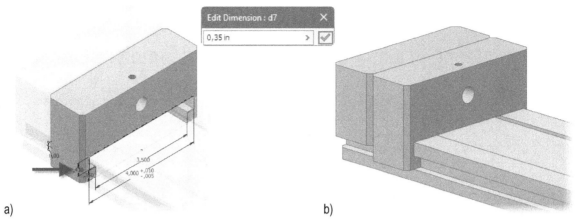

a)   b)

Fig. 113

A new value of dimension will be included after the model gets updated, or after returning to the main level of assembly. Because you do not have to make any other changes to the model of the jaw, you can immediately return to the main level of the assembly, which automatically updates the edited model.

12. Finish editing and return to the main level of the assembly. Click on **Return** icon on the right side of the **3D Model** tab. Now, the height of the retaining wall and the jaw are equal and the gap between the hook and the groove is removed, as shown in Fig. 113b.

13. Save the model. Do not close an assembly file.

The jaw already has its 2D technical drawing. The changes which were just done will be automatically applied to the drawing when you open it – the drawing is automatically updated at the time of its opening.

14. Open the file **DPV_6S_02.dwg**, located in the folder **... \Designs\DPV_6S**. This program will automatically update the geometry and dimensioning of your part. Updated view showing a notch in the jaw is presented in Fig. 114.

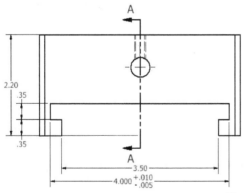

Fig. 114

15. Save and close the drawing file. Return to work with the 3D model. End of exercise.

Exercise summary

Now, you can place already existing components to the assembly and apply the basic constraints in order to determine the location of the inserted components relative to other components. Moreover, you know how to measure the distance between the planes and how to make changes in dimensions of the parts within the assembly level. In the next exercise, you will learn how to work in a cross–section of assembly and you will create a new part in the context of an assembly, in relation to existing parts. You will also use assembly constraints between the solid part and the part which is still a sketch.

Exercise 5
Part modeling in a cross-section of the assembly. Clamping screw

In this exercise, you will create a clamping screw. You will apply the technique of working in a cross-section of the whole assembly, which will help in creating important details. In the previous exercise, you have set the constraints between solid parts. Now, you will use other opportunities of applying constraints: before creating a 3D model of the clamping screw, you will apply constraints to set the correct position of the main sketch of the clamping screw. This will validate the screw design and help make some corrections before transforming it into the 3D solid model. In Fig. 115a, there is shown a sketch of the clamping screw which was set in the right position and Fig. 115b shows the finished clamping screw (rest of the parts are shown in the cross–section).

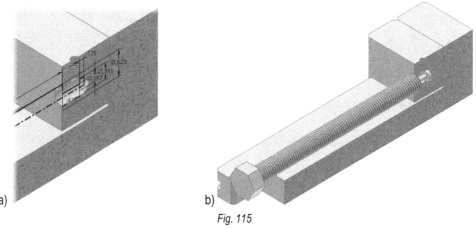

a)   b)

Fig. 115

In addition, by doing this exercise you will get familiar with new tools for sketching and solid modeling.

Designing of a new part – the clamping screw – you will start with turning on a cross-section of an assembly. The clamping screw should have a suitable shape of a front tip which will give you a possibility to use a fixing screw in order to prevent protrusion of the clamping screw from the jaw. As a result, you get the opportunity of loosening and clamping of the jaws using clamping screw. To make it easier to draw a sketch of the correct shape of the tip of the clamping screw, you can temporarily cut the whole assembly by plane, on which will be located the axis of the clamping screw. As an intersection plane, you will use a plane of symmetry of the jaw.

The first step is to set a new "home" view of **ViewCube**, which will help you to quickly obtain the desired setting model in 3D space.

1. Set a new, main view of the **ViewCube**. Assuming that the assembly file, saved in the previous exercise, is open, set the model view as in Fig. 116a, by clicking the appropriate corner of **ViewCube**.

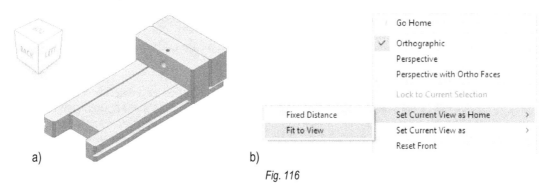

a)   b)

Fig. 116

Confirm this setting as the new main view. Right-click any wall of the **ViewCube**, and then select **Set Current View as Home> Fit to view**, as in Fig. 116b. From now on, clicking on the icon of a cottage, located above the **ViewCube**, will set a model in this view.

 2. Make a visual intersection of assembly model using the symmetry plane of the jaw. On the **View** tab in the **Visibility** panel, click on **Half Section View** icon. The program is waiting for you to select the section plane. Click **YZ Plane**, located in the **Origin** folder of the component **DPV_6S_02:1**, as in Fig. 117a.

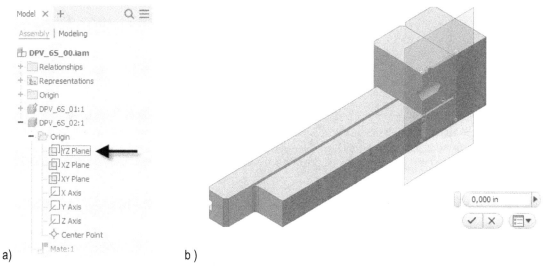

a)   b)

Fig. 117

The program will create a preview of the intersection of the assembly model as in Fig. 117b. In the edit field of a mini toolbar, confirm the offset value equal to **0** inches. A ready cross-section is presented in Fig. 118a.

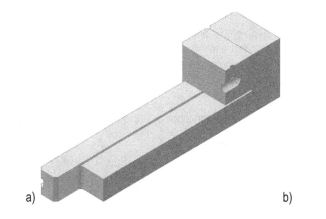

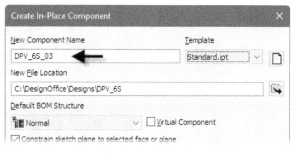

a)   b)

Fig. 118

 3. Create a new part in the assembly file. On the **Assemble** tab in the **Component** panel, click on **Create** icon. In the **Create In-Place Component** dialog box enter the file name of the new part: **DPV_6S_03**. Make sure that the template to create a new part is **Standard.ipt** and determine the location for the new part file in the folder **DPV_6S**. The correct settings in the dialog box are shown in Fig. 118b.

Click **OK**. The program is waiting for you to select the base plane for the new part. Click again **YZ Plane** of the component **DPV_6S_02:1**, located in the **Origin** folder, as in Fig. 117a. This program creates a new, empty component and is waiting for the decision of the user. Other components are grayed out, as in Fig. 119a.

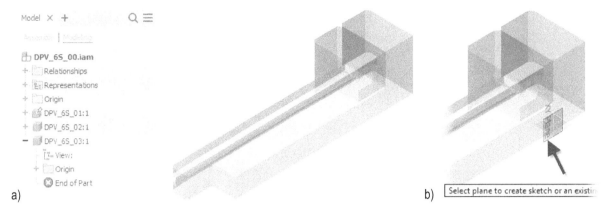

a)   b)   Select plane to create sketch or an existin

Fig. 119

4. Create the sketch of the first shape of the new part. In the **3D Model** tab, on the **Sketch** panel, click on **Start 2D Sketch** icon. The program displays a set of planes of the coordinate system of the new part and is expecting to indicate a plane to put the new sketch on. Click **XY Plane**, shown in Fig. 119b – if necessary, set the model in the main view. After selecting the plane, the program sets the model in a view as in Fig. 120.

Fig. 120

The clamping screw is a rotating part – you will form it by revolving the profile around an axis. For this purpose, the screw will use a sketch which is only half of the screw cross section and the axis of rotation. First, you will sketch the approximate profile of the screw, which then will be dimensioned to achieve the desired size of the screw. By working in the context of an assembly, and additionally, in the assembly cross–section, you can easily determine the shape of the tip of the screw, be seeing where the hole is placed for setting a screw, where the pressure plane is, etc.

5. Draw a sketch of the clamping screw, as in Fig. 121. All lines should be horizontal or vertical lines.

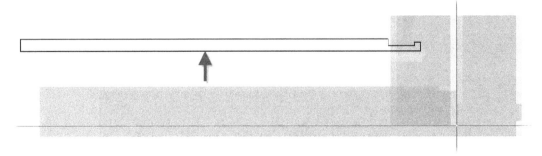

Fig. 121

6. Change the bottom line of the sketch from solid into centerline which makes it as an axis of rotation. Mark the line indicated by the arrow in Fig. 121 and then on the **Sketch** tab in the **Format** panel click on **Centerline** icon. This program will convert the indicated line into the center line, as in Fig. 122. This change will facilitate the dimensioning of the sketch of a rotating feature and accelerate the creation of the revolved part.

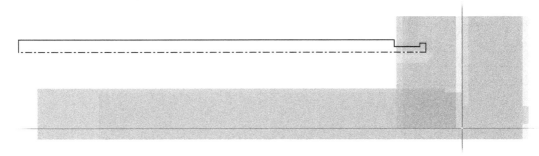

Fig. 122

7. Dimension the sketch. On the **Sketch** tab in the **Constraint** panel, click on **Dimension** icon. Place dimensions of the sketch elements, such as in Fig. 123. For diameter dimension you should indicate a horizontal line, then the axis of rotation and the position of the dimension. Dimension values can be given in decimal and fractional notation.

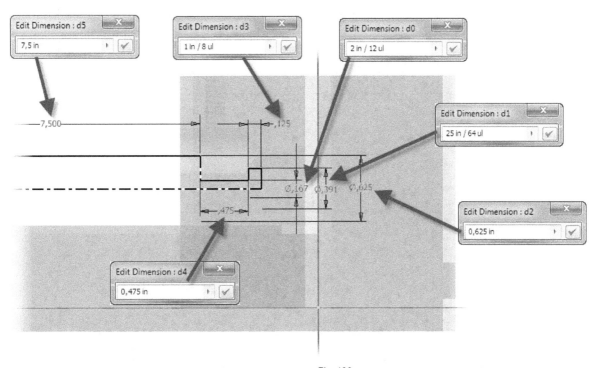

Fig. 123

In this exercise, specific dimensions have been given. However, when working in the context of an assembly, you can easily determine the size of the planned part, by making measurements of existing parts with which your new part will collaborate.

The current state of the dimensioned sketch is shown in Fig. 124.

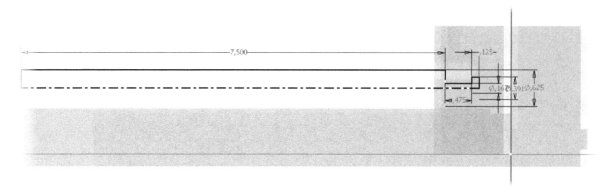

Fig. 124

To fully constrain the sketch, you are still missing two dimensions, which define the position of the sketch relative to the origin of the coordinate system. It is recommended to place the sketch of the revolving parts in one of the planes of the part's coordinate system and the rotation axis is one of the axes of the coordinate system. This makes using the symmetry plane in various situations much easier, without having to define additional planes. To set the sketch of the screw in the symmetry of the part coordinate system, move the starting point of the rotation axis of the sketch to the center point of the sketch coordinate system. For this purpose, you can use the coincident constraint.

8. Move the start point of the axial line into the center point of the coordinate system. On the **Sketch** tab in the **Constrain** panel, click on **Coincident Constraint** icon. Select the points indicated by arrows in Fig. 125a. The effect of the applied constraint is shown in Fig. 125b.

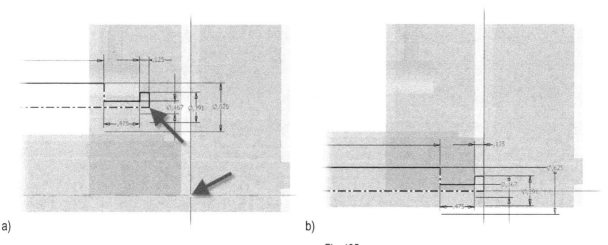

a)   b)

Fig. 125

9. Finish your sketch. Press and hold the right button of your mouse and pull towards: "**at 6 o'clock**". Release the button. For a moment, the program displays the name of the command **Finish Sketch 2D**.

10. Set the home view of a model. Click the house icon above the **ViewCube** to set the model view as in Fig. 126a.

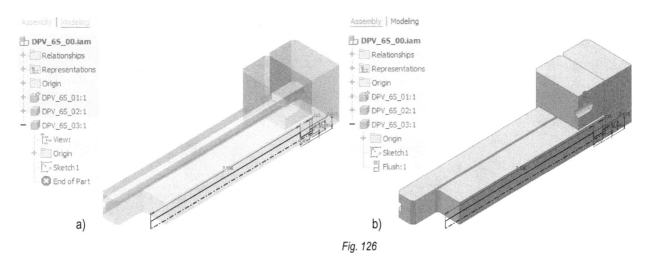

Fig. 126

The sketch of the screw, and therefore the entire screw, is located "inside" the body of the drill-press vise. Now, you will set the screw in the target position using the assembly constraints. However, before that, you must exit the edit part mode. You will return to the edit mode later to complete the model of the screw.

 11. Finish the edit of the screw and return to the level of the main assembly. Press and hold the right button of the mouse and pull towards: "**at 6 o'clock**". For a moment, the program displays the name of the command **Finish Edit**, and then finishes editing and returns to the level of the main assembly. The rest of the components are no more grayed out in the browser and on the screen, as in Fig. 126b.

When working in a cross-section mode you can also use assembly constraints, which will provide a precise orientation of components to each other. Now, you will set the target position of the clamping screw using the **Mate** constraint.

12. Place the screw in the target position. On the **Assembly** tag in the **Relationships** panel, click on **Constrain** icon. The program displays **Place Constraint** box, where the default constraint is set to **Mate** type, and **Mate** solution. The program is waiting for you to select two objects to constraint them.

You will constrain the bolt axis with the axis of the hole. As a first object, select the sketched axis of the screw, denoted by 1 in Fig. 127a. As a second object, select the axis of the hole in a jaw, denoted by 2. The program will display the axis of the hole when you hover on the cylindrical surface of the hole.

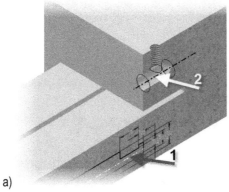
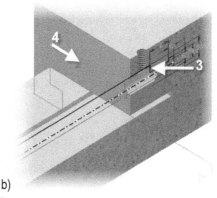

Fig. 127

After selecting the second object, the program will display the preview of the effect of using the constraint, aligning the screw axis to the axis of a hole. Click **Apply** to confirm the constraint. Now, the screw is positioned as in Fig. 127b.

The program is now waiting for you to select another pair of objects to constrain. You are expected to place the clamping surface of the screw on the face of the jaw. For this purpose, you will constrain the edge of the sketch, which will form the screw clamping surface after applying a revolve feature to the face of the jaw.

The **Mate** type of constraint offers the possibility of constraining the sketched line and the plane. This constraint allows the sketched line to slide on the face of the jaw.

As a first object select the edge, denoted by 3 in Fig. 127b. As a second object, select the plane of the jaw face, denoted by 4. The program displays a preview of the applied constraint. This is the last constraint - click **OK**. in the **Place Constraint** dialog box. Correctly positioned sketch of clamping screw is shown in Fig. 128a.

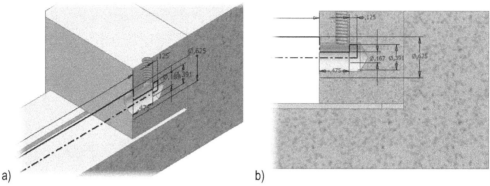

a)   b)

Fig. 128

Set model view, as in Fig. 128b. In that kind of a view, it is easy to make sure if the sketch of a screw is appropriately positioned in relation to other parts of the assembly, and if it has the proper dimensions.

13. Restore the main view of the model. Click the house icon above the **ViewCube** or press **F6**.

Now, you will finish the screw design. You will go back into edit mode and create a revolve feature, based on the existing sketch. This feature creates the main shape of the clamping screw. Then, you will create a hexagonal head of a screw, which will allow you to clamp the jaws with the key.

14. Enter the edit-part mode. In the browser, click twice the component **DPV_6S_03:1** or double-click the sketch of the screw in the graphics window. The program makes other assembly components, on the screen and in the browser, becomes grayed out.

15. Create the screw by revolving the sketch. On the **3D Model** tab in the **Create** panel, click on **Revolve** icon. Alternatively, you can use the function of the gestures by dragging pressed, right button of the mouse towards: "**at 3 o'clock**".

Since there is only one sketch which forms a closed loop, and one of the lines is an axial line, the program automatically selects the loop and the axis for performing a revolve feature, as in Fig. 129a.

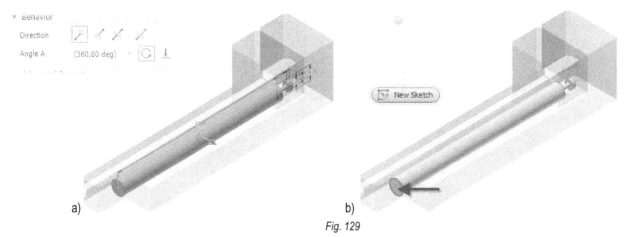

a)   b)

Fig. 129

Confirm the operation. Click **OK**. A ready revolved feature is shown in Fig. 129b.

The last element of the clamping screw is a hexagonal head, which will be created by applying the extrude feature. As a first step, you should create a sketch plane for the sketch of a head.

16. Create a sketch of the screw head. Move the cursor towards the plane of the base of the cylinder, denoted by the arrow in Fig. 129b to mark it and then press the right button and pull towards: "**at 6 o'clock**". For a moment, the program displays the name of the command **New Sketch**, then starts the sketching mode on that plane and sets a view as in Fig. 130a.

17. Draw a hexagon. On the **Sketch** tab in the **Create** panel, click on **Polygon** icon. In the **Polygon** dialog box, select **Circumscribed** type and make sure that you have number **6** in the edit field. As a center point of polygon choose the center-point of the projected circle, and next stretch the polygon, like in Fig. 130a.

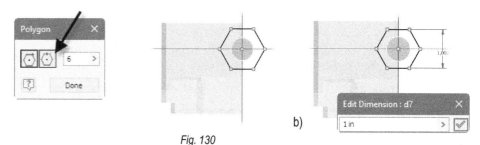

a)   b)

Fig. 130

Click **Done** to complete the polygon.

18. Dimension the polygon. On the **Sketch** tab in the **Constrain** panel, click on **Dimension** icon. Alternatively, you can use the gestures' function by pressing the right button of the mouse and dragging it towards: "**at 7.30 o'clock**". Set the size of the polygon to **1.0 inch**, by inserting a dimension between two parallel sides, as in Fig. 130b.

19. Finish the sketch. Press and hold the right button of the mouse and pull towards: "**at 6 o'clock**". Release the button. For a moment, the program will display the name of the command, then will finish the sketch and set the model in isometric view like in Fig. 131a.

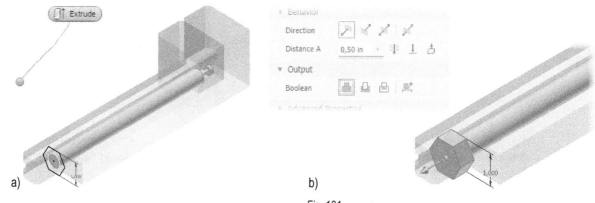

a)   b)

Fig. 131

20. Create a hex head using the extrude feature. Press and hold the right button of your mouse and pull towards: "**at 1.30 o'clock**". Release the button. For a moment, the program will display the name of the command that is located in this place, as in Fig. 131a then will run command **Extrude**.

There are two loops in the sketch. Select both loops, so that program creates the preview of a hexagonal head. Set extrusion distance, or height of the screw head, to **0.50 inch**. The correct settings are shown in Fig. 131b.

Click **OK**. to confirm. Ready bolt's head shows Fig. 132a.

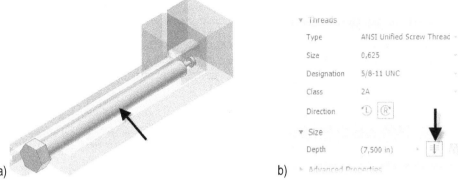

a)   b)

Fig. 132

The last element of the screw design is a screw thread. You will create a screw thread on the entire length of the cylindrical surface using 0.625 inches.

21. Create a thread. On the **3D Model** tab in the **Modify** panel, click on **Thread** icon.

The program displays a **Thread properties** panel with the enabled **Face** button, waiting for you to select a surface on which the thread will be placed. Make sure that the **Full Depth** option is on. Select the cylindrical surface indicated by the arrow in Fig. 132a. The program retrieves the cylinder diameter and proposes a thread **5/8-11 UNC**, which can be read on the **Threads** section, as in Fig. 132b. Click **OK**. A finished screw thread is shown in Fig. 133.

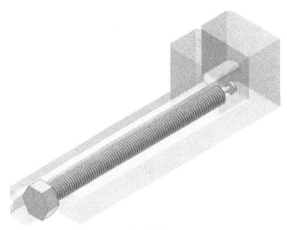

Fig. 133

You have finished the design of a clamping screw. The final step is to describe the parts by supplementing them with iProperties. Before that, as in the previous models, you will write down the part file, as the program will automatically fill in the **Part Number** property.

*In this exercise, you have learned how to create new features: **Revolve** and **Thread**. Their icons in the browser determine the type of the item. Like for the previously known features, to edit these features just right-click on the item in the browser and select **Edit Feature**.*

22. Save the file. Click **Save** icon in quick access toolbar. The name and location of the file were set on the beginning of this exercise in the **Create In-Place Component** dialog box.

23. Assign additional data to the part, and select material. In the browser right-click on file name **DPV_6S_03:1** and select **iProperties** from a menu. In the **DPV_6S_03 iProperties** dialog box go to the **Project** tab and enter in the appropriate fields, the data presented in Fig. 134a.

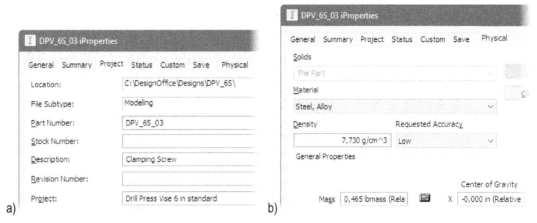

a)   b)

Fig. 134

Select your material for the part. Go to the **Physical** tab and from **Material** drop-down list select **Steel, Alloy**. The program will assign the material and calculates the physical parameters of the part that is visible on the **General Properties**, as in Fig. 134b.

After selecting the material, click **OK**.

Now, you can finish edit, return to the main level of the assembly, and disable the cross-section of the assembly.

24. Finish edit the clamping-screw model. On the **3D Model** tab in the **Return** panel, click on **Return** icon. Alternatively, press and hold the right mouse button and pull it towards: "**at 6.00 o'clock**". Release the button. Return to the level of the main assembly collapses edited component and turn off gray out of other components in the browser and on the graphics screen. After finishing editing, the screw gets also cut by the cutting plane of the assembly, as in Fig. 135a.

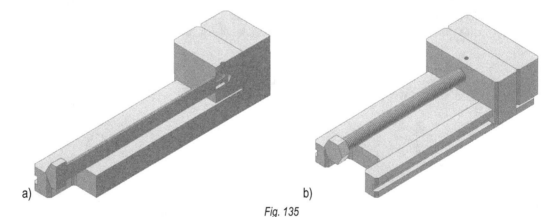

a)   b)

Fig. 135

25. Turn off the cross-section of the assembly. On the **View** tab, in the **Appearance** panel, click on **End Section View** icon. Now, the model of the vise looks like in Fig. 135b.

26. Save the final assembly file. Do not close the assembly model. End of the exercise.

Exercise summary

*In this exercise, you have learned about new modeling tools and methods of working in the assembly environment. You were introduced to the new possibilities of applying **Mate** type assembly constraints. In the next exercise, you will do the last part of the vise. The new part will be built using the edge projection technique. You will also check how the new part will adopt when you edit the referenced edges.*

Exercise 6
Modeling of the adaptive part in assembly. Screw support

In this exercise, you will learn about using the technique of modeling parts in the context of assembly, utilizing projection edges of other parts to the active sketch currently modeled part. Projected geometry can be associative to the original geometry that is projected – when the parent sketch is modified then the projected geometry will update itself to reflect the changes. In addition, the projection edge causes constraint of the new part relative to parts from which geometry has been projected. In this exercise, you will design support for clamping screw, based on the edges of the body, highlighted in Fig. 136a. Ready support is shown in Fig. 136b.

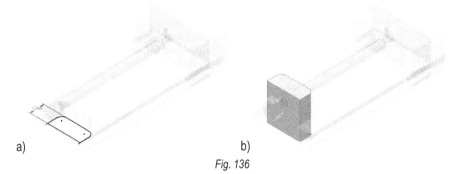

a)   b)

Fig. 136

 1.   Create a new part in the assembly file. Assuming, that the assembly file is open, on the **Assemble** tab in the **Compo-nent** panel, click on **Create** icon. In the **Create In-Place Component** dialog box, enter the name of a new part **DPV_6S_04**. Make sure that the template for creating a new part is **Standard.ipt** and define the localization a new part's file in subfolder **DPV_6S**. Correct settings in this dialog box are shown in Fig. 137a.

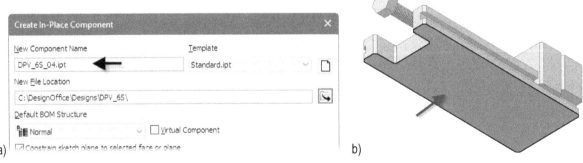

a)   b)

Fig. 137

Click **OK**. The program is now expecting you to indicate the plane for the new part. Rotate the model and select the bottom face of the body, indicated by the arrow in Fig. 137b. This program creates a new, empty component and is waiting for the next decision of the user. Rest of the components become grayed out.

2.   Create a new sketch. On the **3D Model** tab in the **Sketch** panel, click on **Start 2D Sketch** icon. The program displays a set of default planes of the coordinate system and is expected to indicate the plane to put on the new sketch. Set the model so that its bottom face is visible and then click on the **XY Plane** as shown in Fig. 138.

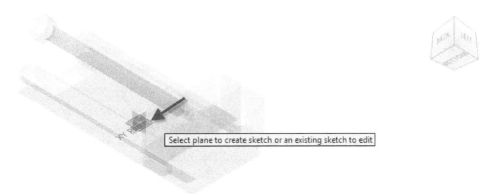

Fig. 138

The program will set the view on the new sketching plane. In this example, the geometry for your new sketch will be obtained by projecting the edges of a cut-out in the body and adding one extra line.

3. Create sketch geometry by projecting the edges. On the **3D Model** tab in the **Create** panel, click on the **Project Geometry** icon. Select five edges of cut-out indicated by the arrows in Fig. 139a.

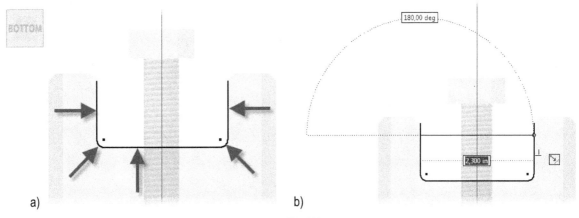

a)   b)

Fig. 139

4. Complete the sketch. Create a close profile by drawing a line connecting two projected edges, as shown in Fig. 139b. If you draw in an isometric view, make sure that the program displays a perpendicularity symbol and the line starts and ends on existing edges.

5. For the new line, set the offset from the opposite parallel line. Place following dimension: **1,00 in**, shown in Fig. 140a.

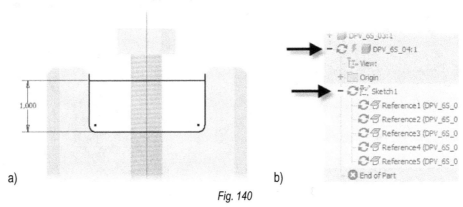

a)   b)

Fig. 140

After applying this dimension your sketch becomes fully constrained. The size of the remaining elements of your sketch is controlled by the sizes of elements from which the edges were "borrowed". If you attempt to add another dimension, it will lead to a display of the message indicating that the sketch is over–constrained. However, if you add this redundant dimension, it will be converted into the drive dimension and it will be presented in parentheses.

6. Finish your sketch and then set the model in home view, by clicking the house icon above the **ViewCube**.

Projecting the edges of the other parts into the sketch of active part, automatically converts an active, ordinary part into the **adaptive** part. Note, that in the browser, the adaptability symbol appears before the icon **DPV_6S_04:1**, and before the icon of **Sketch1**, as in Fig. 140b, which means that this part is adaptive. In the explication of **Sketch1**, there are five projected adaptive edges of the vise body. The right button options allow you to turn off the adaptability, to end connection with the reference edge or to delete the projected edge.

7. Create the main shape of the part using the extrusion feature. This program will automatically select the closed profile for extrusion and propose the distance of extrusion equal to the last-entered value. To determine the correct height of extrusion you will measure the distance between the base of a vise and the top face of a jaw.

Measure the height of the draw for extrusion. Click the arrow icon on the right side of the **Distance A** field, shown in Fig. 141a, then click on **Measure** in a menu.

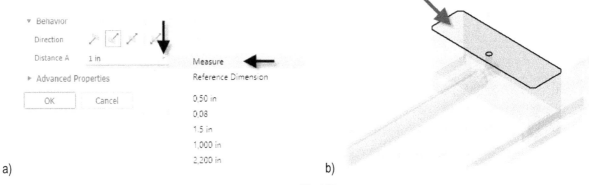

a)   b)

Fig. 141

Select the top face of the jaw, indicated by the arrow in Fig. 141b. Next, rotate the model and select the bottom face of the base, indicated by an arrow in Fig. 142a.

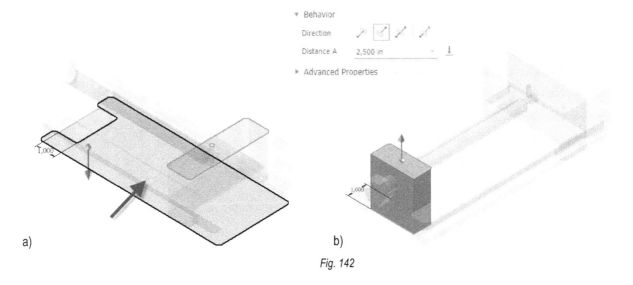

a)   b)

Fig. 142

The program will measure the distance and will put the result in the edit field. Make sure that the measured distance and draw direction are as shown in Fig. 142b. Click **OK**. Ready extrusion feature is shown in Fig. 143a.

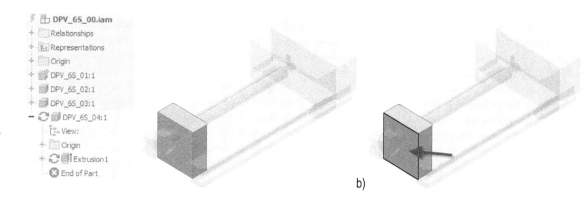

a)   b)

Fig. 143

Note, that adaptability icon has also appeared before **Extrusion1** feature icon in the browser, which means that this shape is adapt itself to the changes caused by projected geometry.

Now, you will create a threaded hole for the clamping screw. In order to precisely locate the hole, you will project the edge of the cylindrical portion of the screw. The center point of the projected circle will be indicated by the point of insertion of the hole. You will start by creating a sketching plane.

  8. Create a sketching plane on the face indicated by the arrow in Fig. 143b. The program sets the view for the sketching plane, as in Fig. 144a.

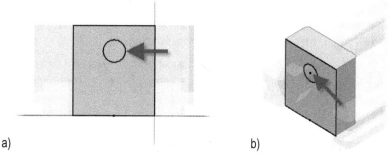

a)   b)

Fig. 144

  9. Project the circular edge of the screw. On the **3D Model** tab in the **Create** panel, click on the **Project Geometry** icon. Move the cursor into the area of the screw head, which will result in displaying different circular edges of the bolt. Click an edge with the largest diameter, indicated by the arrow in Fig. 144a.

  10. Finish sketch after circular edge projection. The program sets the model again in an isometric view.

  11. Create a threaded hole. On the **3D Model** tab in the **Modify** panel, click on **Hole** icon. The program displays a **Hole** properties panel and is waiting to select a location of the new hole. Select the center point of the projected circle, indicated in Fig. 144b.

Then, in the hole properties panel, shown in Fig. 145a, turn on the option to create a tapped hole, denoted by 1, select the standard ANSI (2), with a diameter size of **0.625** inches (3), threaded on full depth (4), through all (5).

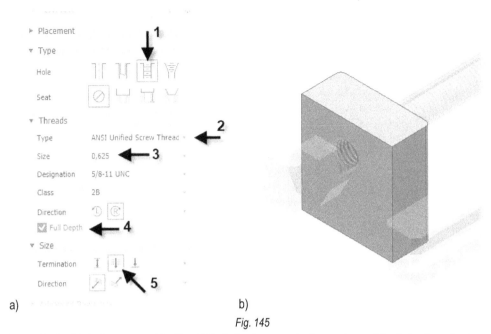

a)   b)

Fig. 145

Click **OK**. A finished hole is presented in Fig. 145b. In the browser, before an icon of the hole, there is also a symbol of adaptively. In this case, the location of the hole may be adapted to change the position of the projected circle.

You can assume that at this moment the expected shape of the new part was achieved and you can finish modeling it. Just complement the properties and the support for clamping screw becomes complete.

12. Save the part file. Click **Save** icon in quick access toolbar. The name and location of the file were set at the beginning of this exercise in the **Create In-Place Component** dialog box.

13. Assign additional data to the part and select material. In the browser right-click on file name **DPV_6S_04:1 1** and select **iProperties** form menu. In the **DPV_6S_04 iProperties**, dialog box goes to the **Project** tab and enter in the appropriate fields, the data presented in Fig. 146a.

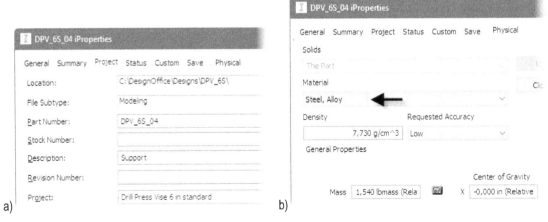

a)   b)

Fig. 146

Select material for the part. Go to the tab **Physical** and from **Material** drop-down list select **Steel, Alloy**. The program assigns the material and calculates the physical parameters of the parts that are visible in the **Physical** tab, as in Fig. 146b. Click **OK**.

Now you finish the edit by returning to the main level of the assembly.

14. Finish editing the clamping screw support model. On the **3D Model** tab in the **Return** panel, click on **Return** icon. Alternatively, press and hold the right mouse button and pull it towards: "**at 6.00 o'clock**". Release the button. The transition to the level of the main assembly collapses edited component and turn off grays out of other components in the browser and on the screen. The assembly model is now represented as in Fig. 147.

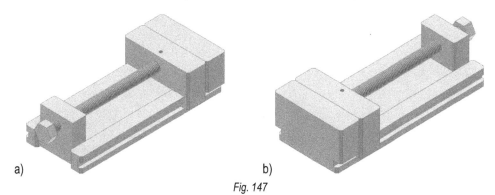

Fig. 147

Now you will check how the adaptability of parts works. You will change the value of the fillet radius of the cut-out in the body of the vise, which should also result in a change of the fillet radius in the support for clamping screw.

15. Set the model in view like in Fig. 147b.

16. Enter edit mode of the body. Click twice on the screen or in the browser, in the body (part: **DPV_6S_01**). The program makes other components grayed out, as shown in Fig. 148a.

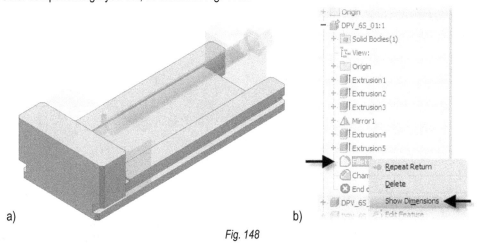

Fig. 148

17. Change the value of the fillet radius. In the browser, right-click **Fillet1** and in the menu select **Show Dimensions**, like in Fig. 148b. The program displays the value of the radius dimension, as in Fig. 149a.

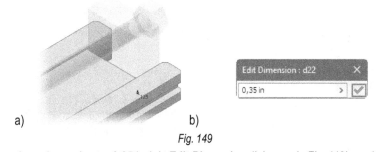

Fig. 149

Click twice in dimension value and enter **0.35** inch in **Edit Dimension** dialog, as in Fig. 149b, and confirm.

---

18. Update the model. Click on **Global Update** icon, located in the quick access toolbar, which will update the fillet radius of the body and then updates fillets in a model of the clamping screw support.

19. Finish editing the body and return to the main level of the assembly. Click on **Return** icon. Returning to the level of the main assembly collapses edited component and turning off grays out of other components in the browser and on the graphics screen. The fillet radius change is now visible on the model of support of clamping screw, like in Fig. 150a.

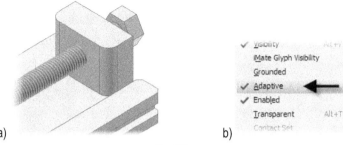

a)   b)

Fig. 150

When you are on the main level of assembly, note that the support clamping screw part is fixed - it cannot be moved in any direction. This behavior is part of adaptive, which is caused by projecting the edges of the body. You can easily disable adaptivity of parts, which will restore the degrees of freedom and prevent automatically adjusting the geometry of the part when the geometry of reference has been changed. After turning off the adaptivity you can add the constraints in the normal way to correctly locate the part in the assembly.

20. Turn off the adaptivity of part. Click the right mouse button in support of clamping screw part, in the browser (**DPV_6S_04**) or on the screen and click **Adaptive** in the menu, as in Fig. 150b, to uncheck the option. This also removes the symbol of adaptivity in the browser.

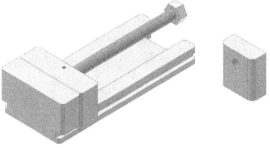

Fig. 151

After turning off the adaptivity you can freely move the support clamping screw, as in Fig. 151b. The support "slides" along the surface of the base plane of the body, as we used the **Mate/Flush** constraints, which was set at the moment of creating the support part.

21. Restore adaptivity of the part. Click the right mouse button in support of clamping screw, in the browser (**DPV_6S_04**) or on the screen and in the menu that appears, click **Adaptive**, which enables the option. The support clamping screw "snaps" into its origin place, and in the browser again appears the adaptivity icon next to **DPV_6S_04** part.

22. Save the final assembly file and edited parts. Do not close the assembly model. End of the exercise.

Exercise summary

You've learned a new technique for modeling parts in the context of the assembly, based on the geometry projection and you have obtained basic information about the adaptivity of the parts. In the next exercise, you insert the standard, retaining screw from the Content Center library and fix the support of clamping screw with the body using a bolted connection.

Exercise 7
Inserting standard part and creating a bolted connection

In previous exercises, you designed all the parts that should be made for the project of our Drill Press Vise. In each mechanical design there are standard parts that are used, which usually are purchased. Autodesk Inventor 2021 offers an extensive library of standard parts, named Content Center, from which you can insert ready-made standard parts.

In addition, the program offers specific utility functions that perform typical machine elements, for example, bolted connection. The components of the bolted connection can also be downloaded from the Content Center. In this exercise, you will insert the standardized set screw from Content Center and you will create a bolted connection which will fix the support for clamping screw with the body. In Fig. 152 an inserted set screw and a bolted connection is shown.

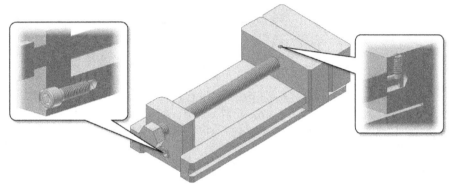

Fig. 152

The set screw will be inserted into an existing hole in the jaw, while the tool for generating bolted connection will perform the necessary holes in the parts being assembled together, in the body and in the support. You will start with the insertion of a set screw into the existing hole.

 1. Insert the set screw from the Content Center. Assuming that you have an open model of the assembly, saved in the previous exercise, in the **Assemble** tab, in the **Component** panel, click on **Place from Content Center** icon. The program displays a **Place from Content Center** dialog box. On the left, there is a structure of the category of the standard parts included in the Content Center. Expand the category **Fasteners**, further **Bolts**, and **Set Screws**. Locate the screw **Slotted Headless Set Screw - Dog Point - Inch**, indicated in Fig. 153.

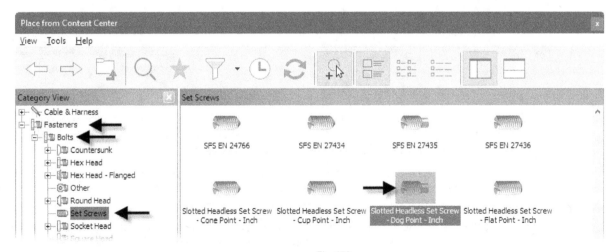

Fig. 153

Double click the screw highlighted in Fig. 153. As a default, the program offers the option of coupling the diameter of the screw to the indicated hole. But first, a preview of default set screw is displayed next to the cursor, as in Fig. 154a.

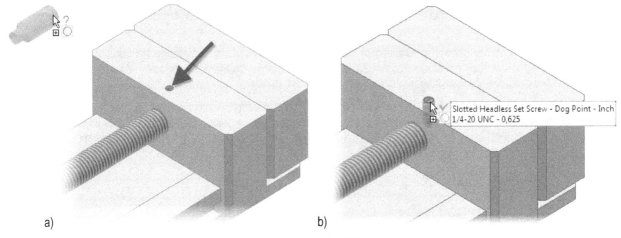

a)   b)

Fig. 154

You want to insert a screw into the hole **1/4 - 20 UNC** with a length of **0.625** inches. Move the cursor to the edge of the hole indicated by the arrow in Fig. 154a. The program detects the diameter of the hole and places the preview of a set screw in a hole, with a suitable diameter, as in Fig. 154b. Click the edge of the hole to confirm the location and diameter of the screw.

Now the program displays an arrow that allows you to determine the length of the screw. If necessary, pull the arrow so that the description of **1.4 - 20 UNC - 0.625** is shown as in Fig. 155a.

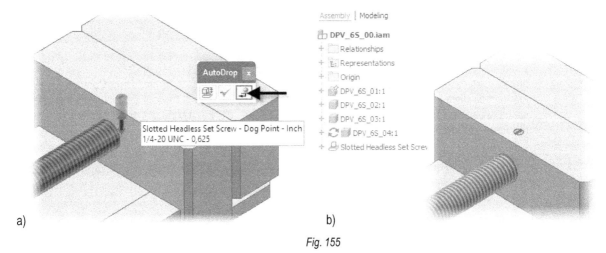

a)   b)

Fig. 155

Submit screw by clicking **Place**, indicated by the arrow in Fig. 155a. This button ends the operation. The inserted screw is shown in Fig. 155b. In the browser, the part placed from the Content Center library has its own icon designation which clearly identifies the type of component – standard part, purchased.

Now you will execute a bolted connection between the support of clamping screw and the body. You will use of screw **Hexagon Socket Head Cap Screw 3/8 - UNC** and you will make a hole with a counterbore in the support of clamping screw.

2. Insert the bolted connection. In the **Design** tab, in the **Fasten** panel, click on **Bolted Connection** icon. The program will display a **Bolted Connection Component Generator** dialog box, in which you will determine the initial options.

From the **Placement** list, select location **Linear**, in the **Type** section select **Blind connection type**, and from the list **Diameter** select **0.375** inches, as in Fig. 156a.

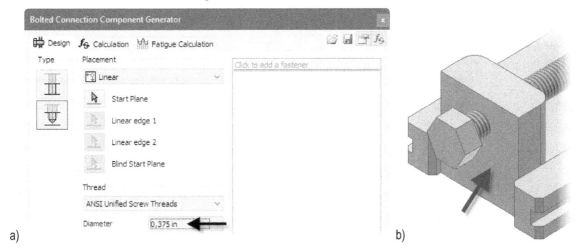

a)   b)

Fig. 156

The program is expecting you to indicate the start plane to insert the screw connection. Select the face of the support, shown in Fig. 156b. After indicating the start plane the program enables the **Linear edge 1** button and is expecting you to indicate the first edge of reference to determine the position of the hole. Select edge, denoted by 1 in Fig. 157a.

In the **Edit** box that appears, enter the **0.5** inches and confirm. For option **Linear edge 2** select the edge denoted by 2, enter a value of **1.15** inch in the **Edit** box and confirm.

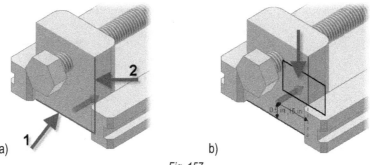

a)   b)

Fig. 157

When you point to the edge, the program enables a **Blind Start Plane** button and expects you to indicate the plane in which the insertion of the blind hole will take place. Select the plane in the cut-out of the body, highlighted in Fig. 157b – just place the cursor over the point where you expect the presence of this plane. After indicating the blind hole plane, the program displays a preview of the holes on the model and in the wizard dialog box, as in Fig. 158a and b.

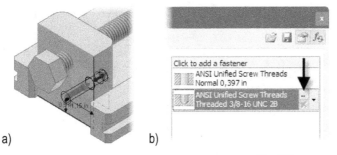
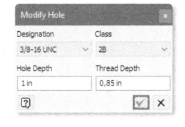

a)   b)   c)

Fig. 158

Set the depth of the blind hole. In the wizard dialog box, click **...** button in the beam of a blind threaded hole, indicated by the arrow in Fig. 158b. In the **Modify Hole** dialog box enter the depth of the hole and thread depth, as in Fig. 158c and confirm.

Set the type of through hole. In the wizard dialog box, in the beam of through hole, click the button indicated by the arrow in Fig. 159a. In the library window, select **ANSI** standard, and then select the hole **ANSI -Socket Head Cap Screw**, as in Fig. 159b.

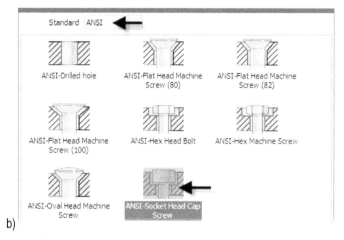

a)   b)

Fig. 159

The program updates the preview of holes in the model as in Fig. 160a. The next step is to select the bolt.

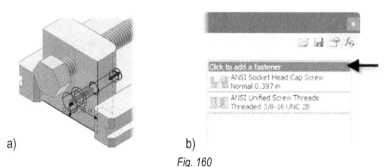

a)   b)

Fig. 160

Select bolt. Click on the beam **Click to add fastener**, shown in Fig. 160b. In the Content Center window select standard **ANSI**, further category **Socket Head Bolts** and select **Hexagon Socket Head Cap Screw - Inch**, as in Fig. 161a.

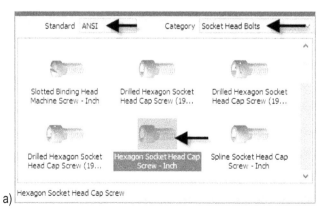
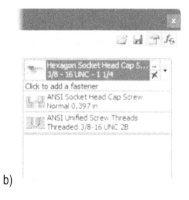

a)   b)

Fig. 161

After selecting the screw, a ready definition of a bolted connection is like in Fig. 161b. At the same time, there is displayed a preview of the bolted connection on the model. Displayed arrows allow for manual adjustment of the proposed length of the bolt and length of the blind hole. Click **OK**. In the **File Naming** dialog box, click **OK**. to accept the default file name and location of the reference file.

A ready bolted connection is shown in Fig. 162a. In the browser, there is a reference subassembly named **Bolted Connection:1**, including parts used in the bolted connection.

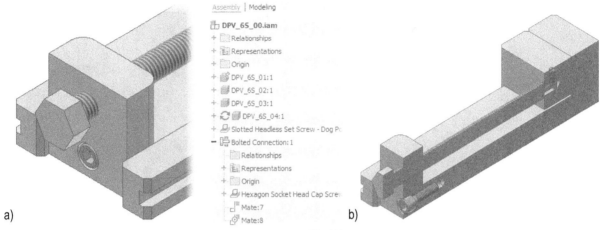

a) b)

Fig. 162

Try yourself to see the details of a bolted connection by enabling a cross–section of a model, like in the exercise *Part modeling in a cross-section of the assembly. Clamping* screw, on page 56. The illustration in Fig. 162b presents a cross-sectional view. Note that the standard parts placed from a Content Center are not cut in cross section.

 3. Turn off the cross–section and save the file of assembly. Do not close an assembly file. End of the exercise.

Exercise summary

You have learned how to insert a fastener from the Content Center. Now, you can also create a basic bolted connection using a specialized wizard. In the next exercise, using assembly constraints, you will check if the designed Drill Press Vise will function correctly.

Exercise 8
Assembly kinematics. Drive constraints

You can assume that the structure of your Drill Press Vise design has been completed. All the components are positioned to reach the position of the clamping vise. The position of the individual components is controlled by assembly constraints which you introduced or were given by the program automatically. Assembly constraints should be selected so as to ensure the possibility of displacement and rotation of components according to the actual function of each component in the assembly. Autodesk Inventor also allows automatic entry of the constraints to force the movement of the components. If the constraints are chosen correctly, you can also trace the kinematic action of the assembly.

In this exercise, you will apply the drive constraint functionality to open the vise. In addition, you will apply the motion constraint which will result in the rotation of the clamping screw. You will start by adding the constraint which is responsible for the opening of the vise.

After inserting the jaw component (**DPV_6S_02**) to the assembly, you defined a mate constraint that mates face of the jaw with the face of the retaining wall. This constraint is responsible for opening/closing the vise and thus you have changed its name to **VISE OPENING**, to make it easier to find this constraint in the browser. To open the vise just enough to change the offset value of VISE **OPENING** constraint from **0** inches to any other value.

1. Open the jaws of the vise by changing the offset value of constraint. In the browse expand the **Relationships** folder, which stores all the applied assembly constraints and double-click the constraint **VISE OPENING**, indicated in Fig. 163a.

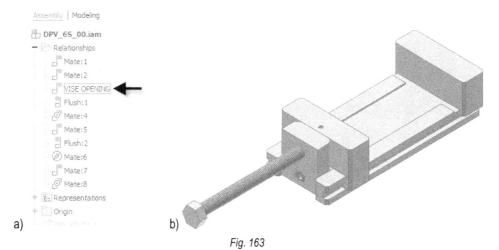

a)   b)

Fig. 163

Enter **6.0** inch in the edit box and confirm. The program will draw away a jaw from the retaining wall as in Fig. 163b.

2. Close the jaws of the vise. Restore an offset value to **0** inches in the edit box of **VISE OPENING** constraint.

    Apart from determining the specific offset values, you can apply the drive constraint functionality, which will result in a smooth changing of the offset values and will present the components in motion.

3. Start the drive constraint. Right-click **VISE OPENING** constraint and select **Drive** in the menu, as in Fig. 164a.

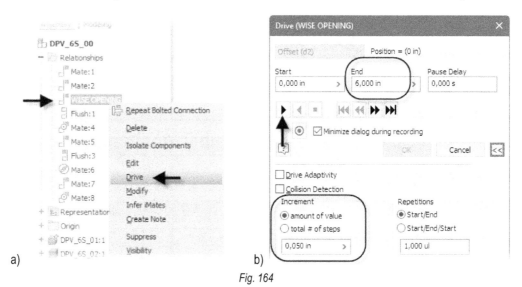

a)   b)

Fig. 164

Click the **>>** button to expand the **Drive** dialog box. You want move the jaw to a distance of a **6.0** inch. In the **End** edit filed, enter the final offset distance equal to **6.0** inch, as in Fig. 164b. In the **Increment** section, enter **0.05** inch, then the movement will be more visible.

Click the **Forward** button, indicated by the arrow in Fig. 164b to start the drive. After reaching the final value, the **Reverse** button will cause the return movement. Click **Cancel** to exit.

Drive constraint presents a smooth opening and closing of the jaws of the vise. However, the clamping screw remains stationary – it only moves with the movable jaw. You will apply now a motion constraint which will rotate the screw when jaws are opened and closed. But firstly, you begin by reviewing the constraints applied automatically, which can interfere with the motion of screw.

When you create a new part in the context of the assembly the program asks you to indicate a flat surface on which it put the sketching plane of the new part. After indicating the surface, the program automatically determines the type of constraint **Mate/Flush**, to the selected plane and the plane of a new part. This constraint is necessary to begin a new part but it can interfere in obtaining the desired behavior of the part within the assembly. After finishing the part, this kind of constraint can be removed or disabled. Disabling a constraint allows you to later turn on the constraint and restore the original position of the parts.

4.   Disable the constraint which is blocking rotation of the clamping screw. Expand the clamping screw node, component **DPV_6S_03:1**, right-click the constraint **Flush:1** and select **Suppress** in a menu, as in Fig. 165a.

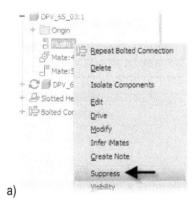 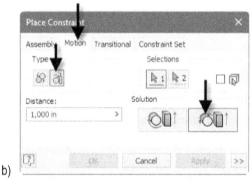

a)   b)

Fig. 165

The symbol of suppressed constraint is now grayed out. In the same way, you can re-enable the constraint. After suppressing the constraint, you can freely rotate the clamping screw.

5.   Define motion constraint. In the **Assembly** tab, in the **Relationships** panel, click on the **Constrain** icon. In the **Place Constraint** dialog box, go to the **Motion** tab and turn on the **Rotation-Translation** type of the constraint and the **Reverse** solution, as in Fig. 165b.

The program is expecting you to select the rotating part as a first part, and the sliding part as a second one. As a first element for the constraint, select the threaded bolt shaft. The program will place the sign of rotational component of the constraint in the axis as in Fig. 166a.

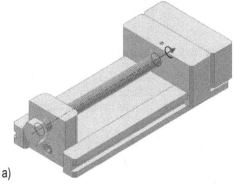 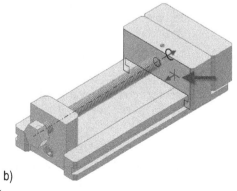

a)   b)

Fig. 166

As a second element for constraint, select the face of a jaw indicated by the arrow in Fig. 166b. After selecting both components, in the **Distance** field, the program will propose the offset linear value, which will take place after turning the screw by one turn. Enter a different value, e.g. **0.09 inch**, as in Fig. 167a. Click **OK**.

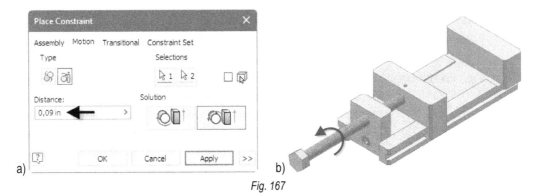

Fig. 167

All constraints have been correctly defined. Now you can test how the vise is working.

6. Start the drive constraint. In the browser, in the **Relationships** folder, right-click the **VISE OPENING** constraints and select **Drive** in the menu. In the **Drive** dialog box, click the **Forward** button. The program will play the movement of the jaw in the range of **0** to **6 inch**, with the rotation of the clamping screw. Click **Cancel**, after checking the behavior of constraints.

7. Save the assembly file. Do not close the file. End of exercise.

Exercise summary

You learned how to apply a basic assembly constraint and how to drive constraints to verify the kinematics of the assembly. This way you can validate concepts of the designed device. In the next exercise, you will organize the contents of the bill of material to ensure that all components of the project have been properly described. The contents of the BOM is the basis to create a parts list.

Exercise 9
Organize content of a bill of material

You can assume, that the project of Drill Press Vise is completed. All parts have been designed and the mechanism is working as expected. Before the creation of drawing documentation, you have to review and arrange the content of the bill of materials. BOM is a database of information about the components of the designed device. On the basis of the BOM, there is a parts list created.

1. Open a **Bill of Materials** dialog box. In the **Assemble** tab in the **Manage** panel click on **Bill of Materials** icon.

The program opens by default the **Model Data** tab, in the **Bill of Material** dialog box, which contains all the information about components of the model. The information comes from data saved in the **iProperties** dialog box of each file. In the **Bill of Materials** dialog box, you can fill in the missing data such as material, description, user attributes, etc. in one common dialog box.

A parts list is created based on the contents of the **Structured** tab or **Parts Only** tab. The default views of the contents of these tabs are disabled. You will go to the **Structured** tab, enable the view and start to organize the contents.

2. Click the **Structured (Disabled)** tab. Right-click in empty space of the dialog box and select **Enable BOM View**, as in Fig. 168.

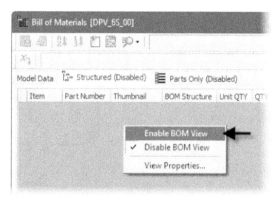

Fig. 168

The program displays the contents of the structured BOM, as in Fig. 169. You can see that the **Part Number** column and the **Description** column are filled in correctly.

 *In the **Bill of Materials** dialog box, you can supplement or change the contents of any not grayed out cells. The change will be saved in the iProperties tab in the part or in the subassembly file.*

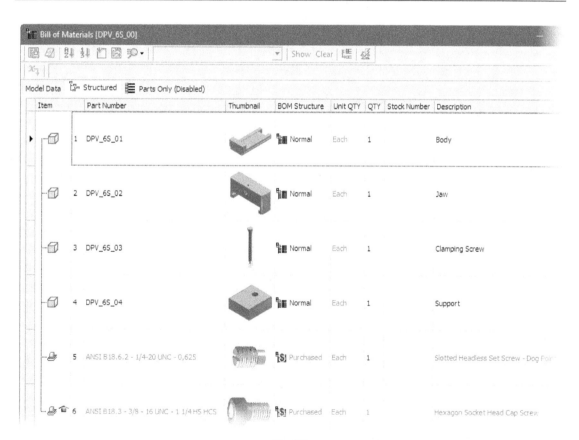

Fig. 169

You will slightly change the contents of the view. You will insert columns: **Material** and **Mass**.

3. Insert column for material. Click **Choose Columns** icon in the toolbar of the **Bill of Materials** window. In the **Customization** window, search for the **Material**, grab and drag it to the right next to **Description** column, as in Fig. 170.

Fig. 170

In a similar way place the **Mass** column, to the right of the **Material** column. Close the **Customization** window. Both of the new columns look like in Fig. 171.

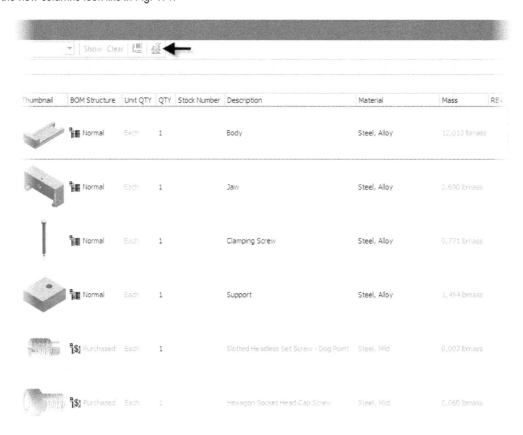

Fig. 171

*If the cell **Mass** includes the value of **N/A** for any row, it is necessary to update the mass properties by clicking on the icon indicated by the arrow in Fig. 171.*

The **Item** column contains the item numbers assigned in the order in which the different parts were made in the model. You can change the contents of the cell **Item** for each row, and then sort the rows or set it in the order in which they should appear in the parts' list, and then renumber them. Now, you will use the second way.

4. Change the order of the rows. You can assume that the **Support** part should be placed above of the **Clamping Screw** part on a list. Grab the first column of the line **Support** before **Item** and drag the row into the place of the row's **Clamping Screw**, as in Fig. 172.

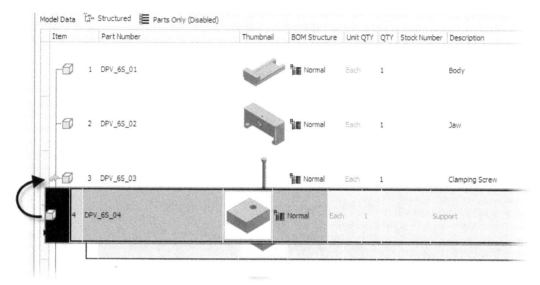

Fig. 172

Now, the order of rows is as in Fig. 173.

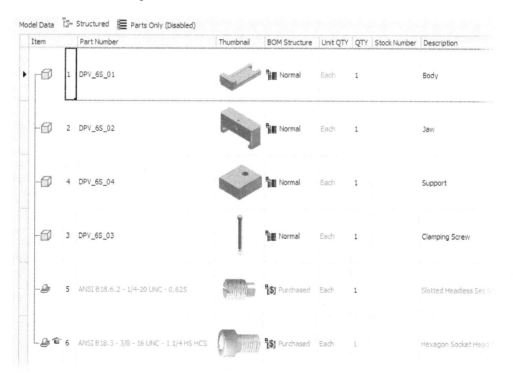

Fig. 173

5. Renumber the contents of the BOM. Click on the **Renumber Items** icon in the toolbar of **Bill of Materials** window. In the **Item renumber** dialog box make sure the **Start value** and **Increment** equal to **1**. Click **OK**. After renumbering the content of the window, it should be as in Fig. 174.

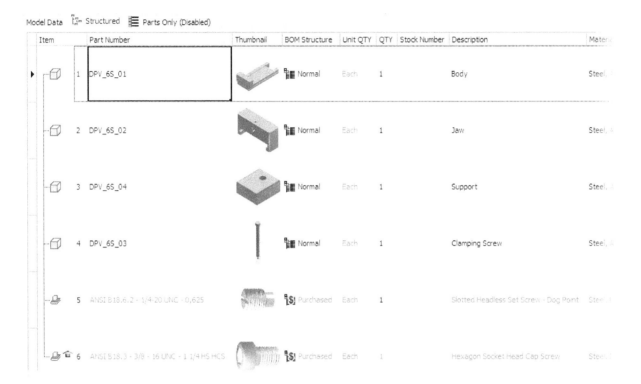

Fig. 174

You can assume that the contents of the window the **Bill of Materials** are now ordered.

 *You can export the contents of the **Bill of Materials** window to an external file, for example, ***. XLS**, for further processing in other departments of the company. To do this, select the icon **Export Bill of Materials** in the toolbar in this window.*

Click on **Done**.

 6. Save the assembly. Do not close an assembly file. End of exercise.

Exercise summary

The correct description of the components of the design is very important. You already know how to make up and organize the contents of a BOM database. In the next exercise, you will learn how to quickly create a visual presentation of the design, e.g. for marketing purposes or to discuss the concept of your product.

Exercise 10
The visual presentation of the project on the screen

The Autodesk Inventor software offers very advanced capabilities of visual presentation of designed products. In this exercise, you will learn about the basic functionality, which will make it easier to prepare a visual presentation of the design concept on the screen. You will learn how to add colors to the entire component or only to selected surfaces of the model. You will learn how to set the model in a perspective view and how to turn on shadows and light reflections. In the end, you will learn how to make a presentation of a model in a predefined scene. In Fig. 175 you can see two variants of the presentation of the vise that will arise in this exercise.

 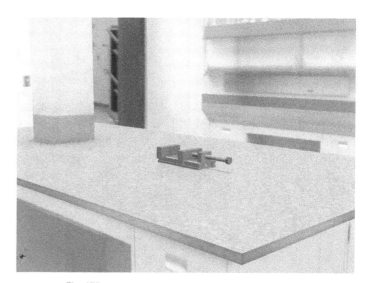

Fig. 175

The following exercises will present other tools for visualization and presentation of a model.

In the previous exercises, you have set the materials which were used to produce different parts of the vise. The standard parts have already assigned a suitable material saved in the Content Center database. Assigned materials allow you to determine the basic physical parameters of the entire project. In addition, together with the physical parameters of the material, the appearance of material is also associated with it. Because selected materials are: **Steel, Alloy** and **Steel Mild** their appearance on the screen is only slightly different – generally they are gray. You can assume, that the finished vise will be painted blue, and the clamping screw will be oxidized. In addition, the guides of the jaw in the body are not covered with paint but are polished. Let's see how to create such a visual representation of the finished product. You will start by assigning appearances.

Autodesk Inventor distinguishes between two levels of assigning appearance to the parts.

- **In the original part file**. In the file level of the part, you can assign a unified appearance across the whole part or assign a different appearance to given surfaces of the part. Appearances assigned in the part file will be visible in all instances of the part in the assembly, in which the part was inserted.

- **In the assembly file**. In the file level of the assembly, you can assign a unified appearance throughout the whole subassemblies or whole parts. You cannot change the appearance of the pieces of parts. Appearances assigned on the assembly level override appearances assigned at the parts level, but without interfering with the original part file - a new look of this part is only in the current assembly.

At first, the new appearance will be assigned to the whole body. You will assign a new appearance to the body of the vise in its original file. You will "paint" the whole body with the exception of rails, which will be polished.

1. Start editing part **DPV_6S_01:1**. Double click in the body on the screen or in **DPV_6S_01:1** in the browser. The model of the body becomes an active component – the remaining parts will be grayed out.

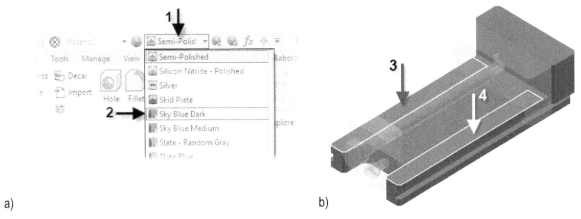

a)   b)

Fig. 176

2. Set the new appearance of the whole body. In the quick access toolbar, expand the list of appearances, indicated by 1 in Fig. 176a and select **Sky Blue Dark** indicated by 2. The whole body turns to a new look.

3. Set a new appearance of guide rails. Press and hold the **CTRL** key and select the two surfaces of the guide rails, as indicated by 3 and 4 in Fig. 176b. Release the **CTRL** key and then right-click and select **Properties**, as in Fig. 177a.

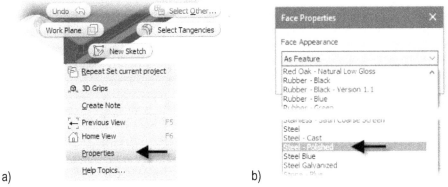

a)   b)

Fig. 177

In the **Face Properties** dialog box select **Steel - Polished** from the drop-down list, as in Fig. 177b. Click **OK**. Now the body is presented as in Fig. 178a.

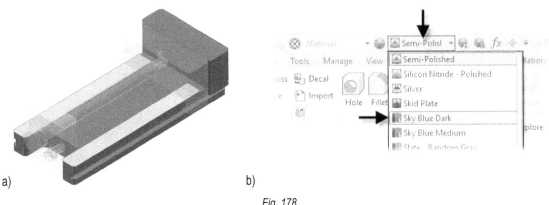

a)   b)

Fig. 178

You can assume that the change in the appearance of the body is done. Now you will change the appearance of the other parts of the vise assembly.

4. Go back to the level of the main assembly. Right-click in empty space and select **Finish Edit**. Alternatively, you can press the right button of your mouse and pull toward: "**at 6.00 o'clock**". You can see that the new look of the body is visible in the assembly.

Now you change the appearance of the jaw and support of clamping screw on the assembly level. Both parts will have the same appearance as the body, but the visual presentation will be valid only at the assembly level.

5. Set new appearance for a jaw and support. Press and hold the **CTRL** key, and then select on the screen or in the browser the jaw (**DPV_6S_02**) and the support (**DPV_6S _04**) parts. Now, expand the list of appearances in the quick access toolbar and select **Sky Blue Dark**, as in Fig. 178b. Both parts will change color.

6. Set new appearance for the clamping screw. Select on the screen or in the browser the clamping screw (**DPV_6S_03**), then expand the list of appearances in quick access toolbar and select **Gunmetal**.

The whole vise has been "painted". The next step is to set a model in perspective view and turning on shading and light reflection. All the basic tools to fine-tune the presentation of the model are located in the **View** tab.

7. Turn on a perspective view of the model. In the **View** tab, in the **Appearance** panel, click on **Perspective** icon, in pull-down of the **Orthographic** icon. Currently, the model looks like in Fig. 179a.

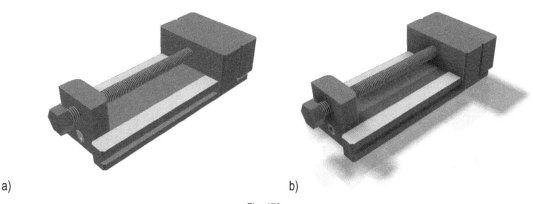

a)   b)

Fig. 179

8. Turn on shading and light reflection. In the **View** tab, in the **Appearance** panel, click on **Shadows** and on **Reflections** icons. The enabled shading and reflections look like in Fig. 179b.

The next step is to change the visual style. In everyday project work is usually used visual style **Shaded** or **Shaded with Edges**. Now you enable **Realistic** visual style, which creates a more realistic picture.

9. Enable realistic visual style. In the **View** tab, in the **Appearance** panel, click on **Realistic** icon, indicated by an arrow in Fig. 180a.

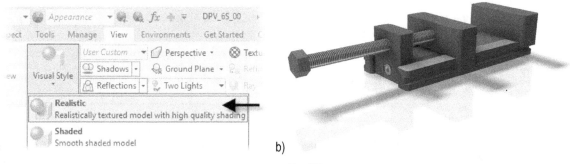

a)   b)

Fig. 180

10. Set the model for presentation. By using the drive constraint functionality, open the jaws of the vise and set the model in the position better presenting the product, e.g. as in Fig. 180b.

The image of the product in such a presentation is closer to the actual look and will help to better evaluate the quality of the project while still on the computer screen. In addition, Inventor provides several predefined visual environments in which the designed product can be presented to show it in its more natural work environment. Now you will turn on one of those environments to show the model of the vise in a different environment – the vise will be placed on the table in a laboratory.

11. Turn on a predefined lighting style. In the **View** tab, in the **Appearance** panel, pull down the list of lighting styles and select **Empty Lab**, as in Fig. 181a.

a)

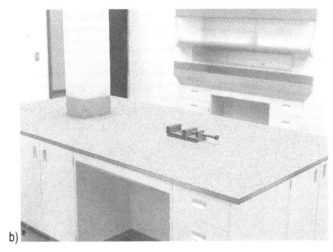
b)

Fig. 181

After loading the lighting style environment, you can see the model of vise placed on the table in the laboratory, as shown in Fig. 181b.

*To save the contents of the screen as an image, go to the **File** tab, select **Export** then selects **Image**, and choose the type of image file. In the options, you can set the resolution of the saved image file.*

You may assume that the project of vise was initially evaluated and approved. The next step is to prepare a presentation material that can be used for marketing purposes and for prepare an instruction montage.

12. Return to **Two Lights** lighting style. In the **View** tab, in the **Appearance** panel, pull down the list of lighting styles and select **Two Lights.**

13. Turn off shading and light reflections. In the **View** tab, in the **Appearance** panel click off the icons **Shadows** and **Reflections**.

14. Turn off the perspective view of the model. In the **View** tab, in the **Appearance** panel, click the **Orthographic** icon, in pull-down of the **Perspective** icon.

15. Close the jaws of the vise, restoring the distance value **0** inches in **VISE OPENING** constraint.

16. Save the assembly file to store the settings for the appearance of the model. End of exercise.

Exercise summary

You already know how to quickly present the project, using the basic visualization tools available in Autodesk Inventor. In the next exercise, you will create an illustration with its own lighting and a video showing the vise in action.

Exercise 11
Rendered picture and the video of a vise

In this exercise, you will use the basic tools offered by the module Inventor Studio. You will create an illustration using additional lighting and you will create a video showing the vise in action. In Fig. 182a, there is an illustration, which will be prepared in the exercise, while Fig. 182b shows one frame from a video.

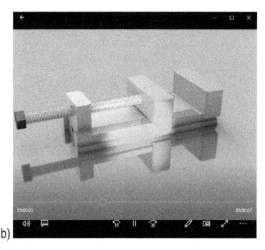

a)   b)

Fig. 182

You will first create a scene which is the basis for preparing the illustration and the video. The scene will include the setting of the camera and lighting style.

1. Set the model in perspective view, turn on shadows and reflections. In the **View** tab, in **Appearance** panel, click on **Perspective** icon and then click icons: **Shadows** and **Reflections**. Set model view as in Fig. 183a.

a)   b)

Fig. 183

2. Turn on the Studio module. In the **Environments** tab, in the **Begin** panel, click the **Inventor Studio** icon. The Inventor Studio view is now enabled in the browser

3. Define setting the camera for the current view. In the browser, right-click the icon **Camera** and then click on the Create **Camera from View** in the menu, as in Fig. 183b. The new setting will be saved as the **Camera1**. When you change the model view, you can easily return to the saved view by clicking on the option: **Set View to Camera** in the right button menu, as in Fig. 184a.

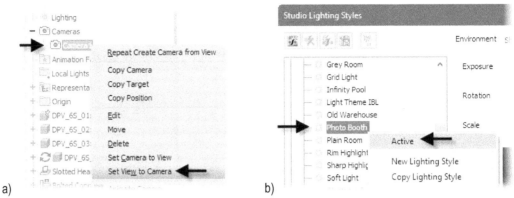

Fig. 184

4. Select and activate the lighting style. In the **Render** tab, in the **Scene** panel, click on **Studio Lightings Styles** icon. In the **Studio Lighting Styles** dialog box on the **Global Lighting Styles** list, right-click the **Photo Booth** style and select **Active** in the menu, as in Fig. 184b. The activated style will appear in the **Local Lighting Styles** list.

5. Turn on the image of the scene in this style. Check **Display Scene Image** box, as in Fig. 185a.

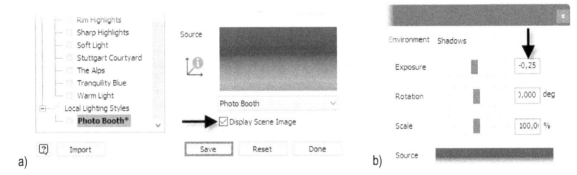

Fig. 185

6. Reduce the exposure scene. Move the **Exposure** slider to the values **–0.25,** as in Fig. 183b. The scene becomes slightly dimmed. Click on **Save** to save this change.

7. Add new light to illuminate the model of the vise. Right-click the **Photo Booth*** style and select the **New Light** in the menu, like in Fig. 186a.

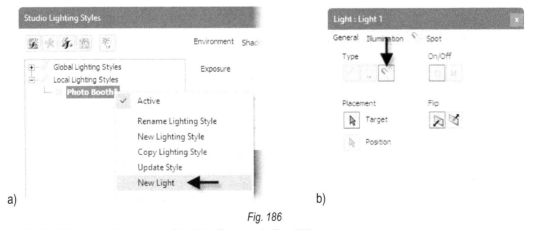

Fig. 186

In the **Light** dialog box, select a type of the light **Spot**, as in Fig. 186b.

In the **Placement** area, the **Target** button is enabled - the program is expecting you now to indicate the target point of the light. Select the face indicated by the arrow in Fig. 187a.

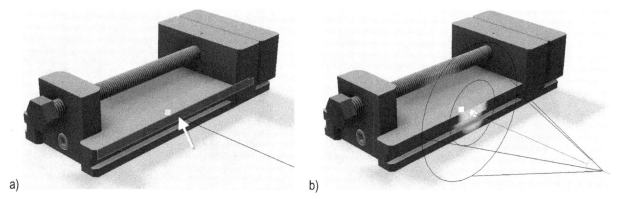

a)   b)

Fig. 187

The program displays a line perpendicular to the selected face and is expecting you to indicate the position of the light source. Select a point on the line, at a certain distance from the face, as shown in Fig. 187b. In the **Light** dialog box, on the **Illumination** tab set the **Intensity** value to **100** and the **Attenuation Compensation** value to a **100**, as shown in Fig. 188a. Click **OK**. in the **Light** dialog box.

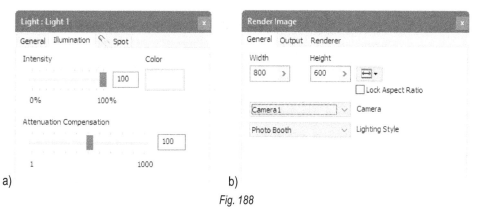

a)   b)

Fig. 188

Click **Done**, in the **Studio Lighting Styles** dialog box.

You have defined the scene and lighting. Now you can render the illustration.

8. Create a rendered illustration. In the **Render** tab, in the **Render** panel, click on **Render Image** icon. In the **Render Image** dialog box, in the **General** tab, set the resolution of the illustration and make sure that the current camera is set on the **Camera1**, and lighting style is set on the **Photo Booth**, as in Fig. 188b.

In the **Render** tab enable the options: **Until Satisfactory**, as in Fig. 189a, and then click on the **Render** button. In the **Render Output** dialog box, you can stop rendering after reaching a satisfactory picture quality, by clicking on the button shown in Fig. 189b.

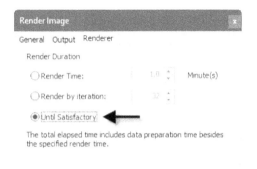
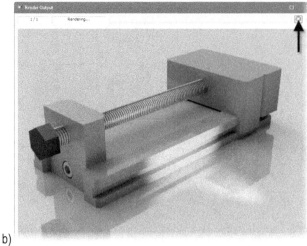

a)   b)

Fig. 189

 9. Save the image. After stopping the rendering, save the image in the project folder, under the name of **Image DPV_6S_00.jpg**. This illustration can be used e.g. for product marketing purposes. Close the **Render Output** window.

Now you will create a video that will demonstrate the vise in action. In the film, you want to show the opening of jaws to the middle position and closing. In addition, the model of your vise will rotate during opening and closing. The entire film will take 10 seconds. The animation will consist of the following events:

Rotate about Y axis									
Vise Opening					Vise Closing				
1 sec.	2 sec.	3 sec.	4 sec.	5 sec.	6 sec.	7 sec.	8 sec.	9 sec.	10 sec.

10. Start preparing the animation. In the browser right-click on **Animations** and then select the **New Animation** in the menu, as in Fig. 190a. The new entry **Animation1** will appear in the **Animations** folder.

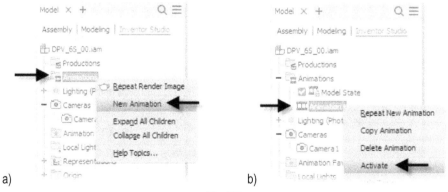

a)   b)

Fig. 190

11. Activate the animation. In the browser, right-click on the **Animation1** and select **Activate** in the menu, as in Fig. 190b. The program will display a window: **Animation Timeline** at the bottom of the screen.

12. Set the length of the animation. Click on the **Animation Options** icon, indicated in Fig. 191a. In the **Animation Options** dialog box set the length of the animation to **10 sec**, as shown in Fig. 191b. Click **OK**.

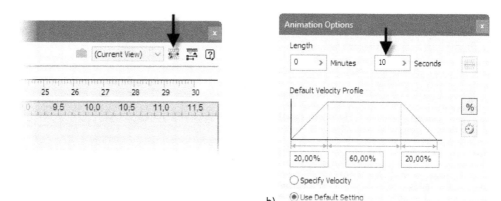

a)   b)

Fig. 191

13. Set the camera, which will be observing the rotation of the vise. In the **Animation Timeline** dialog box, expand the list of views and select the **Camera1**, as in Fig. 192a.

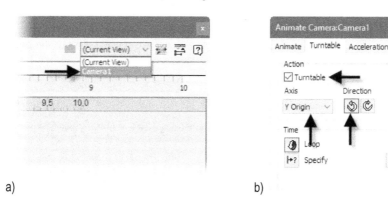

a)   b)

Fig. 192

14. Define the rotation of the model. In the **Render** tab, in the **Animate** panel, click on the **Camera** icon. In the **Animate Camera** dialog box, go to the **Turntable** tab, turn on the option **Turntable**, and set the axis **Y** as the axis of rotation, set the direction and the end time to **10,0 sec.**, as in Fig. 192b. A turntable symbol will appear on the model, as in Fig. 193a.

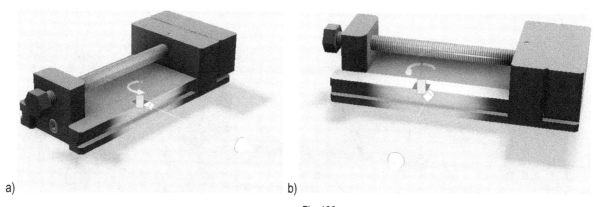

a)   b)

Fig. 193

Click **OK**. The program will set the end view of animation on the screen, at 10 sec, as shown in Fig. 193b. In the expanded **Animation Timeline** window, a line of the event will be visible, as in Fig. 194.

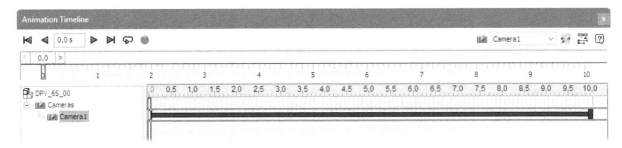

Fig. 194

15. Make a preview of the current state of animation. In the **Animation Timeline** window, click **Go to Start** button to return to the beginning of the timeline and then click on the **Play Animation**. After watching the preview of the animation, click on **Go to Start** again.

You can achieve the effect of opening and closing the jaws by animating the assembly constraint **VISE OPENING**. You will create an event involving the opening of the jaws which will take 5 sec. You will get the animation of jaws closing by creating a mirror of events that define the opening of the jaws.

16. Define jaws' opening animation. In the **Render** tab in the **Animate** panel, click on **Constraints** icon. In the **Animation Constraints** dialog box, there is an enabled **Select** button for selecting a constraint. Expand the contents of the component: **DPV_6S_01:1** and select constraint **VISE OPENING**, indicated in Fig. 195a.

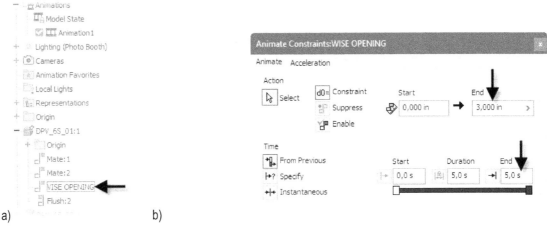

a)   b)

Fig. 195

In the **Animation Constraints** dialog set the final value of the offset to **3.0 inch**, and set end time of an animation to **5.0 sec**, as in Fig. 195b. Click **OK**. The program will set the model view at the end of this event, as shown in Fig. 196.

Fig. 196

In the expanded **Animation Timeline** window there is visible a line of the new event, as in Fig. 197.

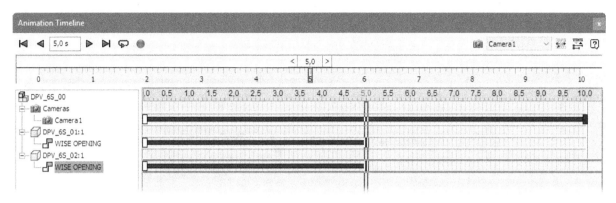

Fig. 197

17. Make a preview of the current state of animation. In the **Animation Timeline** window, click on **Go to Start** button to return to the beginning of the timeline and then click on **Play Animation**. After watching the preview of the animation, click on **Go to Start** again.

18. Define jaws' closing animation. In the **Animation Timeline** window, right-click the line of **VISE OPENING** constraint animation and select **Mirror** in the menu, as in Fig. 198.

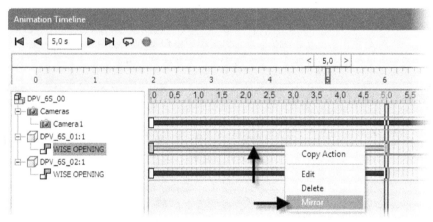

Fig. 198

The program automatically creates a mirror image animation setting from a previous event, as in Fig. 199.

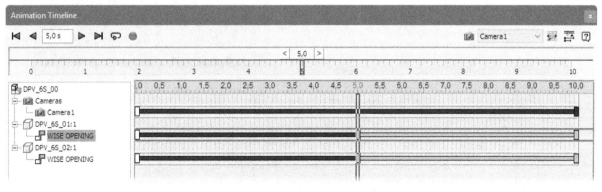

Fig. 199

19. Make a preview of the whole animation. In the **Animation Timeline** window, click on **Go to Start** button to return to the beginning of the timeline and then click on the **Play Animation**. After watching the preview of the animation, click on the **Go to Start** again.

You can assume that the animation is completed. The last step is to render the movie. Rendering speed will depend on the performance of your computer.

20. Create a movie. In the **Render** tab, in the **Render** panel, click on **Render Animation** icon. In the **Render Animation** dialog box, on the **General** tab, set the image size and make sure that the camera set on the **Camera1**, view, and lighting style is **Photo Booth**, as in Fig. 200a.

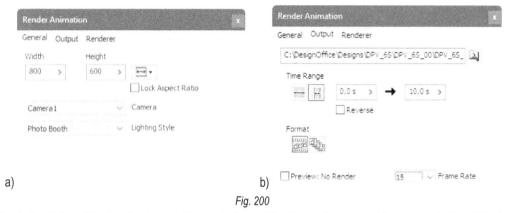

a)   b)

Fig. 200

On the **Output** tab, set the location to save the movie file, set the time and number of frames, as in Fig. 200b. Select a video file format and enter a file name: **Video of Vise DPV_6S_00**. On the **Renderer** tab enable **Render by iteration** option, as in Fig. 201a, to perform several iterations of each frame.

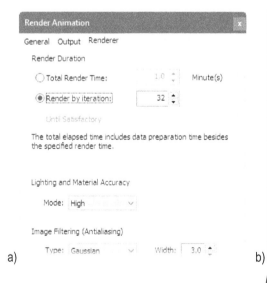

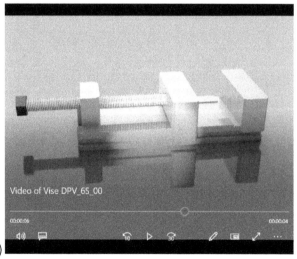

a)   b)

Fig. 201

Click the **Render** button. The program will start the process of rendering 151 frames of a movie. Each frame will be rendered 32 times to get better quality.

21. After completion of rendering, close the windows **Render Output**, and then **Render Animation**.

22. Exit the Inventor Studio module. Click on **Finish Inventor Studio** icon, to the right of a **Render** tab.

Your video can be viewed in your favorite media player, as in Fig. 201b. The movie can be used e.g. for product marketing purposes.

23. Turn off shadows and reflections. On the **View** tab, in the **Appearance** panel click icons: **Shadows** and **Reflections**.

24. Turn off a perspective view of a model. On the **View** tab, in the **Appearance** panel click on **Orthographic** icon.

25. Save the assembly file. End of exercise.

Exercise summary

You already know how to do a rendered illustration of designed product and know how to create a simple video which shows the operation of the designed device. These skills will help you to present intentions of the projects and create the appropriate information materials. In the next exercise, you will learn how to prepare a presentation of exploded assembly, which can be widely used in providing information about the designed device.

Exercise 12
Creating a presentation file

Presentation file can be useful in technical documentation, in order to show the device or components in disassemble form, the installation instructions, or to create a video presentation of the assembly process. In this exercise, you will create a presentation file for the vise model. Presentation file will include two views: **Assembled** and **Exploded**, shown in Fig. 202 and a video illustrating the assembly/disassembly process. In the next exercises, the views from the presentation file will be used to create an exploded view in the drawing of the product.

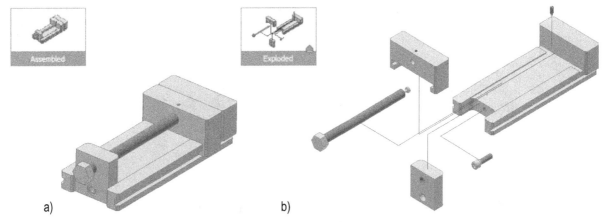

a)   b)

Fig. 202

Presentation file is a separate file with extension ***.ipn**. To create a presentation file program, use a special template.

1. Start creating a presentation file. In the **My Home** window, click on the **Presentation** button, indicated in Fig. 203.

Fig. 203

After loading the template file, the program displays the **Insert** window, by default. Choose the assembly file **DPV_6S_00.iam**, as in Fig. 204, and click **Open**.

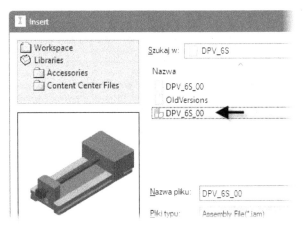

Fig. 204

Before taking further actions, let's look at the user interface in the presentation mode, shown in Fig. 205.

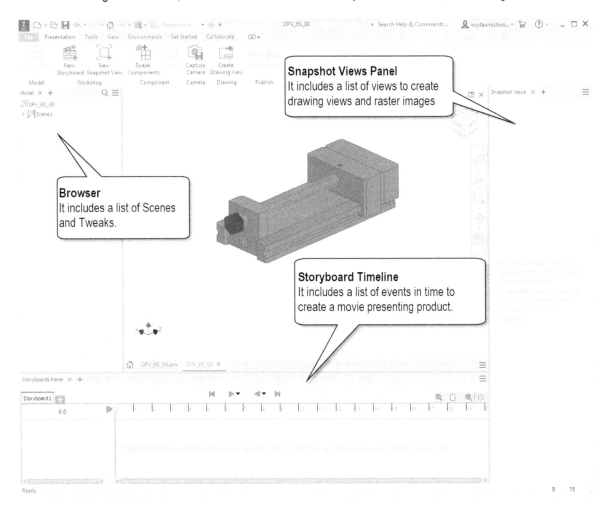

Fig. 205

By default, the program displays the **Storyboard Timeline** to create a presentation of disassembly of the product, from which you can create a video clip. Based on scenes from the video, you can create a static view to draw documentation or for presentation.

Now, you will create a video presentation of the disassembling of the vise by making a manual tweak of parts, and then you will create two static views. The component for tweak can be selected from the model or in the browser. The first component you will select in the browser.

   2. Remove the set screw. Expand the browser node **Scene 1 > DVP 6S_00.iam**, then select the component: **Slotted Head Set Screw** and then right-click on the graphics area and select the **Tweak Components** from the menu, as in Fig. 206a.

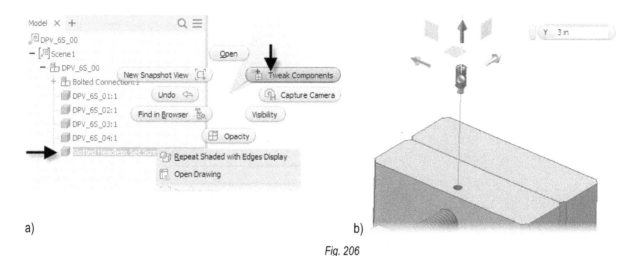

a)   b)

Fig. 206

Pull the arrow Y of the manipulator up and enter the offset distance by **3** inches in the edit box, as in Fig. 206b. Press **ENTER** to confirm. The **Tweak** is saved in the browser, like in Fig. 207a.

Now, you will eject the clamping screw and will put the additional offset from the axis.

3. Remove the clamping screw. On the **Presentation** tab, in the **Component** panel click on the **Tweak Components** icon. Select the clamping screw and pull the Z arrow of the manipulator towards the Z direction and enter the offset distance **10** inches in the edit box, as in Fig. 207b.

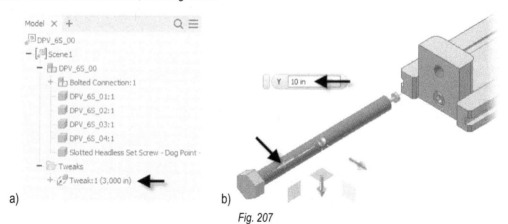

a)   b)

Fig. 207

Next, pull the X arrow in the distance of **–4 inch**, as in Fig. 208. Enter the exact distance in the edit box.

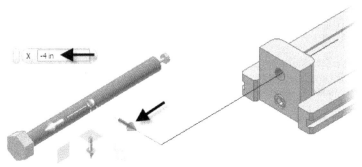

Fig. 208

Press **ENTER** to accept the tweaks.

4.   Remove the support mounting screw. On the **Presentation** tab, in the **Component** panel click on the **Tweak Components** icon. Select the mounting screw and pull the Z arrow of the manipulator in the –Z direction and enter the offset distance **–4** inches, as in Fig. 209a.

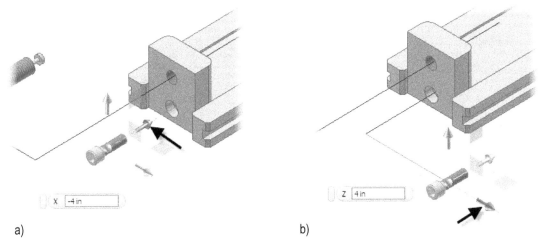

a)   b)

Fig. 209

Next, pull the arrow X in the X direction to the distance of **4** inches, as in Fig. 209b and press **ENTER**. Currently, the exploded view is presented like in Fig. 210.

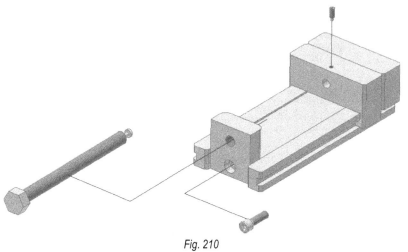

Fig. 210

5. By yourself, follow the tweak of support of the pressure screw to the distance **Z= –5** inches and **Y= 4** inch. The correct position of the support after removal is shown in Fig. 211.

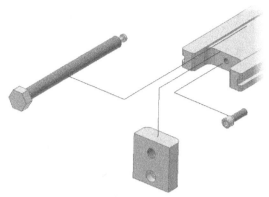

Fig. 211

6. The last part to tweak is a jaw. Move the jaw to the distance **Z= 13** inch from a retaining wall and move it up to the distance of **Y= 6** inch, as in Fig. 212.

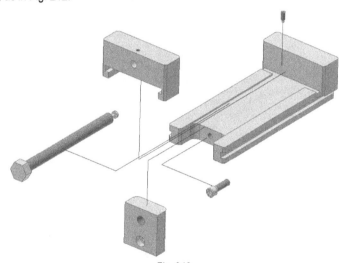

Fig. 212

The program has registered nine events in the timeline panel, as in Fig. 213.

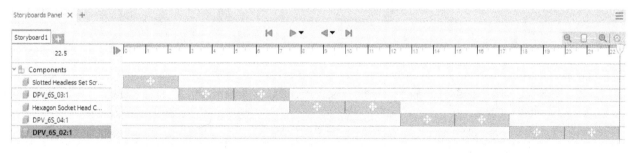

Fig. 213

Each event takes 2.5 sec. The whole presentation of the disassembly takes 22.5 sec. The program offers the possibility of moving events in the timeline panel and allows shortening or lengthening the event to fit the needs of the presentation better. In the timeline panel, simply grab the event box and extend, shorten or move to another position.

▷ ▼ **7.** Watch a video presentation of disassembly of the vise. Click on the **Play Current Storyboard** button in the timeline panel.

During playback, some components may not be visible because the presentation was created for the initial model view. You can set the starting and final camera view now so that all components will be visible in the video presentation.

⫷ **8.** Set the starting view of the camera. Make sure that the time indicator is located at the beginning of the presentation. If necessary, click on the **Back to Storyboard Beginning** button in the timeline panel. Adjust the view of the assembled model to the screen, as in Fig. 214.

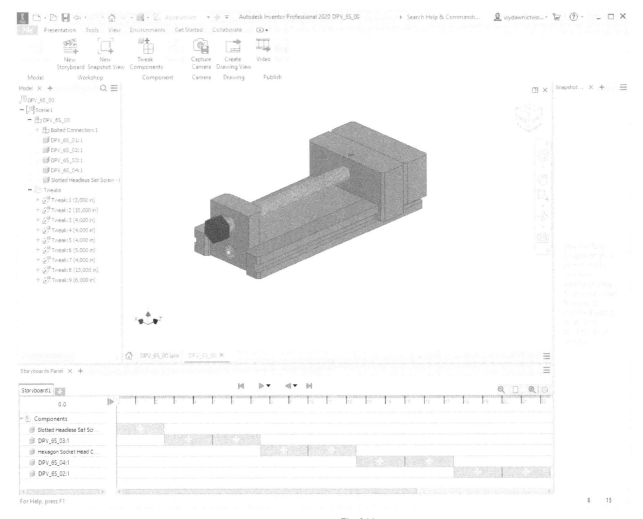

Fig. 214

  9. Save the camera position for the start of the presentation. On the **Presentation** tab, in the **Camera** panel, click on the **Capture Camera** icon.

⫷ **10.** Set the final view of the camera. Make sure that the time indicator is located at the end of the presentation. If necessary, click on the **Forward to Storyboard End** button in the timeline panel. Adjust the view of the disassembled model to the screen, as in Fig. 215.

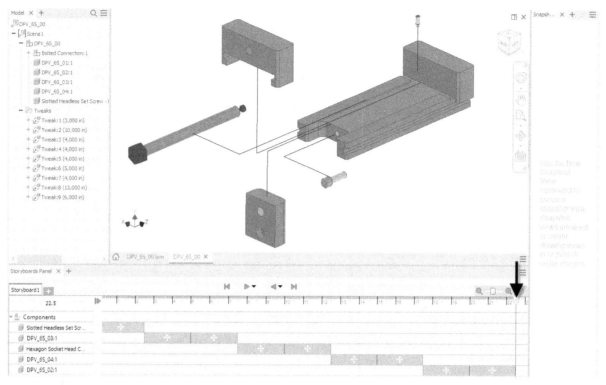

Fig. 215

 11. Save the camera position of the last moment time of the presentation. On the **Presentation** tab, in the **Camera** panel, click on the **Capture Camera** icon. The program places the camera view event at the end of the presentation, as in Fig. 216.

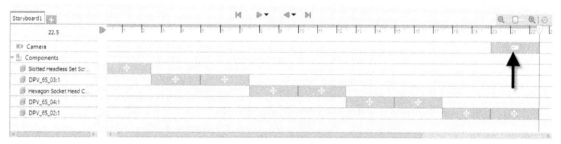

Fig. 216

You can assume that the final view of the model should be reached in **2.5 sec**. of presentation. To obtain it, just move the camera view event box to the beginning of the timeline.

12. Move the camera view. Grab and drag a camera view box, indicated by the arrow in Fig. 216, to the position shown in Fig. 217.

Fig. 217

13. Watch the video presentation of disassembling the vise after adding the camera view event. Click on the **Play Current Storyboard** button in the timeline panel. Now, for the first 2.5 sec. the vise model should be moved to the final location. The rest of the disassembling will be carried out after obtaining the final view.

14. Set the view of the model in its original position. Click on the **Back to Storyboard Beginning** button in the timeline panel.

    You can assume that the presentation of the disassembling process of the vise is ready. Now you will create two views, which can be used to create technical drawings, presenting the vise in assembled and in the disassembled state.

15. Save the view of the assembled vise. On the **Presentation** tab, in the **Workshop** panel, click on the **New Snapshot View** icon. The new view will be placed in the panel **Snapshot Views**, as in Fig. 218a. Change the name of this view to the **Assembled**, as in Fig. 218b, editing field under the illustration view.

a)   b)

Fig. 218

The second view presents a disassembled vise. To create this view, go to the end of the video presentation.

16. Set the view of the vise in a full disassembling state. Click on the **Forward to End Storyboard** button in the timeline panel.

17. Save the view of the disassembled vise. On the **Presentation** tab, in the **Transform** panel, click on the **New Snapshot View** icon. The new view will be placed in the panel **Snapshot Views**, as in Fig. 219a. Change the name of this view to the **Exploded**, as in Fig. 219b, editing field under the illustration view.

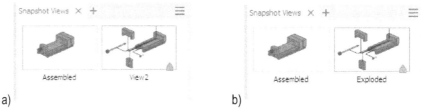

a)   b)

Fig. 219

Now you can improve each of the views. In this example, you will re-center the position of the views. To do this, you will need to enter the edit view mode. This will turn off the timeline panel.

18. Enter edit mode of the **Assembled** view. Double-click on the illustration view in the panel **Snapshot Views**. The active view is highlighted with the border, as in Fig. 220a.

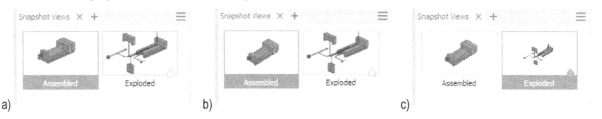

a)   b)   c)

Fig. 220

19. Center the view, if necessary. Click a corner cube common to the faces: **BACK**, **LEFT** and **TOP**. On the **Presentation** tab, in the **Camera** panel, click on the **Update Camera** icon. The centered view will be shown in the illustration view in the **Snapshot Views** panel, as in Fig. 220b.

20. In a similar manner, adjust the **Exploded** view. Double-click on the illustration view in the panel **Snapshot Views**, and then center the view of the disassembled vise and click on the **Update Camera**. The adjusted view is shown in Fig. 220c.

    Returning to the operating mode of the timeline occurs after selecting an icon: **Finish Edit View** in the **Exit** panel.

21. Save the presentation named **DPV_6S_00.ipn**, in **DPV_6S** folder and close it. End of exercise.

Exercise summary

You know how to create a simple presentation of the assembly/disassembly process, which can be used in technical drawings, assembly instructions or for the presentation of design intent. In the next exercise, you will create drawing documentation of the designed vise.

Exercise 13
Technical drawing of the assembly. List of parts and numbering

You can assume that the design of Drill Press Vise has been finished and accepted. Next step is to prepare technical documentation of design. In this exercise, you will create a technical drawing of the assembly, which will contain a list of parts and item numbers. The drawing will be prepared using the default configuration of the software. In Fig. 221 you will see a drawing that will be created in this exercise.

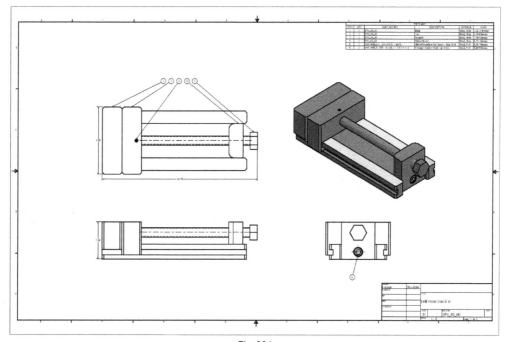

Fig. 221

---

*Before starting this exercise, complete **Exercise 9. Organize content of a bill of** material, on page 80.*

---

1. Start creating a new drawing file. On the **Get Started** tab, in the **Launch** panel, click on the **New** icon. In the **Create New File** dialog box, select the template **Standard.dwg**, highlighted in Fig. 222a, and click on **Create**.

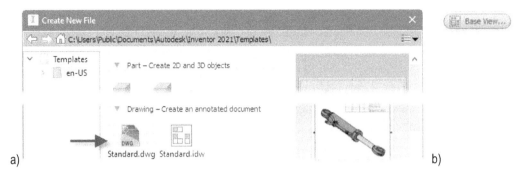

Fig. 222

After selecting a template file, the program will create the 2D drawing mode and will automatically display the drawing sheet in the form of **D**, containing default frame and title block.

You will put three orthogonal drawing views, one isometric view, parts list, and item numbers/balloons. To determine the base view, you will use the tool that allows you to select any view of the model. Default, the program offers the option to create multiple drawing views when you run the **Base view** command.

2. Create the three orthogonal views of the vise assembly and one isometric view. On the **Place Views** tab, in the **Create** panel, click on the **Base** icon. Alternatively, press and hold the right mouse button and pull towards: "**at 12.00 o'clock**". Release the button. For a moment, the program displays the **Base View**, as in Fig. 222b, and then runs the command.

The program "connects" the side view (the **FRONT)** of the assembly to the cursor, as in Fig. 223a. Click on the **View-Cube** arrow from right to set the side view: **RIGHT**, as in Fig. 223b.

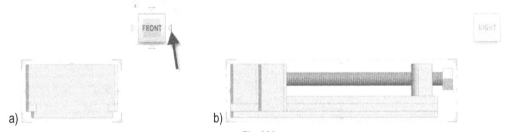

Fig. 223

Make sure that in the **Drawing View** dialog box, the view scale is **1:1**, as in Fig. 224a. Go to the **Display Options** tab and select the options: **Thread Feature**, **Tangent Edges**, and **Interference Edges**, as in Fig. 224b, which will display the thread and some edges in the drawing view.

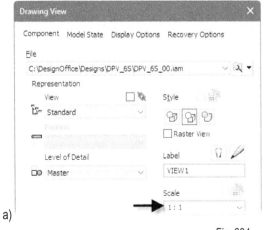

Fig. 224

Move the dialog box so it won't obscure the drawing area, then drag the cursor above the base view, as in Fig. 225, and confirm the localization of the top view.

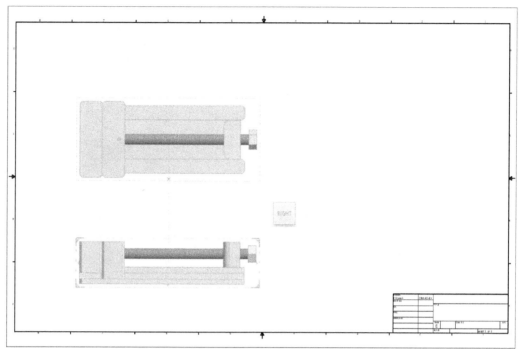

Fig. 225

Then move the cursor to the right of the base view, as in Fig. 226, and then click to confirm back view.

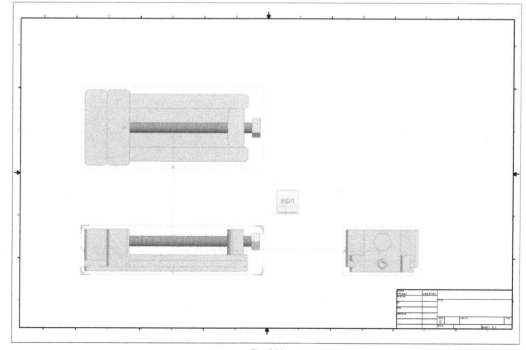

Fig. 226

The last view is an isometric view. Move the cursor above the back view, as in Fig. 227, and then click to confirm the isometric view.

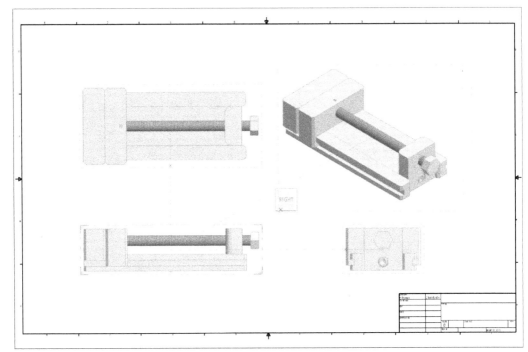

Fig. 227

To finish, right-click and select **OK**. The program will generate four drawing views shown in Fig. 228.

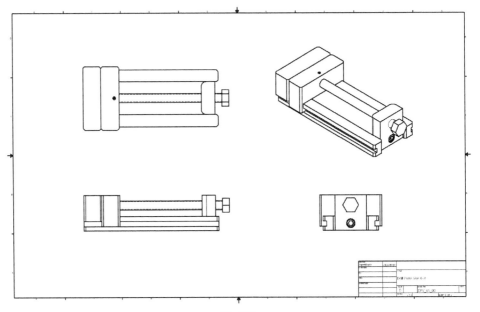

Fig. 228

It is worth noting that the drawing title block was automatically filled with the name and part number from the firstly placed drawing view.

3. Change the look of an isometric view to **Shaded**. Select the view, right-click and select the **Edit View** in the menu, as in Fig. 229a.

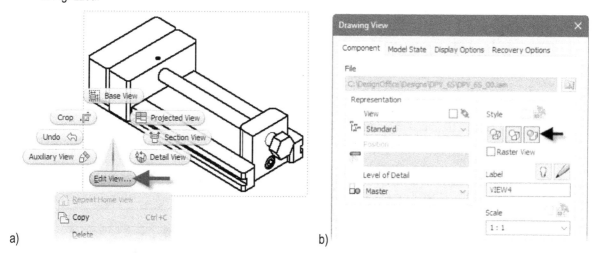

a)　　　　　　　　　　　　　　　　　　b)

Fig. 229

In the **Drawing View** dialog box enable **Shaded** option, indicated by the arrow in Fig. 229b, and click on **OK**. Now, an isometric view is shaded, as in Fig. 230.

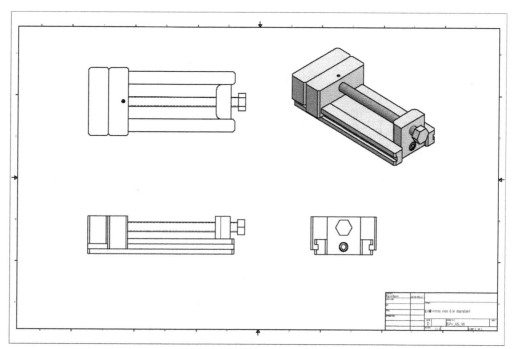

Fig. 230

4. Complete the drawing views with the centerlines. Right-click on the base view and select the **Automated Centerlines** in the menu. In the **Automated Centerlines** dialog box, enable the generation of the centerlines for **Revolved Features** parts and enable **Axis Parallel** view, as indicated in Fig. 231a.

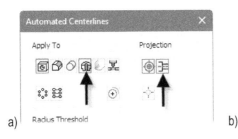
a)

b)

Fig. 231

Click on **OK**. The program generates centerlines of the bolt, as in Fig. 231b. Repeat this for the other two orthogonal views. If necessary, you can also manually add centerlines, using the tools contained in the **Symbols** panel, on the **Annotate** tab.

5. Create bounding box dimensions. On the **Annotate** tab, in the **Dimension** panel, click on the **Dimension** icon. Finished centerlines and dimensions are shown in Fig. 232.

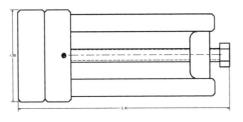
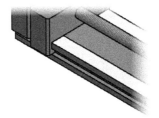

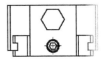

Fig. 232

6. Insert the list of parts. On the **Annotate** tab, in the **Table** panel, click on the **Parts List** icon. The program displays the **Parts List** dialog box and is waiting for you to select the source view to read the contents of the BOM database. Click on any of drawing views, and then click **OK**. in the **Parts list** dialog box. Place the parts list in the upper right side of the sheet, grabbing the upper right corner of the frame. The finished list of parts is shown in Fig. 233a.

This list consists of the default style parts list, stored in a library of styles and standards. You can modify the list of parts styles editing its local definition in the drawing or you can edit the list of parts directly in the drawing. Now, you will edit the list of parts directly in the drawing to add two columns.

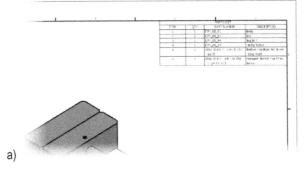
a)

b)

Fig. 233

7. Add the columns: **MATERIAL** and **MASS** to the list of parts. Right-click on the parts list and select **Edit Parts List** in the menu, as in Fig. 233b. In the **Parts List** dialog box, click on **Column Chooser** icon, shown in Fig. 234a.

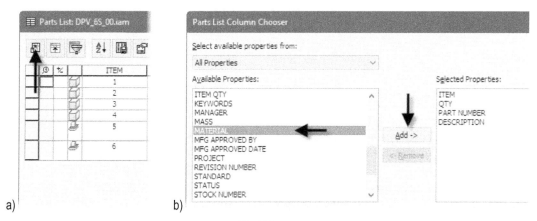

a)   b)

Fig. 234

In the **Parts List Column Chooser** window locate the **MATERIAL** position on the **Available Properties** list and click on **Add ->,** as in Fig. 234b. Then, locate the item **MASS** and click on **Add ->**. Click **OK**. Additional columns will now be presented, as in Fig. 235.

ITEM	QTY	PART NUMBER	DESCRIPTION	MATERIAL	MASS
1	1	DPV_6S_01	Body	Steel, Alloy	12,013 lbmass
2	1	DPV_6S_02	Jaw	Steel, Alloy	2,690 lbmass
3	1	DPV_6S_04	Support	Steel, Alloy	1,454 lbmass
4	1	DPV_6S_03	Clamping Screw	Steel, Alloy	0,771 lbmass
5	1	ANSI B18.6.2 - 1/4-20 UNC - 0,625	Slotted Headless Set Screw - Dog Point	Steel, Mild	0,007 lbmass
6	1	ANSI B18.3 - 3/8 - 16 UNC - 1 1/4 HS HCS	Hexagon Socket Head Cap Screw	Steel, Mild	0,060 lbmass

Fig. 235

Click **OK**. Supplemented list of parts looks like in Fig. 236.

PARTS LIST					
ITEM	QTY	PART NUMBER	DESCRIPTION	MATERIAL	MASS
1	1	DPV_6S_01	Body	Steel, Alloy	12,013 lbmass
2	1	DPV_6S_02	Jaw	Steel, Alloy	2,690 lbmass
3	1	DPV_6S_04	Support	Steel, Alloy	1,454 lbmass
4	1	DPV_6S_03	Clamp Screw	Steel, Alloy	0,771 lbmass
5	1	ANSI B18.6.2 - 1/4-20 UNC - 0,625	Slotted Headless Set Screw - Dog Point	Steel, Mild	0,007 lbmass
6	1	ANSI B18.3 - 3/8 - 16 UNC - 1 1/4 HS HCS	Hexagon Socket Head Cap Screw	Steel, Mild	0,060 lbmass

Fig. 236

8. Correct the column widths. Grab the boundary line of the column and drag to the left or to the right to adjust the column's width to the contents. Matched widths are presented in Fig. 237.

ITEM	QTY	PART NUMBER	DESCRIPTION	MATERIAL	MASS
			PARTS LIST		
1	1	DPV_6S_01	Body	Steel, Alloy	12,013 lbmass
2	1	DPV_6S_02	Jaw	Steel, Alloy	2,690 lbmass
3	1	DPV_6S_04	Support	Steel, Alloy	1,454 lbmass
4	1	DPV_6S_03	Clamp Screw	Steel, Alloy	0,771 lbmass
5	1	ANSI B18.6.2 - 1/4-20 UNC - 0,625	Slotted Headless Set Screw - Dog Point	Steel, Mild	0,007 lbmass
6	1	ANSI B18.3 - 3/8 - 16 UNC - 1 1/4 HS HCS	Hexagon Socket Head Cap Screw	Steel, Mild	0,060 lbmass

Fig. 237

You can set up multiple styles of the lists of parts, in the Style Library, in which you will store the information about the selected columns and their widths and other settings. As a result, the list will immediately be created correctly, according to the selected style. For more information about creating your own styles refer to the help system.

9. Add balloons by using the automatic option. On the **Annotate** tab, in the **Table** panel, click on the **Auto Balloon** icon. The program displays the **Auto Balloon** dialog box and is waiting for you to select the view of the source from which will be reading the numbering data. Click on any views in the drawing, since all the views come from the same file. Then, the program is expected to identify the components that are to be ballooned. Select the whole top view using the window selection tool, as in Fig. 238a.

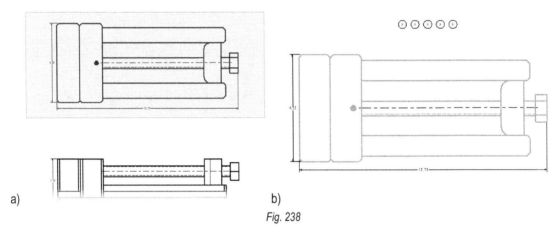

a)   b)

Fig. 238

In the **Auto Balloon** dialog, in the **Placement** area, click on the **Select Placement** button, and then select the location for balloons above the top view, as in Fig. 238b. Click **Apply**. The program will create the balloons, as in Fig. 239a.

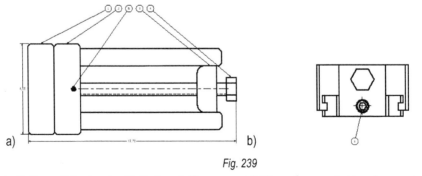

a)   b)

Fig. 239

The **Auto Balloon** dialog box is still displayed. There are no balloons for a socket head cap screw. Click on the view again, and then click the screw head shown in the back view. In the **Auto Balloon** dialog box click on the **Select Placement** and place a balloon for the screw below the view as in Fig. 239b. Click **OK**.

Now, you can assume that the technical drawing of the vise assembly is ready.

10. Save the drawing file in the folder **...\DesignOffice\Designs\DPV_6S**. By default, the program will suggest a name for the drawing file as the same name as the assembly file's name, which was formed the first drawing view: **DPV_6S_00**. Extension of drawing: **DWG**. End of exercise.

Exercise summary

You can create some drawing views of the assembly model, supplemented by centerlines and dimensions. You can add balloons and insert the list of parts for the assembly drawing. In the next exercise, you will create the exploded drawing of the vise.

Exercise 14
Technical assembly drawing with an exploded view

In this exercise, you will create a drawing showing the vise in a disassembled state, with the description of the individual components. You will create one exploded view of the vise and you will adopt the style of the balloons to the needs of this drawing. In addition, you will create a list of purchased parts. The finished exploded drawing is shown in Fig. 240.

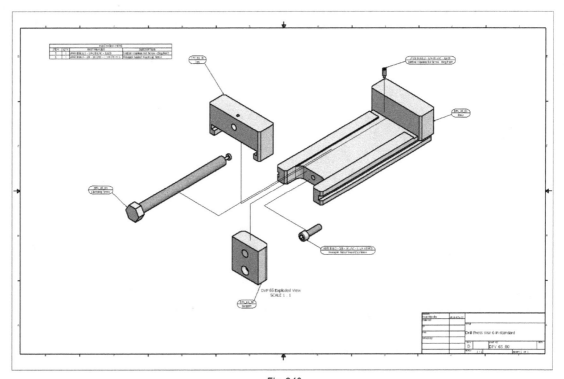

Fig. 240

*Before starting this exercise, complete the **Exercise 12. Creating a presentation**, on page 97.*

 1. Start creating a new drawing file. On the **Get Started** tab, in the **Launch** panel, click on the **New** icon. In the **Create New File** dialog box, select the template **Standard.dwg**, highlighted in Fig. 241a, and click on **Create**.

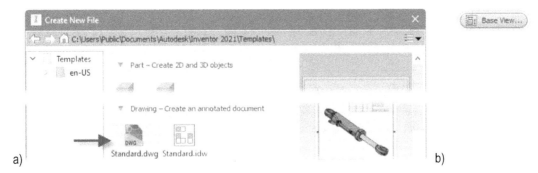

Fig. 241

After selecting a template file, the program moves to create the 2D drawing mode and automatically displays the drawing sheet in the form of **D**, containing the default frame and the title block.

You will place one drawing view based on the saved view **Exploded** in the **DVP 6S_00.ipn** file.

2.   Create an exploded view. On the **Place Views** tab, in the **Create** panel, click on the **Base** icon. Alternatively, press and hold the right mouse button and pull towards: "**at 12.00 o'clock**". Release the button. For a moment, the program displays the **Base View**, as in Fig. 241b and then runs the command.

In the **Drawing View** dialog box, click on the **Open an existing file** icon, indicated by the arrow in Fig. 242a, and select the file **DVP_6S_00.ipn**, saved in **DVP_6S** folder. Set the options for displaying and describing the view as in Fig. 242b.

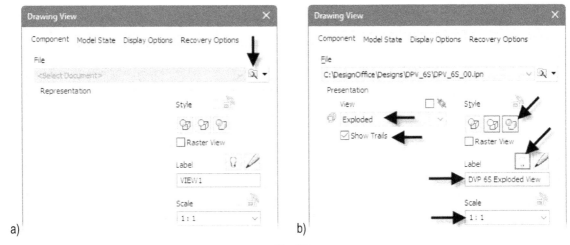

Fig. 242

Set the exploded view like in Fig. 243, then right-click and select **OK**, to confirm.

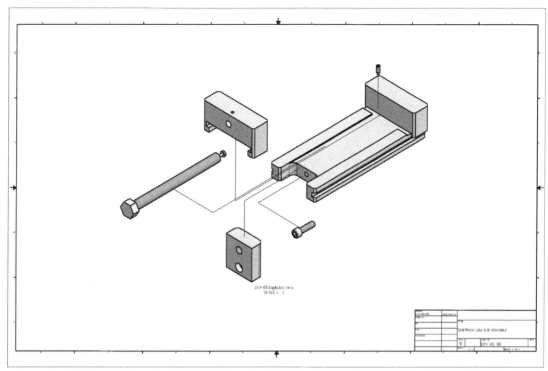

Fig. 243

Now you will create a drawing description using balloons. Before, you will create a new local style of balloons, which you will use to create the description of the components. The new balloon style will contain the part number and description, instead of the item number.

3. Create a local style of balloons. On the **Manage** tab, in the **Styles and Standards** panel, click on the **Styles Editor** icon. In the **Style and Standard Editor**, expand the **Balloon** node, right-click the style **Balloon (ANSI)** and select **New Style**, as in Fig. 244a.

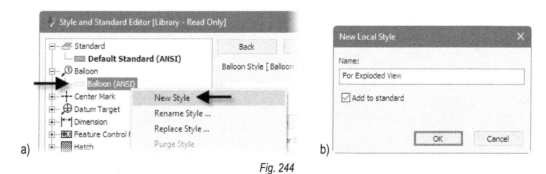

Fig. 244

In the **New Local Style** dialog box enter new style name as in Fig. 244b and click **OK**.

In the **Balloon Formatting** area, pull down the list of balloon shapes and select **Circular – 2 Entries**, indicated in Fig. 245a.

Fig. 245

Next, click the **Property Chooser** button, indicated in Fig. 245b. In the **Property Chooser** dialog box set the properties **PART NUMBER** and **DESCRIPTION** as a **Selected Properties**, as in Fig. 246a. Click **OK**.

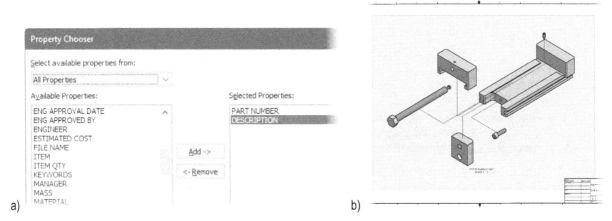

Fig. 246

In the **Style and Standard Editor** dialog box click **Save and Close** button.

4. Create a description of the components in the drawing. On the **Annotate** tab, in the **Table** panel, click on the **Auto Balloon** icon. The program displays the **Auto Balloon** dialog box and is waiting for you to select the view of the source from which will be read the numbering data. Click on exploded view and next select the whole view using the window selection tool, as in Fig. 246b.

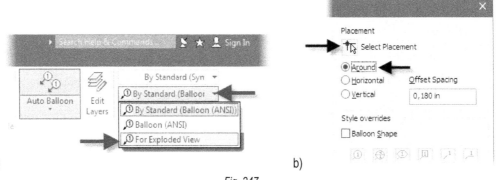

Fig. 247

Select the style of balloons and the localization. In the **Format** panel, pull down the list of balloon styles and select **For Exploded View** style indicated in Fig. 247a. In the **Placement** area, select **Around** option, shown in Fig. 247b and then click **Select Placement** button.

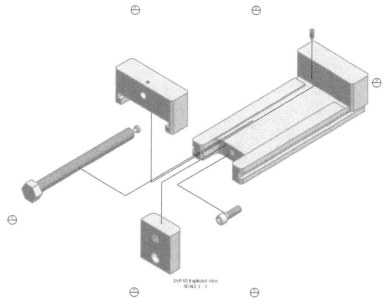

Fig. 248

By moving the mouse, you can to arrange the balloons around an exploded view, as in Fig. 248. Click to confirm the position. Click **OK**. to complete. The program places balloons filled with part numbers and descriptions of the components as in Fig. 249.

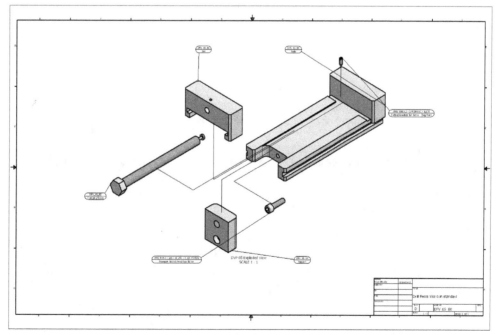

Fig. 249

The balloons can now be moved manually to achieve the desired appearance of the drawing.

Now, you will put on the drawing list of the purchased parts. To do this, you will modify the list of parts using the filters.

 5. Insert the list of parts. On the **Annotate** tab, In the **Table** panel, click on the **Parts List** icon. The program displays the **Parts List** dialog box and is waiting for you to select the source view to read the contents of the database BOM. Click on the exploded view, and then click **OK**. in the **Parts list** dialog box. Place the list of parts in the upper left side of the sheet as in Fig. 250a.

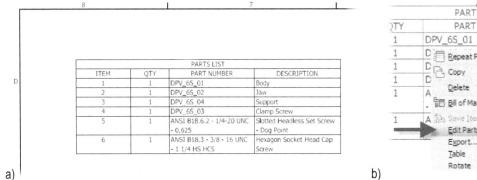
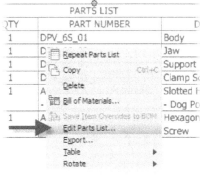

a)   b)

Fig. 250

6. Edit the list to include only the purchased components. Right-click on the list of parts and select the **Edit Parts List** in the menu, as in Fig. 250b. In the **Parts List** dialog box, click on the **Filter Settings** icon, shown in Fig. 251a.

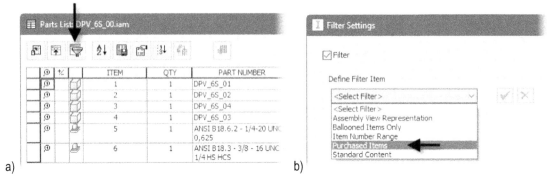

a)   b)

Fig. 251

In the **Filter Settings** dialog box, select the **Purchased Items** on the list, as shown in Fig. 251b, and then enable **Purchased Items Only**, and click on the **Add Filter**, as in Fig. 252a.

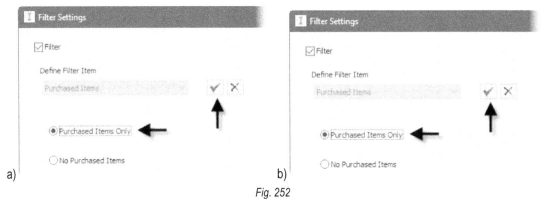

a)   b)

Fig. 252

The new filter appears in the list of filters, as in Fig. 252b. Click **OK**. The contents of the **Parts List** window will be restricted to purchased items, as in Fig. 253a.

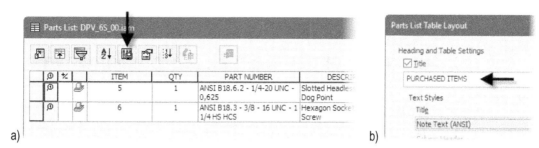

a)   b)

Fig. 253

Change the title of the list. Click on the **Table Layout** icon, shown in Fig. 253a. In the **Parts List Table Layout**, enter a new title, as in Fig. 253b. Click **OK**.

Click **OK**. in the **Parts List** dialog box. The contents of the list are now shown in Fig. 254.

PURCHASED ITEMS			
ITEM	QTY	PART NUMBER	DESCRIPTION
5	1	ANSI B18.6.2 - 1/4-20 UNC - 0,625	Slotted Headless Set Screw - Dog Point
6	1	ANSI B18.3 - 3/8 - 16 UNC - 1 1/4 HS HCS	Hexagon Socket Head Cap Screw

Fig. 254

A completed drawing including an exploded view, descriptions and list of purchased components is shown in Fig. 255.

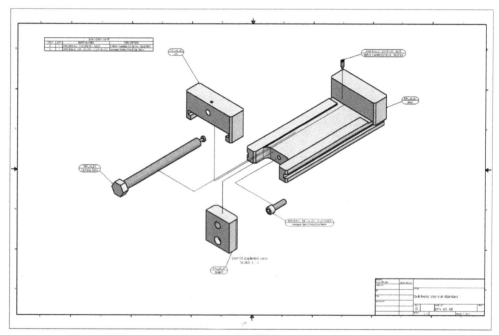

Fig. 255

7. Save the drawing in folder **...\DesignOffice\Designs\DPV_6S** using the name: **DPV_6S_00_Exploded**. File extension: **DWG**. End of exercise.

Exercise summary

Now, you know how to prepare a drawing presenting an exploded view of the designed product. You already know how to create different styles of balloons and how to apply filters to obtain a restricted list of parts. In the next exercise, you will create technical drawings for the remaining parts of the projected vise. In these drawings, you will learn how to apply new drawing elements which have not been used yet, such as breaking view, break out view and detail view.

Exercise 15
2D drawings of parts. Break out, breaking and detail views

In this exercise you will create technical drawings of the vise body, clamping screw and clamping screw support. You know how to create a drawing of the part containing the orthogonal views and dimensioning if you have completed *Exercise 2.The technical drawing of the part. The jaw*, on page *26*. In this exercise, you will focus on the creation of drawing elements, which have not yet done before. Drawing elements like dimensioning, descriptions and symbols you will complete by yourself. In this exercise, you will prepare drawings shown in Fig. 256.

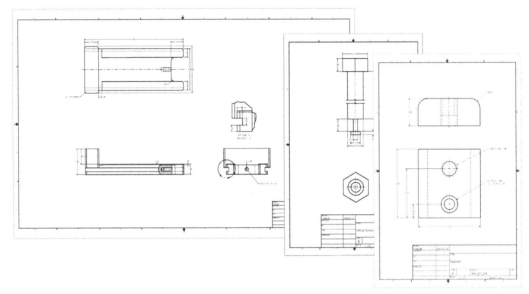

Fig. 256

You will start with the technical drawing of the vise body, in which you will put break out view and detail view.

1. Create a new technical drawing of the vise body based on **DPV_6S_01.ipt** file saved in folder **...\DesignOffice\Designs\DPV_6S**. The drawing should be done on sheet form **D**, in scale **1:1**, with disabled hidden edges. Additionally, enable thread features in the **Display Options** tab, as in Fig. 257a. Create orthogonal views shown in Fig. 257b.

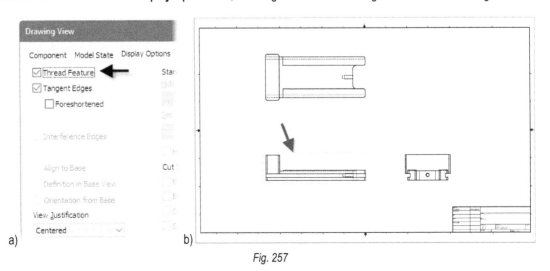

Fig. 257

Now, you will create the break out in the base view, which will show a threaded hole. You will start with the sketch of the break out border.

2. Create a sketch of the boundary of a break out. The sketch should be associated with a particular view. Click in the area of the base view, to display a frame with a dashed line around the view, as in Fig. 257. Then, on the **Place View** tab, in the **Sketch** panel, click on **Start Sketch** icon. The program will turn on the sketch mode in the selected view. The center of the coordinate system of the sketch should be placed in the center of the base view.

3. Using a spline draw a closed shape of a break out boundary. On the **Sketch** tab, in the **Create** panel, click on the **Spline Interpolation** icon. Draw a shape shown in Fig. 258a. To close a loop just connect endpoint of the spline with the starting point. You can also draw a rectangle or any other closed shape.

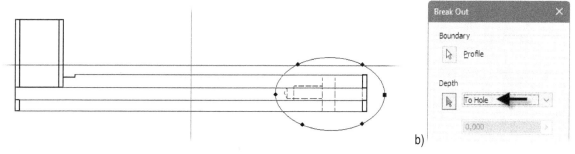

a)   b)

Fig. 258

4. Finish the sketch. Now you can create a break out.

5. Create a break out. On the **Place Views** tab, in the **Modify** panel click the **Break Out** icon. If there is still an active base view then the program automatically recognizes a closed loop, for use as a boundary for a break out, and displays the **Break Out** dialog box. If a base view is not active just click it. Now you should determine the depth of the break out. On the **Depth** list, select **To Hole** option, as in Fig. 258b. When you choose the option select the hole in the side view, indicated by an arrow in Fig. 259a.

a)   b)

Fig. 259

Click **OK**. in **Break Out** dialog box. The program creates a break out as in Fig. 259b. Now you will create a detail showing the groove of jaw guides.

6. Create a detail view. On the **Place Views** tab, in the **Create** panel, click the **Detail** icon. The program is expecting you to indicate the view. Click in the middle of the side view shown in Fig. 260a.

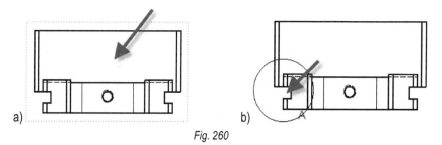

a)   b)

Fig. 260

The program displays a **Detail** dialog box, in which you can set the parameters of the detail view. The program is expecting you to indicate the range of detail. Click in the center of the groove, indicated by the arrow and drag to set the range of detail as in Fig. 260b. Click to confirm the border of the detail view and place the detail view above the side view, as in Fig. 261a.

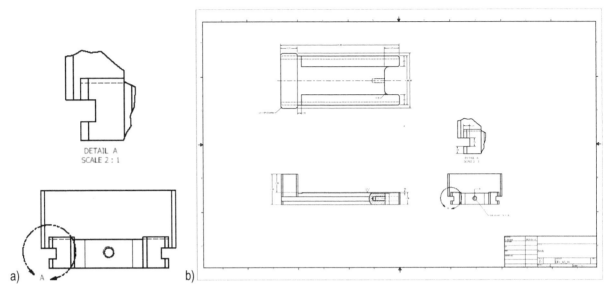

a)   b)

Fig. 261

7. Based on previously acquired skills complete the technical drawing of the vise body by the centerlines, dimensioning, mechanical symbols, etc., according to the needs. Use the dimensioning derived from model sketches whenever possible. If necessary, complete the dimensioning manually. The finished technical drawing of the vise body is shown in Fig. 261b.

8. Save the drawing file in folder **...\DPV_6S**. By default, the program will suggest a name for the drawing which is the same name as the part file name, which formed the first drawing view: **DPV_6S_01**. Extension of drawing: **DWG**.

9. Create a new technical drawing of the clamping screw. This drawing should include two views in scale **2:1**, on sheet form size **B**. After selecting the drawing template, the program uses by default sheet form size **D**. Right-click in the browser **Sheet:1** and select **Edit Sheet** in the menu. In the **Edit Sheet** dialog box select form size **B** form **Size** list and set the **Portrait** orientation of a sheet, as in Fig. 262a.

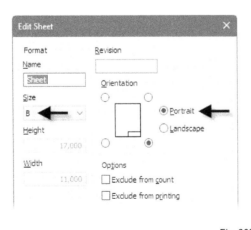

a)

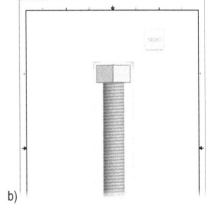

b)

Fig. 262

Click **OK**. The program changed the size and frame of a sheet.

10. Create two orthogonal drawing views of the screw based on file **DPV_6S_03.ipt** stored in the folder **...DesignOf-fice\Designs\DPV_6S**. Set the views scale to **2:1**, and select **FRONT** as an orientation of the base view, like in Fig. 262b. Place the view as in Fig. 263a. As you can see the view goes beyond a frame of the sheet. To better fit the contents of the drawing to a sheet you will use a break view.

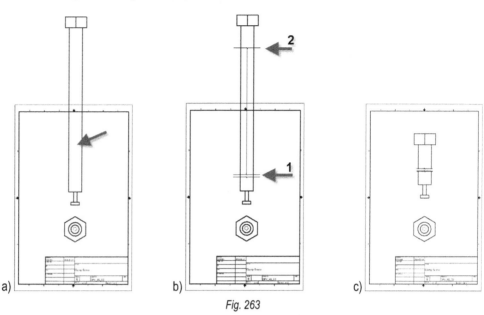

Fig. 263

11. Create a break view. On the **Place Views** tab, in the **Modify** panel, click **Break** icon. The program is expecting you to indicate a drawing view for breaking. Click in the middle of the view indicated by the arrow in Fig. 263a. The program displays a **Break** dialog box, where you can set options for break view. The program is expecting you to indicate the boundary points of the break.

Extend the range of the break between points marked by 1 and 2 in Fig. 263b. When you select the second point the program executes a break. Drawing view with the break is shown in Fig. 263c (after moving the view down).

12. Based on previously acquired skills, complete the technical drawing of the clamping screw by the centerlines, dimensioning, mechanical symbols, etc., according to your needs. Use the dimensioning derived from model sketches whenever possible. If necessary, complete the dimensioning manually. Note that the program placed the dimension of the screw length without subtracting break size which is expected behavior. The finished technical drawing of the clamping screw is shown in Fig. 264a.

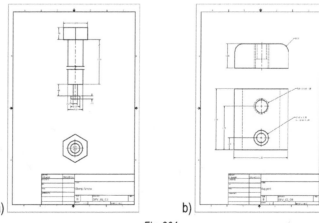

Fig. 264

13. Save the drawing in folder **…\DesignOffice\Designs\DPV_6S** with the name: **DPV_6S_03**. File extension: **DWG**.

14. At the end of this exercise create by yourself a technical drawing of the support for the clamping screw. To create a drawing, select the file **DPV_6S_04.ipt** stored in the folder **…\DesignOffice\Designs\DPV_6S**. Assume the scale of **2:1**, the sheet size **B**. In this drawing you should to manually place most of the dimensions because the 3D model was formed mostly by a projection of the edges of the other part. The finished drawing of the support is presented in Fig. 264b.

15. Save the drawing in folder **…\DesignOffice\Designs\DPV_6S** with the name: **DPV_6S_04**. File extension: **DWG**.

Close all opened files of the models and drawings. End of exercise.

Exercise summary

You know how to create drawing views that contain breaks, break out's and details. You can assume that the first project whose goal was to design a drill press vise DPV_6S, has been completed. In the end, you have a set of 3D models and technical drawings of all assemblies and parts.

Doing the exercises of a first project you learned the basic techniques of modeling parts and assemblies, you know how to work in the context of the assembly and how to prepare a technical drawing of the design. In the following exercises, you will learn how to easily get a new version of the design based on an existing design, while maintaining appropriate relationships between 3D and 2D files.

Exercise 16
Creating a new version of the vise based on the current version

You can assume that you have to do another version of the machine vise, indicated as **DVP_6S_M**, which is slightly different from the vise **DVP_6S**. The new version will be modified so the corps of the vise can be attached to a tabletop. Also, in the new version the clamping screw head will be changed from hexagonal to cylindrical. Other components of the vise can be used without change from model **DVP_6S**. In addition, you must create an illustration and a video presentation of the new version of the vise for marketing purposes.

In this exercise, you will create a new version of the vise based on your existing version of the vise. You will learn how to create a copy of the design while maintaining relationships between files. Fig. 265a shows the current version of the vise **DVP_6S** and Fig. 265b shows the new design – **DVP_6S_M**.

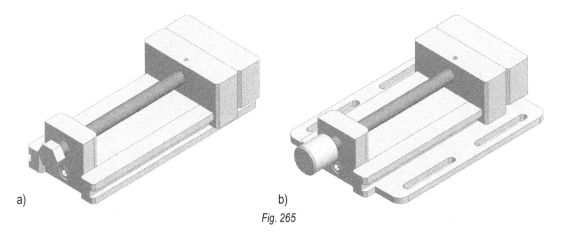

a)   b)

Fig. 265

To produce a new version of the vise you should create: a new model of the body, a new drawing of the body, a new model of the clamping screw, a new drawing of the clamping screw, a new model of the assembly and a new assembly drawing. The rest of the 3D models and drawings can be taken without change from the model **DVP_6S**. In order to obtain files of a new version, you will create a copy of an existing design, renaming necessary files.

In the Autodesk Inventor 2021 the entire process of creating a copy of the design consists of two phases:

- Creating copies of models and drawings, taking into consideration changes in the names of files and maintain relationships among files;

- Entering construction modifications in copied files of 3D models and drawings.

As a result, copies of drawing files are automatically updated, and the original files of the previous version will not be affected. In the end, you will have to view the new drawing files and update or complement dimensioning, descriptions and annotations.

To create a copy of an existing design you will use the **Design Assistant 2021** utility program, which is normally installed with Autodesk Inventor 2021. This program ensures the proper procedure of the copying process while maintaining proper relationships between files.

The new version of the vise and all the new files will be placed in the folder **DVP_6S_M**. Files used in a new version but applied without any changes remain in the original location.

Copying model files, renaming files, and maintaining file relationships should only be performed using the Design Assistant 2021 program or any program from the Autodesk Vault 2021 family.

---

 1. Run the **Design Assistant 2021** program. Click **START > Autodesk Inventor 2021> Design Assistant 2021**. The program will display a blank window in the **Properties** mode.

 2. Open the main assembly file of the vise – **DVP_6S_00.iam**. Click the **Open** icon and open file **DVP_6S_00.iam** which you can find in the **…\Designs\DPV_6S** folder. In **Properties** mode the content of the **Design Assistant 2021** window is like in Fig. 266.

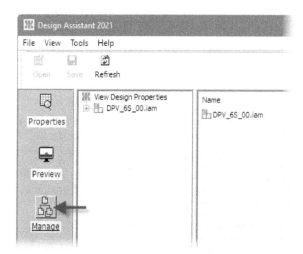

Fig. 266

In the **Properties** mode, you can revise, supplement and copy of the file properties. The administrative operations carried out in the design, such as renaming the file or copying the design are implemented in the **Manage** mode.

 3. Switch to the **Manage** mode. Click on **Manage** icon shown in Fig. 266. The program displays a structure of the **DVP_6S_00** assembly file, like in Fig. 267.

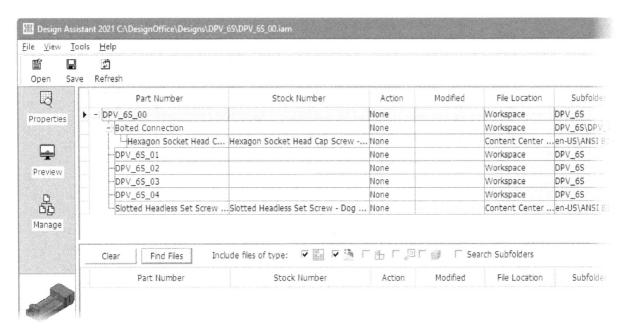

Fig. 267

In the new version of the vise you will change the body of the vise, and thus the assembly model. Therefore, you have to create copies of the vise assembly and the body part files. New files should be placed in the new folder: **DVP_6S_M**.

4.   Select the files you want to copy. At the row of the **DVP 6S_00** file, right-click in the **Action** column, and in the menu that appears, select **Copy**, as shown in Fig. 268a.

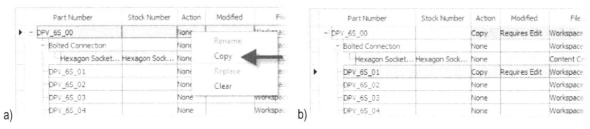

Fig. 268

The program will place, in the **Action** column, marking operations: **Copy**. Also, select to create a copy model of the body **DVP_6S_01**. Now both files are marked as files to be copied, as in Fig. 268b.

5.   Create a new folder for copies of the files. Select the rows of both files to be highlighted in light blue. Right mouse clicks in the column **Subfolder** and, in the menu that appears, select **Change Path**, as in Fig. 269a. In **Browse For Folder** dialog box create a subfolder **DVP_6S_M**, located in the folder **... \Designs**, as in Fig. 269b.

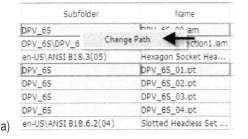
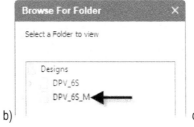

Fig. 269

Highlight the folder and click **OK**. The path to the file copies will be as shown in Fig. 269c.

6.   Rename the copied file. Right-click the **DVP 6S_00** in the **Name** column and in the menu select **Change Name**, as in Fig. 270a.

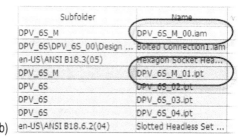

Fig. 270

In the **Open** window, in the **File Name** field, enter a name for the copied file: **DVP_6S_M_00** and click **Open**. Repeat this operation for **DVP_6S_01** file by entering the name of the copied file **DVP_6S_M_01**. Now the new file names will be visible in the **Name** column, as in Fig. 270b. Notice that at the same time the content if the **Part Number** column is updated automatically.

You may assume that the operation of duplicating files of 3D models has been prepared. In a similar manner, you will prepare an operation to create a copy of related files: technical drawing of a vise assembly, technical drawing of a vise body and other related files.

At this point, you have prepared the copy operation for the assembly file and body part file. The copy of the clamping screw file you will do later in the exercises to get to know the method to replace an existing file with a copy.

7.   Find the associated files: drawings files and presentations files. Select the model's files to find all related files. Press the **CTRL** key and select the rows of files: **DVP_6S_M_00** and **DVP_6S_M_01** have been highlighted in light blue. In the bottom section of the window, select related **DWG** files and **IPN** files type, as in Fig. 271.

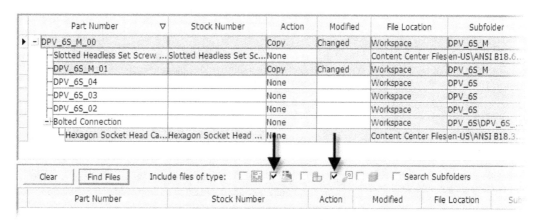

Fig. 271

After selecting the file types, click the **Find Files** button. Click **OK**. in the message box. The program will find four related files: a presentation file, a technical drawing of the assembly, an exploding drawing of a vise and technical drawing of the part, as shown in Fig. 272.

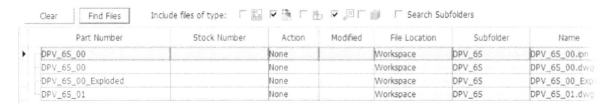

Fig. 272

Proceeding as files of 3D models, create copies of these four files in the new folder. First, select what action to take on found files.

8. Mark files to make a copy. For all four files, right-click in the **Action** column and select **Copy** in the menu. The **Copy** indicator will appear in the **Action** column in rows of all marked files, as in Fig. 273a.

a)   b)

Fig. 273

9. Change the destination folder for copies of related files. Be sure that the rows of all related files are still highlighted in light blue. Click the right mouse button in the **Subfolder** column and then select **Change Path** in the menu. In the **Browse For Folder** window, locate the subfolder **... \Designs\DPV_6S_M** and click **OK**. The new subfolder will be included in the location of all the related files as in Fig. 273b.

10. Rename the related copied files. In the line of each file, right-click in the **Name** column and in the menu that appears select **Change Name**. In the **Open** window, in the **File Name** field, enter the new name of the file copy, as in the **Name** column in Fig. 274. At the same time, the content of the **Part Number** column will be updated.

Fig. 274

At this point, you have been completed all the preparatory operations of creating a copy of design including its associated files. After finishing the preparation activities, the contents of a **Design Assistant** window should present itself as in Fig. 275.

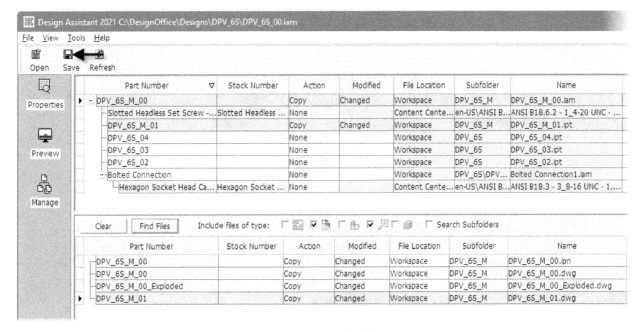

Fig. 275

11. Confirm the operation. Click the **Save** icon, located in the toolbar of the **Design Assistant 2021** window, as shown in Fig. 275. Click **OK.**, in a message window.

12. Close the **Design Assistant 2021** window.

 13. In the Autodesk Inventor 2021 software open the assembly model of a new version of vise **DVP_6S_M_00.iam**, located in **...\Designs\DPV_6S_M** folder. On the screen appears the assembly model of the vise as in Fig. 276a.

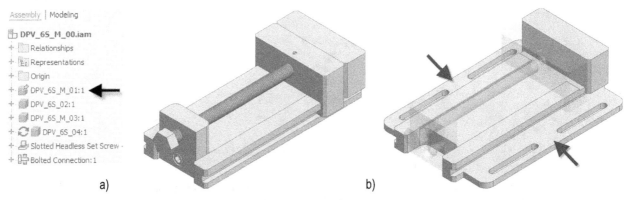

Fig. 276

Notice, that in the browser the body of the vise is also marked as **DVP_6S_M_01**. Now you will change the geometry of the model, adding to the main body new features for mounting the vise on the tabletop.

14. Move to the editing of the body – double-click the body. The program will be grayed out all other components and enable for editing model of the body in the context of the assembly. Create a fastener shown in Fig. 276b. You may apply any values for dimensions of this element.

 15. Finish editing of the body after entering modifications. Now, the vise looks like in Fig. 277.

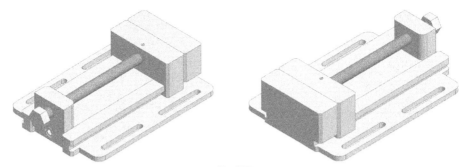

Fig. 277

It turns out that you forgot about the clamping screw. In the new version of the vise, the hexagonal head of the bolt should be replaced with a cylindrical head, for manual clamping jaws without a key.

This is a typical situation, usually, it is not possible to foresee all the files you want to copy. In this case, you will make a copy of a set of files for its model and drawing, then replace the existing part with its copy in the assembly model. The entire operation can be performed during execution of a replecment component command – „on the fly".

16. Replace the existing clamping screw with its copy. In the browser, right-click the component **DPV_6S_03:1** and select **Component –> Replace**, in the menu, as in Fig. 278a.

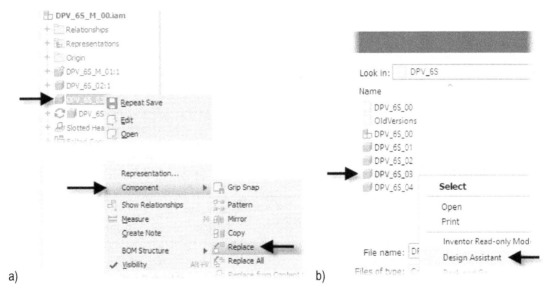

a)   b)

Fig. 278

Create "on the fly" a copy of part and the associated drawing. In the **Place Component** window, locate the **DPV_6S_03** file of the part, in the folder **DPV_6S**, then right-click the part file and select **Design Assistant** in the menu, as in Fig. 277b. The program opens the **Design Assistant** window containing one item – a file **DPV_6S_03.ipt**.

In the **Design Assistant** window, select the file to create a copy of the screw, change the subfolder to **DPV_6S_M** and enter a new name for the file of the screw: **DPV_6S_M_03.ipt**. The changes required are shown in Fig. 279.

Part Number	Stock Number	Action	Modified	File Location	Subfolder	Name
DPV_6S_M_03		Copy	Changed	Workspace	DPV_6S_M	DPV_6S_M_03.ipt

Fig. 279

Now you have to find associated drawing file. In the bottom of the window, select the icon **DWG**, and then click the **Find Files** button. The program finds three files, which use the current part file of the screw. Create a copy of the technical drawing file of the clamping screw only. Mark the row to create a copy of the drawing file, enter a new subfolder name **DPV_6S_M**, and enter a new name for the drawing file **DPV_6S_M_03.dwg**, as shown in Fig. 280.

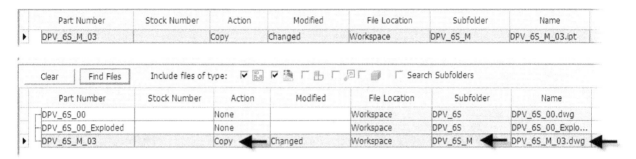

	Part Number	Stock Number	Action	Modified	File Location	Subfolder	Name
▶	DPV_6S_M_03		Copy	Changed	Workspace	DPV_6S_M	DPV_6S_M_03.ipt

Clear	Find Files	Include files of type: ☑ ☑ ☐ ☐ ☐ ☐ Search Subfolders					
Part Number	Stock Number	Action	Modified	File Location	Subfolder	Name	
DPV_6S_00		None		Workspace	DPV_6S	DPV_6S_00.dwg	
DPV_6S_00_Exploded		None		Workspace	DPV_6S	DPV_6S_00_Explo...	
▶ DPV_6S_M_03		Copy	Changed	Workspace	DPV_6S_M	DPV_6S_M_03.dwg	

Fig. 280

Click **Save** to confirm the copy operation, click **OK**. and then close the **Design Assistant** window - you're back in the **Place Component** dialog box.

Navigate to the folder **DVP_6S_M**, locate the file **DVP_6S_M_03.ipt**, as in Fig. 281a, and click **Open**.

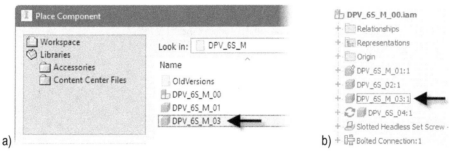

a)   b)

Fig. 281

The file of the clamping screw will be replaced with a new one, which is clearly visible in the browser, as in Fig. 281b. Now the geometry of the new screw must be modified.

17. Move to the editing of the clamping screw – double-click the clamping screw. The program will be grayed out all other components and enable for editing model of the screw in the context of the assembly, as in Fig. 282a.

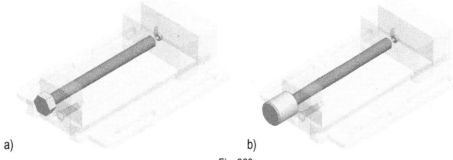

a)   b)

Fig. 282

Remove the features which form the hexagonal head (Extrusion1) of the screw and create a cylindrical knob with a diameter of **1.35** inch and high of **1.5** inches. Create chamfer edges of a cylinder with a value of **0.075** inches. The finished cylindrical knob is shown in Fig. 282b.

18. Finish editing the clamping screw after entering modifications. The newly completed version of the vise looks as is does in Fig. 283a.

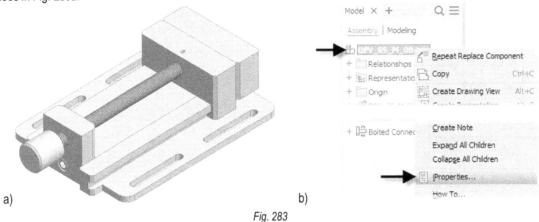

a)   b)

Fig. 283

You can assume that the geometry of the new version of the vise has been changed. Now you need to make corrections in the description of the components of the new version, contained in **iProperties**. The program takes most of the property's values from the previous version to the new version. You will need to change the descriptions of the assembly file, as well as, the descriptions of the body and clamping screw.

19. Change the description of the new version of the vise. In the browser right-click on file name **DPV_6S_M_00.iam** and select **iProperties** in the menu, as in Fig. 283b. In the **DPV_6S_M_00 iProperties**, go to the **Project** tab and enter in the appropriate fields, the data presented in Fig. 284a.

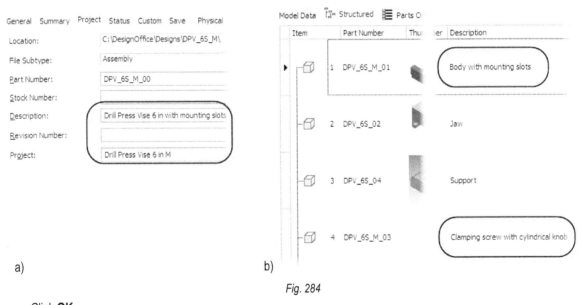

a)   b)

Fig. 284

Click **OK**.

Now, you will perform the changes in the descriptions of the body and clamping screw but in the **Bill of Materials** dialog box.

20. Modify the descriptions of the new body and clamping screw. On the **Assemble** tab, in the **Manager** panel click the **Bill of Material** icon. Move to the **Structured** tab and edit description of the body and clamping screw, as in Fig. 284b. Click **Done**.

21. Save the assembly file. Click **Yes** to confirm the saving of the edited part files.

Now, let's see how the changes look in the contents of the assembly drawing of the **DVP_6S_M_00** vise, the exploded drawing, the drawing of the body and the drawing of the clamping screw.

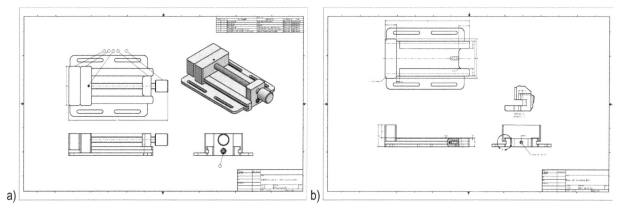

a) b)

Fig. 285

 22. Open the file **DVP_6S_M_00.dwg**, located in the folder **...\Designs\DPV_6S_M**. The program opens and regenerates the assembly drawing of the vise. After adjusting the starting points and the location of the existing dimensions the drawing looks like in Fig. 285a. It is worth to note that in the title block there is entered a part number and description of the new version of the vise and on the parts list, there are part number **DVP_6S_M_01** of a new body and the part number **DVP_6S_M_03** of a new clamping screw along with a new description. The rest of the parts have the same as in the **DVP_6S_00** vise.

 23. Open the file **DVP_6S_M_01.dwg**, located in the folder **...\Designs\DPV_6S_M**. The program opens and regenerates the drawing of the body, as in Fig. 285b.

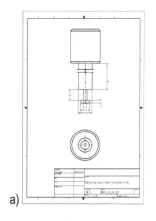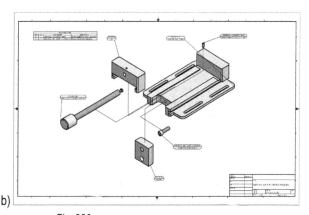

a) b)

Fig. 286

 24. Open the file **DVP_6S_M_03.dwg**, located in the folder **...\Designs\DPV_6S_M**. The program opens and regenerates the drawing of the clamping screw, as in Fig. 286a.

 25. Open the file **DVP_6S_M_00_Exploded.dwg**, located in the folder **...\DrillPressVises \DPV_6S_M**. The program opens and regenerates the drawing of the exploded presentation of the vise, as in Fig. 286b (after adjustment of the anchor points of the balloons).

 All drawings must be completed with the necessary dimensions and descriptions, taking into account the changes in the design of the vise.

In the new assembly file, in the Inventor Studio environment, there is stored information about the parameters of rendering the illustration and about animation settings, copied from the original assembly file. You can easily do a rendered illustration and video presentation for a new version of the vise, without the need to re-set the parameters of the existing scene and animation.

26. Turn on the Inventor Studio module. On the **Environments** tab, in the **Begin** panel, click the **Inventor Studio** icon. The program remembers the camera and lighting style used in the original file.

27. Turn on the shadows and reflections. On the **View** tab, in the **Appearance** panel, click on the **Shadows** and **Reflections** icons.

28. Create a rendered illustration. On the **Render** tab, in the **Render** panel, click the **Render Image** icon. In the **Render Image** dialog box, on the **General** tab, set the resolution of the illustration and make sure that the current camera is **Camera1**, and lighting style is set to **Photo Booth**. In the **Render** tab enable options **Until Satisfactory** and then click **Render** button. In the **Render Output** dialog box, you can stop rendering after reaching a satisfactory picture quality. After stopping the rendering save the image in the project folder, under the name of **Image DPV_6S_M_00.jpg**. This illustration could be perhaps used for product marketing purposes. Close the **Render Output** window. An illustration of a new version of the vise may look like in Fig. 287.

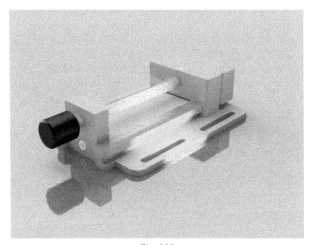

Fig. 287

29. Now, you can also render a video for the new version of the vise, based on the saved animation settings from the original assembly file **DVP_6S_00.iam**. Try it yourself.

30. Save and close all opened files. End of the exercise.

Exercise summary

You know how to easily get a new version of the design based on an existing design while maintaining appropriate relationships between 3D and 2D files without having to re-create the 2D drawings and thus reduce the amount of work to do.

Exercise 17
A task: do it yourself

Based on the **DVP_6S_M_00.iam** model create a new version of drill press vise named **DVP_6S_MI_00**, shown in Fig. 288. Create a 3D model and complete drawing documentation, illustration files, and a video. In this new version, following new files will appear – 3D models of jaw inserts and a rod for clamping screw, as well as their drawings and additional fasteners. Only the support of the clamping screw will remain unchanged - the rest of the files will be given new names and will be modified.

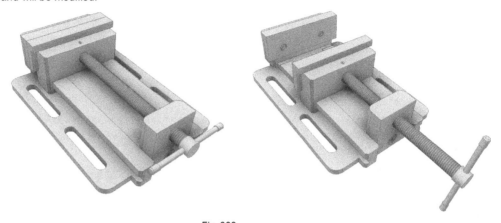

Fig. 288

Fig. 289 shows the selected drawings and a rendered illustration of the new vise **DVP_6S_MI_00**.

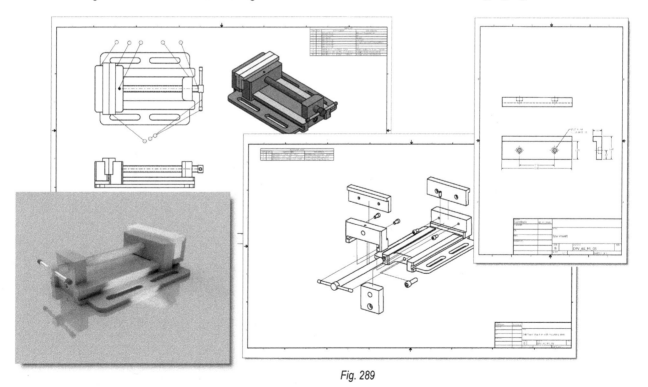

Fig. 289

Good luck!

Summary of Example No 1

If you correctly followed all the exercises contained in this example, you can:

- Modeling simple singular mechanical parts in a separate part file or in the context of an assembly.
- Compose parts in the assembly and control their mutual position.
- Insert standard parts from the Content Center and create bolted connections.
- Drive the assembly constraints to verify the kinematics of the assembly model.
- Prepare a basic visual presentation of a designed product containing rendered illustrations and video animation.
- Prepare an exploded presentation of the product.
- Create technical drawings of the project, including the basic views, dimensions, descriptions, parts list.
- Create drawings with exploded views for presentations or assembly instructions.
- Create a new product design based on an existing design with associated drawings, rendered illustrations, and video presentations
- Carry out basic administrative operations on files with maintaining files relationships.

You've learned the fundamental principles of designing in Autodesk Inventor 2021 software. Now, you can delve into the more difficult issues bound to the tools available in the program and get to know in detail the features that have already been used in this manual.

In further examples you can learn about other interesting functionalities of the Autodesk Inventor 2021 software: creating parametric libraries and basics of iLogic.

EXAMPLE NO 2. LIBRARY OF COMPONENTS

When designing different products, a big improvement in everyday work is the use of libraries of components that are usually purchased from external suppliers or produced on-site as company standard components. Such a component is simply inserted into the model, and in addition, it has all the necessary descriptions that will appear properly in the BOM and allow easy to order this component from the supplier.

In this chapter, you will learn how to easily prepare library components. You will create two components: footer and handle. The footer will be designed in one version only, while the handle will be available in several dimensions' versions. For this reason, the footer will be modeled as a regular single part, while the handle will be created as an iPart – a special Inventor part model associated with a version table. Both library parts will be saved in library folders, for easy application in designed products and will be marked as a purchased part for easy filtering in BOM. The library parts prepared here will be used in the next example - in the design of a parametric metal housing.

The library parts should be stored in a special library folder that automatically assigns a read-only attribute to the files. For this reason, you will start by modifying the project definition file - you will prepare folders for library parts. In addition, you will add special iPart parts folder, which will be a hidden folder and it will be used for store versions of iPart component.

Exercise 18
Supplementing the configuration of the project file

In this exercise, you will add paths to the library components folders to the project file. You will create the main library folder named **Accessories**, shown in Fig. 290a. In this folder, you can then create other library subfolders for different types of components.

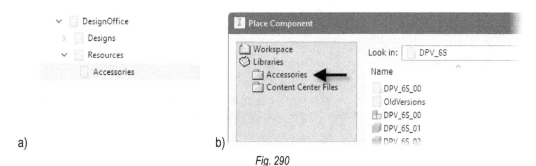

a)   b)

Fig. 290

The library folder will be visible in the file opening window or in the file save window, as in Fig. 290b. In this folder, you can place additional subfolders for specific types of parts, such as **Footers**, **Handles**, etc.

1. Make sure all files are closed. Enter the edit mode of the project file. On the **Get Started** tab, in **Launch** panel, click the **Projects** icon.

2. Create a library of accessories. Highlight **Libraries** and click the plus sign like in Fig. 291.

Fig. 291

Enter the library name: **Accessories** and create **Accessories** subfolder in the **Resources** folder, like in Fig. 292.

Fig. 292

To confirm the library, click in the empty area of the **Projects** window. Now you will add a hidden folder for the iPart component version files. This folder will not be visible when you insert a component into the assembly but is important for work an iPart component libraries.

For hidden folder enter the same library name and folder name, proceeded by the _ character, like in Fig. 293.

Fig. 293

To confirm the library, click in the empty area of the **Projects** window. The correct definition in the project file of the main library **Accessories**, for purchased and company standard parts, is presented like in Fig. 294.

Fig. 294

Library defined in this way will serve both components that have only one version, as well as iPart components that have many versions.

3. Confirm changes to the project file – click **Save** then **Done**.

    End of exercise

Exercise 19. Library component as a single part. Footer

139

Exercise 19
Library component as a single part. Footer

In this exercise, you will create a model of rubber footer that can be used as a support of box, case, etc. On Fig. 295a is shown the ready footer, while on Fig. 295b you can see an example of the footer application - four supports in the bottom of the metal case.

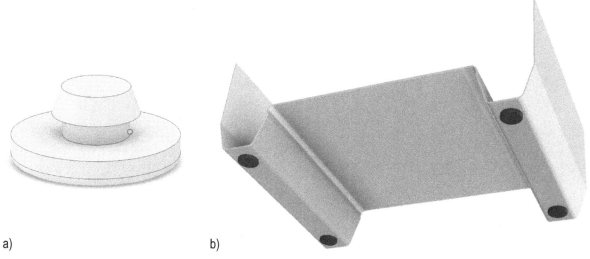

a)　　　　　　　　　　b)

Fig. 295

We assume that the footer is purchased and has the catalog designation of the supplier: **F-035**, related to the width of the assembly gap. The dimensions of the footer are shown in Fig. 296.

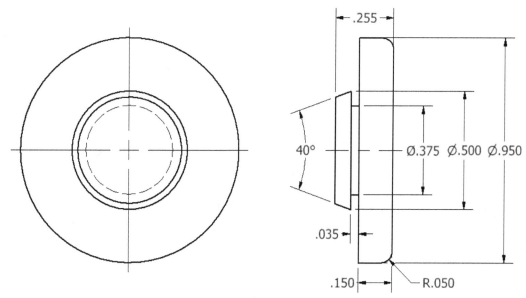

Fig. 296

1.　Start a new part file. Click the **Part** icon in the **My Home** window, indicated in Fig. 297.

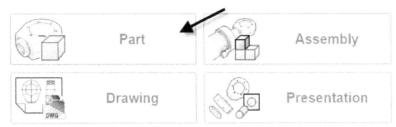

Fig. 297

 2. Start a new sketch. Click the **Start 2D Sketch** icon in the **Sketch** panel on the **3D Model tab**. Select the **XY Plane** to place a new sketch, as in Fig. 298a.

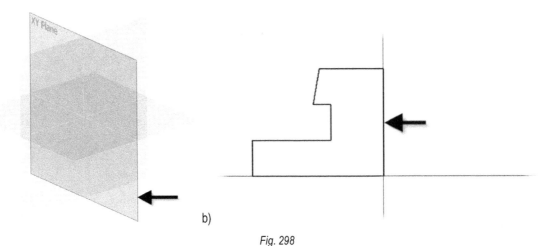

a)   b)

Fig. 298

 3. To create the footer, you will use a revolve feature. Draw a footer sketch, shown in Fig. 298b.

 4. Change the vertical line of the sketch from a solid line into centerline. Select the line indicated by the arrow in Fig. 298b and then, on the **Sketch** tab in the **Format** panel, click **Centerline** icon. This way the program will convert the indicated line into the center line, as in Fig. 299a. This change will facilitate the dimensioning of the sketch of rotating feature and accelerate the creation of the revolved part.

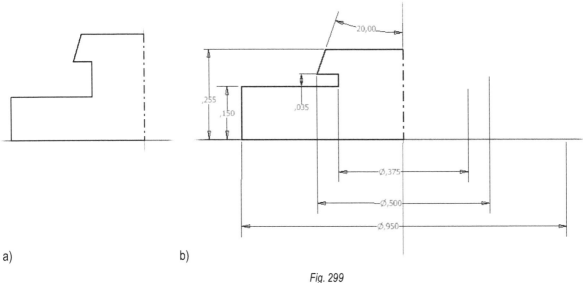

a)   b)

Fig. 299

5. Dimension the sketch. On the **Sketch** tab in the **Constraint** panel, click on **Dimension** icon. Place dimensions of the sketch elements, like in Fig. 299b. For diameter dimension, you should indicate a solid line, axis of rotation and the position of the dimension. Dimension values can be given in decimal and fractional notation. The sketch should be fully constrained.

6. Finish the sketch. Press and hold the right button of your mouse and pull towards: "**at 6 o'clock**". Release the button. For a moment, the program displays the name of the command: **Finish Sketch 2D**

7. Create the footer by revolving the sketch. On the **3D Model** tab in the **Create** panel, click on **Revolve** icon. Alternatively, you can use the function of the gestures by dragging pressed, right button of the mouse towards: "**at 3 o'clock.**

Since there is only one sketch which forms a closed loop, and one of the lines is an axial line, the program automatically selects the loop and the axis for performing a revolve feature, as in Fig. 300a.

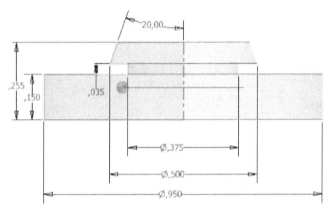

Fig. 300

Confirm the operation. Click **OK**. Ready, a revolved feature is shown in Fig. 301a (isometric view).

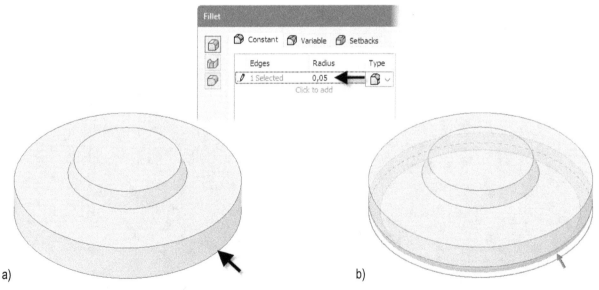

a)   b)

Fig. 301

8. Create a fillet of the edge of the footer. On the **3D Model** tab, in the **Modify** panel, click on **Fillet** icon. Select edge indicated by the arrow in Fig. 301a. Enter a value of fillet radius of **0.05 inch**. The program shows a preview of a fillet, like in Fig. 301b. The arrow can be used to manually change the radius of the fillet. Click **OK**.

You can assume that the footer will always be placed in the assembly using the **Insert** constraint. In the library components, it is a good practice to use **iMate** constraint which is half part of a full constraint definition. The other half of the constraint is defined on another component which should be mounted with the first one. When the part with the iMate constraint will be put into the assembly the program look for the second half of iMate definition on other components and will automatically join both components. In this model, you will create such a half constraint for further use.

9. Define iMate constraint. On the **Manage** tab, in the **Author** panel, click the **iMate** icon. In the **Create iMate** dialog box, select **Insert** constraint, indicated in Fig. 302a.

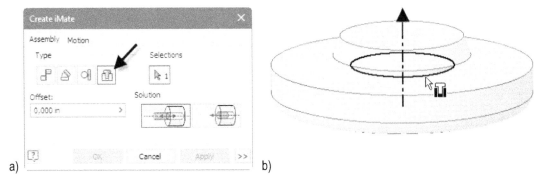

a)   b)

Fig. 302

To create an iMate constraint, click the edge indicated in Fig. 302b. This edge will connect to the edge of the hole in the component to which the footer will be placed. When inserting, the program will search for the second half of the same type of constraint definition and with the same name. For this reason, it is worth giving a unique name to this iMate constraint.

Expand the bottom part of the **Create iMate** dialog box and enter the name: **FOOTER**, like in Fig. 303a.

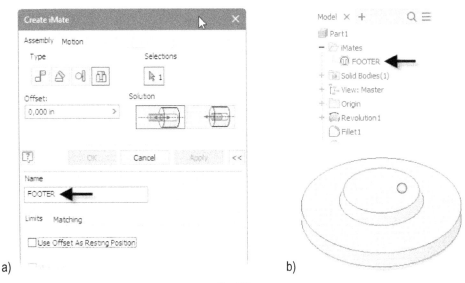

a)   b)

Fig. 303

Click **OK**. The iMate constraint is visible on the model as iMate Glyphs and in the browser, in the **iMates** folder, like in Fig. 303b.

The footer is almost ready. It is still necessary to set the footer material, assign description information and save the part file in the library folder.

10. Assign additional iProperties data to the part, and select material. In the browser, right-click on **Part1** and select **iProperties** from a menu, like in Fig. 304a.

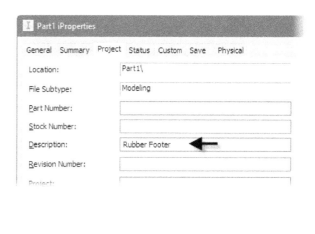

a)   b)

Fig. 304

In **iProperties** dialog box, go to the **Project** tab and enter the name of the part in the **Description** field, like in Fig. 304b.

Go to the tab **Physical** and from **Material** drop-down list select **Rubber**. The program assigns the material and calculates the physical parameters of the parts that are visible on the **Physical** tab, as in Fig. 305a.

a)   b)

Fig. 305

Click **OK**.

You will now mark this component as **Purchased** as a default BOM structure. This designation makes it easier to filter components purchased in BOM.

11. Assign the **Purchased** attribute. On the **Tools** tab, in the **Options** panel, click the **Document Settings** icon. In the **Document Settings** dialog box, go to the **Bill of Materials** tab and select **Purchased** in the **Default BOM Structure** list, like in Fig. 305b. Click **OK**.

It can be considered that the footer is ready for saving. We assume that the file name of this component is the same as the name in the supplier's catalog, which will facilitate the ordering process. The footer model should be saved in the library folder, which will protect it from accidental editing.

 12. Save file. Click the **Save** icon in the **File** menu. In the **Save As** dialog go to the **Accessories** folder and create a subfolder **Footers** there. Then go to the new folder and save in them the file of the footer model. Enter the name of the file: **F-035.ipt**, like in Fig. 306.

Fig. 306

Click **Save**. Click **Yes** in the message window. The first library component is ready.

End of exercise.

Exercise 20
Library component as iPart. Handle

In this exercise, you will learn the basics of creating an iPart parts library. You will create a handle that can be used to move devices. We will assume that in our projects we will use four versions of the same type of handle. Individual versions will differ only in length. In Fig. 307a, all versions of the handle are shown, and Fig. 307b shows the use of holders in the metal console model.

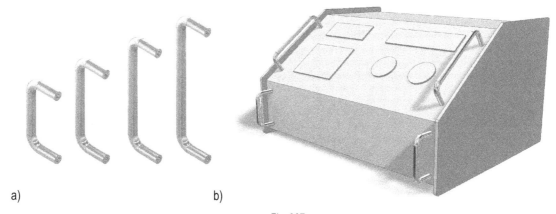

a)   b)

Fig. 307

In order not to create many separate files, you can create one parametric iPart model in which the table for dimensions of each version of the handle will be included. When inserting a handle, you can select a specific version and the program will generate the appropriate model.

1. Start a new part file. Click the **Part** button in the **My Home** window, indicated in Fig. 308.

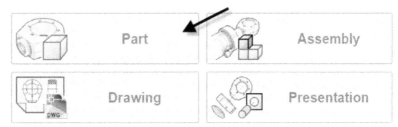

Fig. 308

2. Start a new sketch. In the **Sketch** panel, on the **3D Model** tab, click the **Start 2D Sketch** icon. Select the **XY Plane** to place a new sketch, like in Fig. 309a.

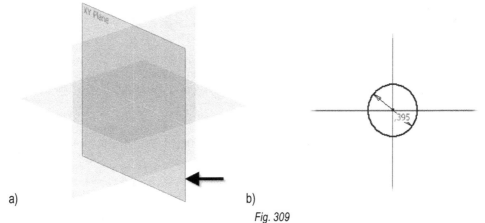

a)   b)

Fig. 309

The handle will be created by sweeping a circle along a C-shaped path. You'll start by sketching a circle.

3. Draw a circle with a diameter of **0.395 in**. Start in the center of the coordinate system, like in Fig. 309b. Finish the sketch.

4. Draw a sketch of the sweep path. Click the **Start 2D Sketch** icon. Select the **YZ Plane** to place a new sketch, like in Fig. 310a.

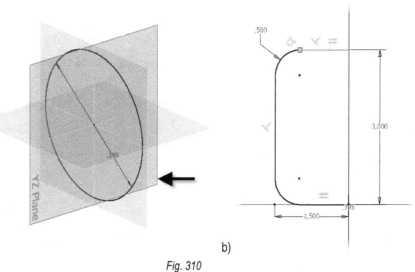

a)   b)

Fig. 310

Draw the sketch shown in Fig. 310b. Start at the center point of the coordinate system. Apply all necessary constraints and dimensions - make sure the sketch is **Fully Constrained**. Finish the sketch. A ready set of two sketches to create a handle shows Fig. 311a.

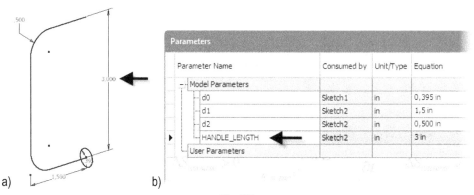

a)   b)

Fig. 311

The dimension with the current value of 3 in, indicated by the arrow on Fig. 311a will be modified to get different versions of the handle. For this reason, it is worth changing the name of this dimension parameter by entering a name that uniquely identifies the dimension. The parameter with the changed name will be automatically applied in the version table when defining an iPart.

 5. Change the parameter name. On the **Manage** tab, in the **Parameters** panel, click the **Parameters** icon. In the **Parameters** window enter the new parameter name: **HANDLE_LENGTH**, in the **Model Parameters** column, like in Fig. 311b. Click **Done**.

 6. Create a handle. On the **3D Model** tab, in the **Create** panel, click the **Sweep** icon. The program displays the **Sweep** properties panel, automatically selects the circle as a closed profile for sweeping and waits for the path selection. Click on the path sketch. The preview of the result of the operation presents Fig. 312a. Click **OK**.

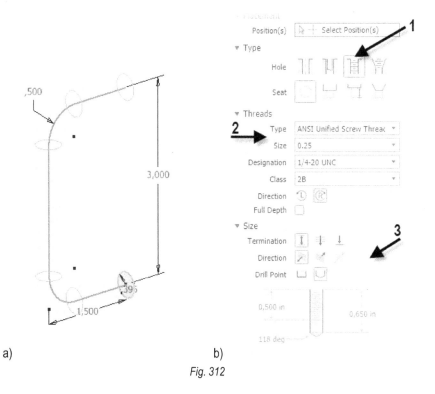

a)   b)

Fig. 312

The last features of the handle are mounting holes. Create two ¼ - **20 UNC** threaded holes, concentrically on both ends of the handle.

7. Create holes. On the **3D Model** tab in the **Modify** panel, click on the **Hole** icon. In the **Hole** properties panel select type of hole **(1)**, thread type and size **(2)**, termination, direction and size of the hole **(3),** as shown in Fig. 312b.

Now you are ready to select insertion points for holes. To create concentric holes, rotate the handle to see planar faces and then place the first hole center on the face, like in Fig. 313a, and click the concentric edge of the handle, indicated by a white arrow in Fig. 313b.

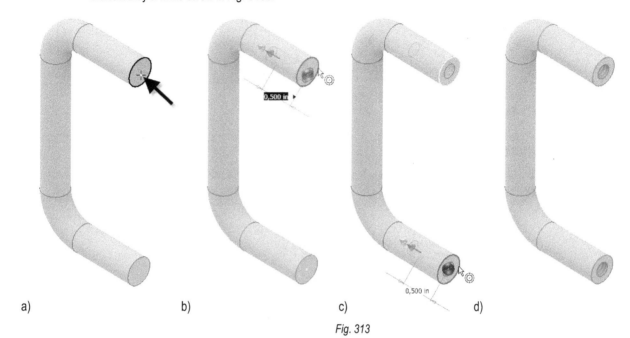

a)   b)   c)   d)

Fig. 313

Create concentric hole on the second end, like in Fig. 313c. Click **OK**. Ready holes are shown in Fig. 313d.

The next step is to assign material and the **Purchased** attribute. We assume that all versions of the handle are made of the same material.

8. Assign the material type and appearance. In the quick access bar, select **Steel** in the list of materials and **Chrome Polished** in the list of appearances, like in Fig. 314a.

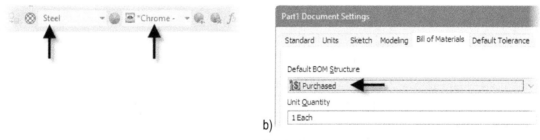

a)   b)

Fig. 314

9. Assign the **Purchased** attribute. On the **Tools** tab, in the **Options** panel, click the **Document Settings** icon. In the **Document Settings** dialog box, go to the **Bill of Materials** tab and select **Purchased** in the **Default BOM Structure** list, like in Fig. 314b. Click **OK**.

You have already created the definition of the base model of the handle. Now you can transform this model into an iPart and create a table for all dimensional versions of the handle.

10. Create an iPart. On the **Manage** tab, in the **Author** panel, click the **Create iPart** icon. The program opens the **iPart Author** window, with a row of the first version, like in Fig. 315.

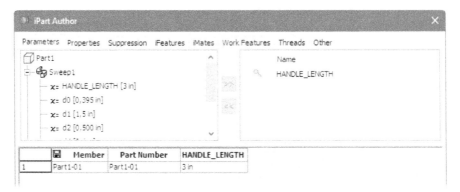

Fig. 315

The program automatically creates a column for a parameter with a custom name, in this case for the parameter **HANDLE_LENGTH**. Now, you will add a column for the iProperties: **DESCRIPTION**.

In the **iPart Author** window, go to the **Properties** tab, select the **Description** property in the **Project** folder and click the button **>>**, indicated in Fig. 316 to move the property to the column area on the right.

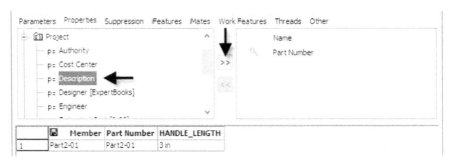

Fig. 316

The new column will appear in the version table of the iPart definition, like in Fig. 317.

Fig. 317

Insert new row for next version of handle. Right-click on existing row and select **Insert Row**, like in Fig. 318.

Fig. 318

Insert three new rows, like in Fig. 319.

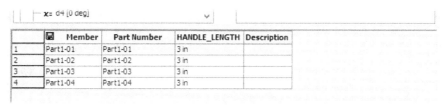

	Member	Part Number	HANDLE_LENGTH	Description
1	Part1-01	Part1-01	3 in	
2	Part1-02	Part1-02	3 in	
3	Part1-03	Part1-03	3 in	
4	Part1-04	Part1-04	3 in	

Fig. 319

Fill in the contents of the columns, like in Fig. 320. The **Member** column contains the file names of the versions.

	Member	Part Number	HANDLE_LENGTH	Description
1	HC-200-03	HC-200-03	3 in	Handle typ C - 3 in
2	HC-200-04	HC-200-04	4 in	Handle typ C - 4 in
3	HC-200-05	HC-200-05	5 in	Handle typ C - 5 in
4	HC-200-06	HC-200-06	6 in	Handle typ C - 6 in

Fig. 320

Now you will select the key column, the content of which will identify the version of the handle when inserting into the assembly. In this example, the key column number 1 can be **Part Number**. You can set several key columns to set the selection according to different parameters.

Set the key column. Right-click the heading of the **Part Number** column and select **Key > 1**, like in Fig. 321.

Fig. 321

The key column will be marked with the key symbol, like in Fig. 322.

	Member	Part Number	HANDLE_LENGTH	Description
1	HC-200-03	HC-200-03	3 in	Handle typ C - 3 in
2	HC-200-04	HC-200-04	4 in	Handle typ C - 4 in
3	HC-200-05	HC-200-05	5 in	Handle typ C - 5 in
4	HC-200-06	HC-200-06	6 in	Handle typ C - 6 in

Fig. 322

You can assume that all versions of the handle have been defined. Click **OK**. The **Table** item will appear in the browser, which includes all versions of the handle, like in Fig. 323a. The part icon has also changed - a small pattern has appeared symbolizing the version table.

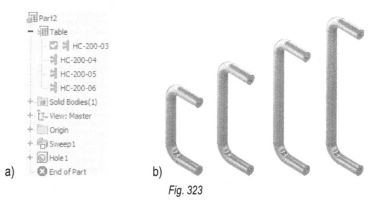

Fig. 323

You can now validate the versions of iPart components by double-clicking the version designation in the browser, under the **Table** item. In total, the program should be able to generate four versions of the handle, like in Fig. 323b. Finally, restore the **HC-200-03** as a default version. The iPart component is ready.

13. Save file. Click the **Save** icon in the **File** menu. In the **Save As** dialog go to the **Accessories** folder and create a subfolder **Handles** there. Then go to the new folder and save in them the file of the handle iPart model. Enter the name of the file: **Handle type C**, like in Fig. 324.

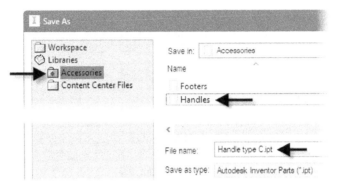

Fig. 324

14. Close the file. End of exercise

Exercise 21
Test of inserting library parts into the assembly

In this exercise, you will check the correctness of the created library parts. You will insert a rubber footer and handles in the empty assembly file, just for test. This exercise explains what is a difference between a static library part and parametric iPart part when inserting it into the assembly.

1. Start creating a new assembly. Click the **Assembly** icon in the **My Home** window, indicated in Fig. 325.

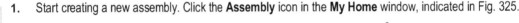
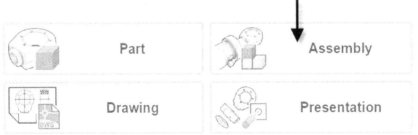

Fig. 325

2. Insert the rubber footers. On the **Assemble** tab, in the **Component** panel, click **Place**. In the **Place Components** window, click the **Accessories** library in the left, go to the **Footers** folder and select the footer model: **F-035.ipt**, like in Fig. 326a. Click **Open**.

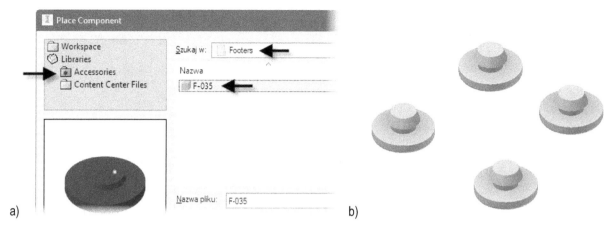

a)

b)

Fig. 326

Place the four footers in the empty area of the screen, like in Fig. 326b.

 3. Insert two handles: one with a length of **4 in** and one with a length of **6 in**. Click the **Place** icon again. In the **Place Components** window, click the **Accessories** library in the left, then enter the **Handles** folder and select the main iPart file: **Handle type C.ipt**, like in Fig. 327a. Click **Open**.

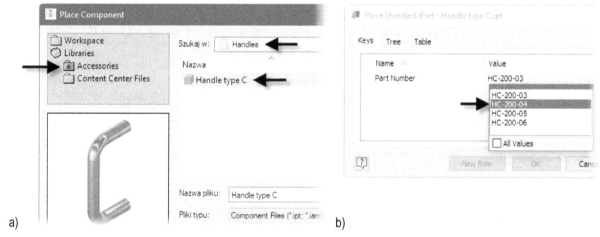

a)

b)

Fig. 327

In the **Place Standard iPart: Handle type C.ipt** window, select the **HC-200-04** version from the **Value** list, like in Fig. 327b, and insert the handle in the empty area of the screen, like in Fig. 328a.

a)

b)

Fig. 328

Then, in the **Place Standard iPart:** window, in the **Value** list, check **All Values** option and select version **HC-200-06**, like in Fig. 328b. Insert the second handle in the empty area of the screen, like in Fig. 329.

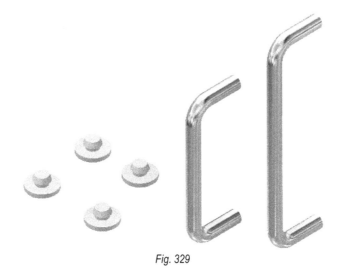

Fig. 329

Click **Dismiss**.

*All files of the versions have been placed in the folder ...**Resources_Accessories\Handles\Handle type C**.*

4. Finally, check how the inserted files are described in the BOM. On the **Assemble** tab, in the **Manage** panel, click the **Bill of Materials** icon. The program will display the **Bill of Material** window with the **Model Data** card active. Inserted components should have the **Purchased** attribute set and the correct designation in the **Part Number** and **Description** columns, like in Fig. 330.

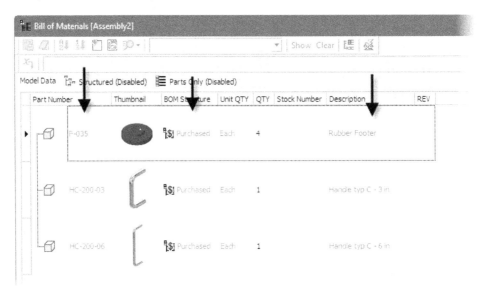

Fig. 330

All values in the BOM window are grayed-out, which means that the component got "read – only" properties – because it has been saved in library folders.

Close the **Bill of Materials** window, and close the file. End of exercise.

Summary of Example No 2

If you correctly followed all the exercises contained in this chapter, you can:

- Configure library folders tailored to your needs for purchased or standardized components
- Create single version library components and correctly describe them for the BOM
- Create parametric iParts components, specify key parameters, descriptions and create a version table
- Plan, execute and enjoy the benefits of component libraries to improve your daily work

In the next chapter, you will apply the library parts created here in the parametric design of the metal case.

EXAMPLE NO 3. PARAMETRIC GENERATOR

If you often create constructively uniform subassemblies of your devices with different dimensions and options, then it is worth considering creating parametric configurators for quickly generating different versions of the sub-assembly. Such a parametric version generator can quickly create a new version file set containing 3D models and an appropriate set of 2D drawings for further work. The new version files will be saved with new names.

In this example, you will create a parametric generator for making a simple metal case that allows you to obtain a model of any size, with or without handles and complete drawing documentation for each version of the case. The generated version of the casing can be further modified in order to obtain a final appearance. In this example, you will learn the basics of designing sheet metal parts, the basics of using parameters in part and in the assembly, and you will learn the basics of programming using iLogic. The approach presented here will show one way to prepare and use the parametric version generator offered by Autodesk Inventor 2021.

On Fig. 331a is shown a model of a metal case with handles, which will be used as a base to create various versions of cases. The two examples are shown in Fig. 331b.

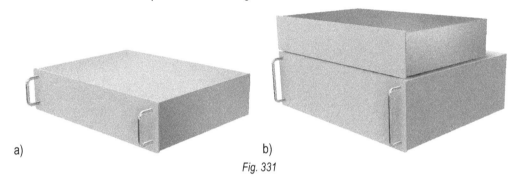

a)   b)

Fig. 331

The initial conditions

Parameters controlling sizes and options

The metal case consists of a sheet metal box and a faceplate. You can assume that you want to control three dimensions of the box. The faceplate will be slightly larger than the width and height of the box. In addition, you will enable or disable handles. The remaining dimensions of the model will depend on the three main dimensions of the box body. On Fig. 332a, there is shown a dialog box form for controlling the dimensions and options of the case which you will create. The three main dimensions of box body controlled by this form are shown in Fig. 332b.

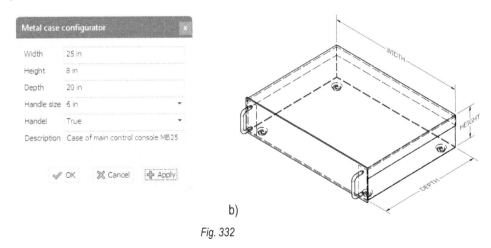

a)   b)

Fig. 332

Folders

In this example, you can assume that subsequent versions of the metal case, including drawing documentation, will be generated using the **iLogic Design Copy** tool. For this reason, it's a good idea to collect generators files containing the assembly model, part models, and drawings in separate folders, and create a separate project file for each generator. In this example, you will create the project file **MetalBox_Gen.ipj**, and put all generator files in the folder **...\ Resources \ Generator \ MetalBox**, like in Fig. 333a.

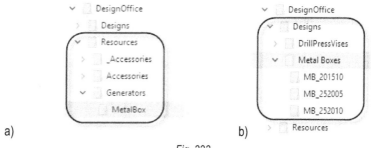

a)   b)

Fig. 333

New versions of the generated metal case will be placed in the **Design** folder, like in Fig. 333b. The illustration shows the folders of the three generated versions of the metal case.

File naming

We will assume that the names of the main assembly files, parts files and drawings files will be composed of two parts. The first part will be the distinguishing feature of the version of the generated model and can be, for example, the order number. The second part of the name will always be constant. The first part of the file name will be automatically added, as a prefix, to all files when the new version of the metal case is generating.

In this example, the metal case generator assembly will contain one assembly file, three part's files, and library files. In addition, four drawings related to 3D models will be created. The structure of the metal case generator may look like in Fig. 334a.

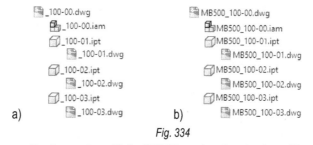

a)   b)

Fig. 334

For example, after generating the version with the **MB500** number, the structure of the resulting set of files will be like in Fig. 334b.

Exercise 22
Create a project file and version generator assembly. Parameters

In this exercise, you will start the project of the version generator. You will create a folder for the generator files and a project definition file. Then you will start a new assembly file.

1. Create a **MetalBox** folder for the version generator files. This folder should be placed in the **... \ Resources \ Generators** folder, like in Fig. 335a.

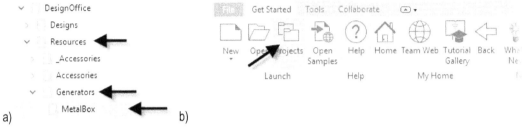

a)   b)

Fig. 335

2. Create a new project file for metal box generator. On the **Get Started** tab, in **Launch** panel, click the **Projects** icon shown in Fig. 335b.

In the **Projects** dialog box click the **New** button. In the **Inventor project wizard** select **New Single User Project** option, shown in Fig. 336. Click **Next**.

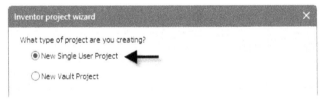

Fig. 336

On the next page of the **Inventor project wizard** specify project file name and location, as shown in Fig. 337. You can choose a different drive to place the main folder of the project.

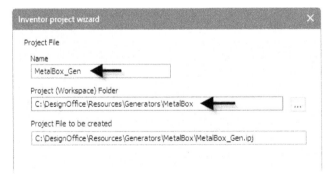

Fig. 337

Click **Next**. Add libraries to the newly defined project file.

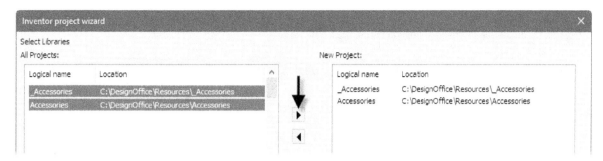

Fig. 338

Select library folders, as shown in Fig. 338 and click the arrow button, to add libraries to the new project file.

Click **Finish** to end the definition of a new project file.

The program creates a project file **MetalBox_Gen.ipj**, in the folder **C:\DesignsOffice\Resources\Generators\MetalBox**. A new project file is placed on the list of projects in the upper part of the **Projects** window, as shown in Fig. 339. The checkmark on the left side of the project name indicates that this is an active project.

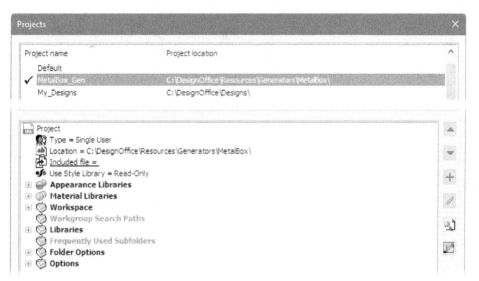

Fig. 339

Click **Done**.

3. Create a new assembly file. In the **My Home** window click the **Assembly** button shown in Fig. 340. The program will create an assembly file based on **Standard.iam** template.

Fig. 340

The new assembly file is currently empty. You can right now save the file, using file name dedicated for this assembly file of version generator.

4. Save the file. Click **Save** icon and enter the file name **_100-00.iam**, like in Fig. 341. Use underscore character to separate the first and second part of the file name.

Fig. 341

You are ready to create a metal case generator. You will start by defining global control parameters, which will be used to drive dimensions of metal box and size and presence of handles.

You can assume that the global parameters that will be placed in the main assembly file will be written in upper-case. In part files, we will, to distinguish, write the names of parameters in lower case letters. In this assembly file, we will create the following parameters: **WIDTH**, **HIGHT**, **DEPTH**, **HANDLE_SIZE,** and **HANDLE**.

5. Define new user parameters. On the **Assemble** tab, in the **Manage** panel, click the **Parameters** icon. In the **Parameters** window, click the **Add Numeric** button at the bottom of the window, like Fig. 342a.

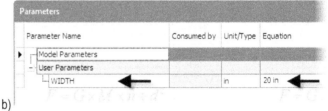

Fig. 342

Enter the parameter name, **WIDTH** and value **20 in**, like in Fig. 342b. Similarly, enter the following parameters: **HEIGHT**, **DEPTH,** and **HANDLE_SIZE**. The parameters entered are shown in Fig. 343a.

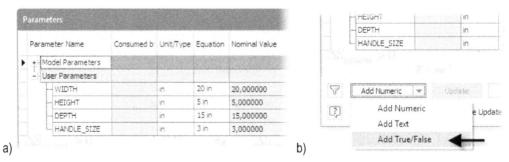

Fig. 343

The last parameter you enter will be a **True / False** type parameter. Pull down the menu by clicking the arrow on the right side of **Add Numeric** and select **Add True / False** on the menu, like in Fig. 343b. Enter the parameter name: **HANDLE** and select **True** in the **Equation** column, like in Fig. 344.

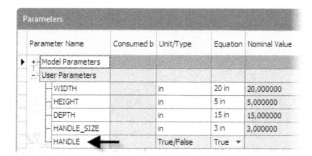

Fig. 344

The handles that can be used in a metal case come in four sizes. For this reason, you can create a list of allowable values for the **HANDLE_SIZE** parameter associated with the handle table.

Create a list of handle lengths. Right-click in the rows of the **HANDLE_SIZE** row parameter and select **Make Multi-Value** in the menu, like in Fig. 345.

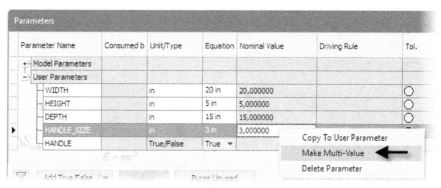

Fig. 345

In the **Value List Editor** window, enter the lengths: **4 in**, **5 in** and **6 in**. Click the **Add button** after entering the new value in the **Add New Items** field. The complete list of acceptable parameter values is shown in Fig. 346a.

a)

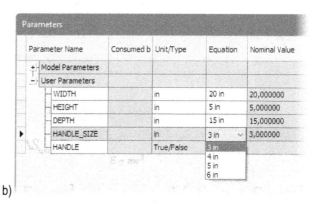

b)

Fig. 346

Click **OK**. The right size of the handle can now be selected from the list shown in Fig. 346b.

You can assume that all required parameters have been defined. Click **Done**.

6. Save the file. Click **Save** icon, but don't close the file if you plan to continue in next exercise.

End of exercise.

Exercise 23
Modeling of the sheet metal bottom of the case

Now you will create a sheet metal bottom of the case. You will learn some basic tools for modeling sheet metal parts, define iMate for fast insertion of footers and will learn how to create a flat pattern of this sheet metal part. The bottom of the case will be created in the context of the assembly and will be a reference for the design of the other parts. In Fig. 347a is shown the finished bottom of the case, which will be created in this exercise. In Fig. 347b, there is shown a flat pattern of this part.

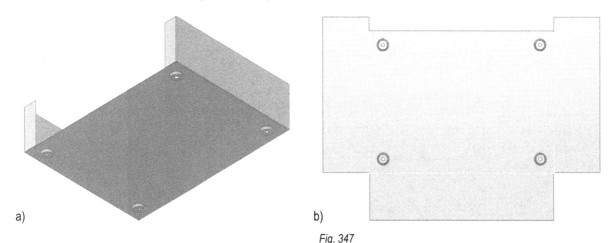

a)   b)

Fig. 347

You are continuing to work with the file **_100-00.iam**. If this file has been closed then you should open it.

 1. Create a new part in the context of the assembly. On the **Assemble** tab, in the **Component** panel, click the **Create** icon. In the **Create In-Place Component** dialog box, enter the file name of the new part and select the template for modeling sheet metal part, like in Fig. 348a.

 In the sheet metal template file, some parameters characteristic for a sheet metal part modeling are already defined. It is good practice to adjust the settings in the sheet metal template to your needs. You can find more information about template configuration in the program's help.

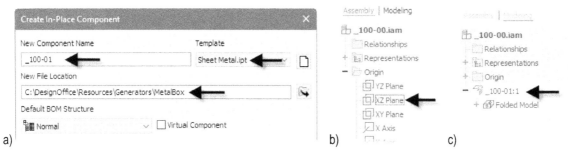

a)   b)   c)

Fig. 348

Make sure that the new part will be placed in the folder **...: \DesignOffice\Resources\Generators\MetalBox**.

Click **OK**. The program is waiting for an indication of the working plane to place the new component. In the **Origin** folder click **XZ Plane**, like in Fig. 348b. The browser will display a new part, which immediately becomes an active part, like in Fig. 348c.

In the Folded Model section of the part, there will be colected a features of the folded part. After creating the flat pattern, a Flat Pattern section will be created, in which the 3D model of flat pattern of the part will be placed.

 2. Set the parameters for modeling the sheet metal part. On the **Sheet Metal** tab, in the **Setup** panel, click **Sheet Metal Defaults** icon. There is already one rule defined in the **Sheet Metal Defaults** window - for a sheet thickness of 0.120 in. Uncheck **Use Thickness from Rule** and enter **0.035 in** in the **Thickness** filed, like in Fig. 349.

Fig. 349

Click **OK**.

It is a good practice to prepare a set of rules in the style and standards library which include sheet thicknesses you use in your designs, material types and methods for calculating the flat pattern for a combination of materials and press brakes. In this example, you only changed the thickness of the sheet, but in real conditions, the new thickness setting, the material type and method of calculation flat pattern should be derived together from the chosen sheet metal rule.

Now you will define the key dimensional parameters that will control the size of this part and later will be associated with the global parameters introduced in the assembly file.

We have assumed that in part files you will enter the parameter names controlling the parts dimensions in lower case letters. In this part file, you will create the following parameters: **width**, **height**, **depth**.

 3. Define new user parameters. On the **Manage** tab, in the **Parameters** panel, click the **Parameters** icon. In the **Parameters** window, click the **Add Numeric** button, like in Fig. 350a.

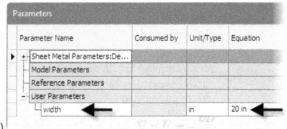

Fig. 350

Enter the parameter name: **width** and the value **20 in**, like in Fig. 350b. Similarly, enter the parameters: **height, depth,** and **handle_size**. All entered parameters and their values show Fig. 351a.

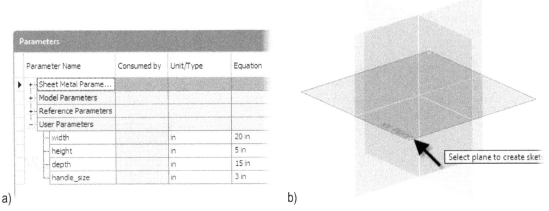

a)   b)

Fig. 351

Click **Done**. Now, you can use these parameters in building your 3D model of the part.

4. Create a sketch for the first sheet metal face. On the **Sheet Metal** tab, in the **Sketch** panel, click **Start 2D Sketch**. Pick the **XY Plane** like in Fig. 351b. Using the **ViewCube**, set the view to the sketching plane like in Fig. 352.

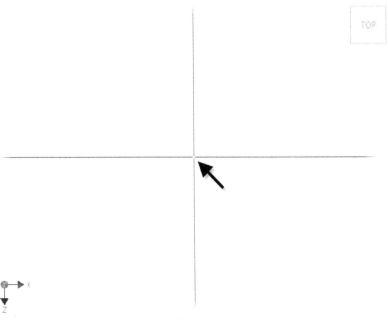

Fig. 352

5. Draw a rectangle from the center point, with size **20 x 15 in**. When entering dimensions, you will enter parameter names instead of numeric values. On the **Sketch** tab in the **Create** panel, click the **Rectangle Two Point Center** icon. As the center point of the rectangle, select the intersection point of the X and Z axes, indicated by the arrow in Fig. 352.

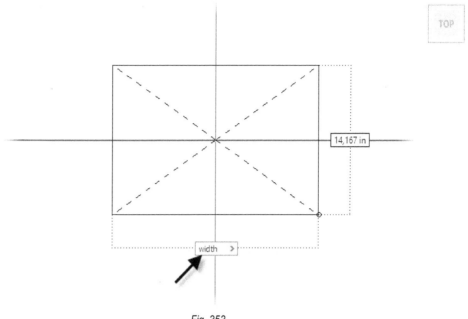

Fig. 353

In the first dimension field of the rectangle, enter the **width**, like in Fig. 353, and press **TAB** to move to the next field. In the second dimension field, type **depth**, like in Fig. 354a.

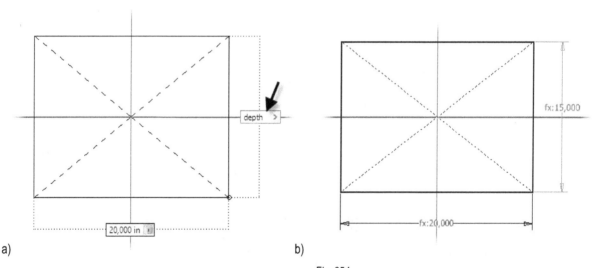

a)   b)

Fig. 354

 Press **ENTER** to confirm dimensions of rectangle. A correctly dimensioned rectangle is shown in Fig. 354b.

6. Finish sketch.

7. Create a main sheet metal face of the base of the metal case. On the **Sheet Metal** tab, in the **Create** panel, click the **Face** icon. Make sure that the face direction arrow points upwards, like in Fig. 355.

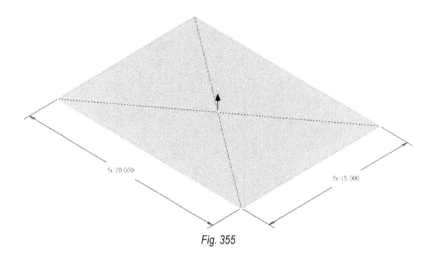

Fig. 355

Click **OK**.

8. Create side and rear flanges using the sheet metal design tools. On the **Sheet Metal** tab, in the **Create** panel, click the **Flange** icon. In the **Flange** window, by default, the edge selection tools is active. Pick three upper edges of the face, indicated in Fig. 356a.

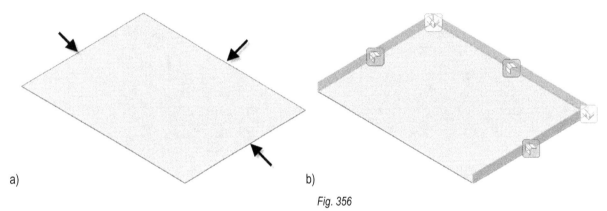

a)   b)

Fig. 356

The program will preview flanges with the default height, like in Fig. 356b. The **height** parameter can be used to determine the height of the side and rear flanges. Enter the **height** in the **Distance** field, like in Fig. 357a.

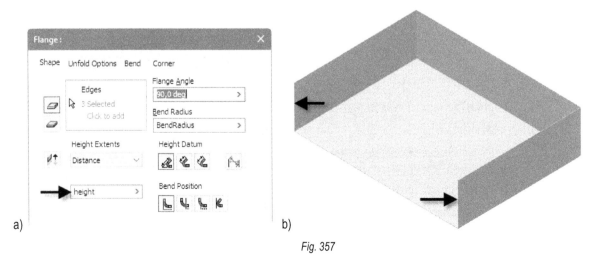

a)   b)

Fig. 357

If you accidentally mark the wrong edge, you can subtract this edge by pressing SHIFT and pointing it again. You can now change the parameters of bending or corners by clicking on the appropriate symbol in the preview.

 The wall height will be corrected later in the design, after assembling the whole assembly and taking into account the height of the feet and the distance from the top cover.

Click **Apply**.

Create two **1.5 in** folds for attaching the front plate. Select the inner edges indicated in Fig. 357b. In the **Flange** window, enter the distance value **1.5 in**, like in Fig. 358a.

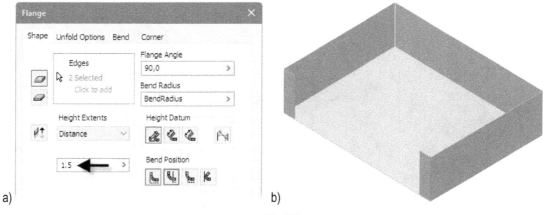

a)   b)

Fig. 358

Click **OK**. Ready flanges are shown in Fig. 358b.

Now you will create four legs that will be created by embossing. Instead of modeling legs from scratch, you can use the iFeature technique and create embossing using the ready shape.

 9. A sketch will be useful for inserting iFeature. Create a sketch on the bottom face. Click the **Start 2D Sketch** icon, rotate the model and pick the bottom face, indicated in Fig. 359a.

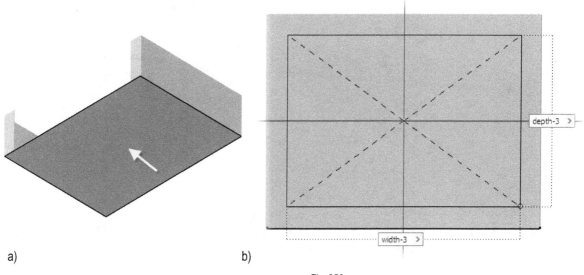

a)   b)

Fig. 359

10. Draw a construction rectangle starting at the center point of the sketch coordinate system. Dimensions of the sketch should be depended from the main parameters of the part. To specify the size of the rectangle, enter in the dimension fields the equations: **width-3** and **depth-3**, respectively, like in Fig. 359b. Finish the sketch.

11. Insert four embosses. You must use the **Punch Tool** tool to insert an iFeature in a sheet metal part. On the **Sheet Metal** tab, in the **Modify** panel, click the **Punch Tool** icon. In the **PunchTool Directory** dialog box, select the **Round Emboss.ide** item, indicated in Fig. 360a, and click **Open**.

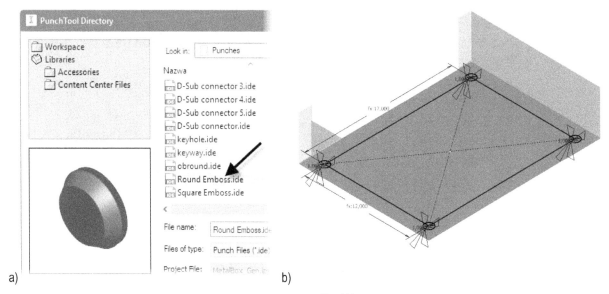

a)   b)

Fig. 360

In the **PunchTool** window, go to the **Geometry** tab, then pick four points for inserting the embosses in the corners of the rectangle, like in Fig. 360b. On the **Size** tab, you can modify the dimensions of the embossing.

Click **Finish**. Ready embosses shows Fig. 361a.

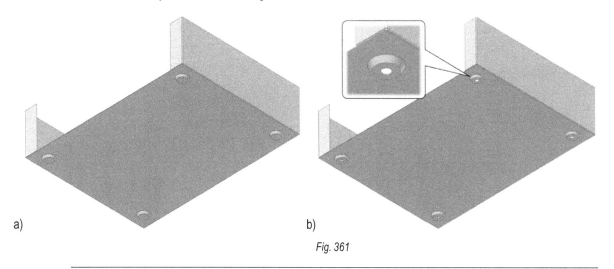

a)   b)

Fig. 361

It is good practice to prepare frequently used shapes as iFeature for quick insertion in the modeled part. You can find more information about iFeature in the program's help.

12. Create four through holes, concentric, with a diameter of **0.375 in**, in the plane face of the embosses. Ready holes are shown in Fig. 361b.

13. Define iMate constraints for automatically inserting elements into holes, e.g. footers (see *Exercise 19*, on page 139) On the **Manage** tab, in the **Author** panel, click the **iMate** icon. In the **Create iMate** window, select the **Insert** constraint, indicated in Fig. 362a.

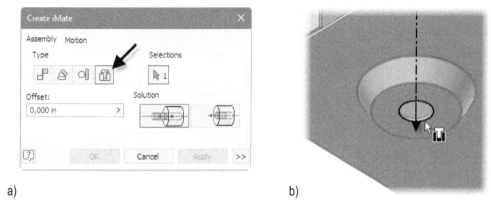

a)   b)

Fig. 362

To insert iMate, click the edge of the first hole, pointed in Fig. 362b. This edge will be connected with the edge of another part to be assembled into that hole, e.g. with an edge of a footer. When inserting, the program will search for the second half of the same type of iMate constraint and with the same name. For this reason, it is worth to give the same name to this constraint like the iMate names in cooperated parts.

Expand the **Create iMate** window and enter the name of the iMate constraint: **FOOTER**, like in Fig. 363a.

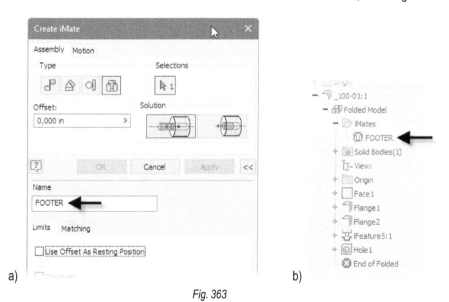

a)   b)

Fig. 363

Click **Apply**. The first iMate constraint is visible on the model as iMate Glyphs and in the browser, in the **iMates** folder, like in Fig. 363b.

Create three more iMates called **FOOTER** in the other three holes, like in Fig. 364a.

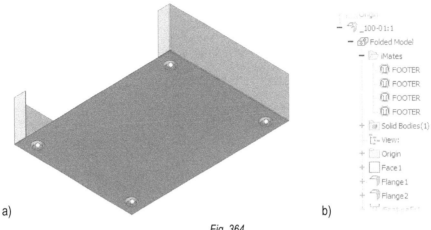

a)   b)

Fig. 364

Each iMate constraint is registered in the **iMates** folder, like in Fig. 364b.

The bottom part of the sheet metal box is almost ready. Now, you will assign material and description to this part.

 14. Assign additional iProperties data to the part, and select material. In the browser, right-click on **_100-01:1** and select i**Properties** from the menu, like in Fig. 365a

a)   b)

Fig. 365

Go to the **Project** tab and enter the name of the part in the **Description** field, like in Fig. 365b. Click **Apply**.

Now, go to the tab **Physical** and from **Material** drop-down list select **Steel, Alloy**. The program assigns the material and calculates the physical parameters of the parts that are visible on the **Physical** tab, as in Fig. 366a.

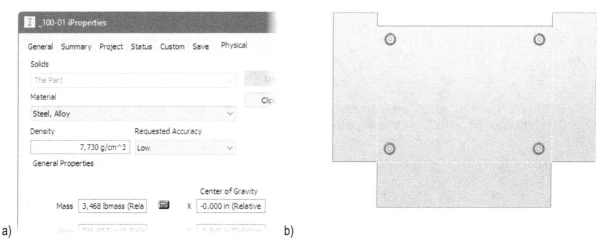

a)   b)

Fig. 366

Click **Apply** and **Close**. You can assume, that the part is finished for the time being.

Now you can make a flat pattern of the folded model of the part. The folded model of the part is saved inside of the part file. After creating a flat pattern, all changes made to the folded model will be transferred to a flat pattern.

 15. Create a flat pattern. On the **Sheet Metal** tab, in the **Flat Pattern** panel, click the **Create Flat Pattern** icon. The program opens a part file in edit mode in the new window and displays the flat pattern, like in Fig. 366b.

In the browser, in the structure of the part, the new item **Flat Pattern** will appear, like in Fig. 367a. Double-clicking this item displays the part unfolds. Double-clicking **Folded Model** displays the model in the folded mode.

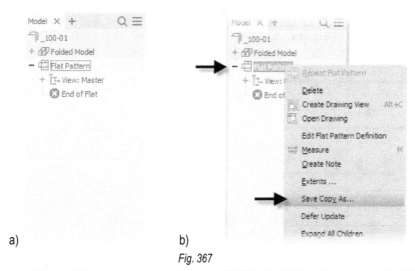

a)   b)

Fig. 367

Flat pattern is also a 3D model. You can save flat pattern as a DXF file for CAM machining, by right-click the **Flat Pattern** and next click **Save Copy As**, as shown in Fig. 367b. Then you can select the file type, folder, and other options depending on the file type chosen.

 16. Close the flat pattern. In the **Sheet Metal** tab, in the **Folded Part** pane, click **Go to Folded Part** icon. The program switches to the folded model environment of the part file. Click **F6** to see a whole part, if needed.

 17. Close the **_100-01.ipt** file. In **File** menu click **Close** icon or click **X** in the upper right corner of the screen. Click **Yes** in the message window to save the file of the part. You are back in the assembly modeling environment.

 18. Save the assembly file, but don't close the file if you plan to continue in next exercise. End of exercise.

Exercise 24
Modeling the cover of the metal case

In this exercise, you will create the top cover of the metal case. The new part will also be created from sheet metal, in the context of the assembly. The ready cover and its flat pattern are shown in Fig. 368.

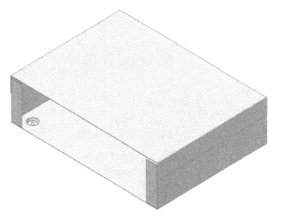

Fig. 368

Continue to work in the **_100-00.iam** file. If this file has been closed, open it.

1. Create a new part in the context of the assembly. On the **Assemble** tab, in the **Component** panel, click the **Create** icon. In the **Create In-Place Component** dialog box, enter the name of the new part file and select the template for modeling sheet metal part, like in Fig. 369a.

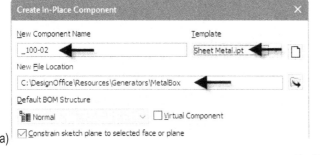
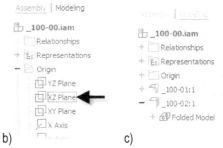

Fig. 369

Make sure that the new part will be placed in the folder **...: \DesignOffice\ Resources\ Generators\ MetalBox**.

Click **OK**. The program is waiting for an indication of the construction plane to place the new component on. In the **Origin** folder pick **XZ Plane**, like in Fig. 369b. The browser will display a new part, which immediately becomes an active part, like in Fig. 369c.

2. Set the parameters for modeling the sheet metal part. On the **Sheet Metal** tab, in the **Setup** panel, click **Sheet Metal Defaults** icon. There is already one rule defined in the **Sheet Metal Defaults** window - for a sheet thickness of 0.120 inches. Uncheck **Use Thickness from Rule** and enter **0.035** in the **Thickness** filed, like in Fig. 370.

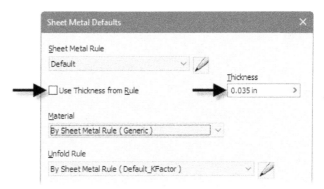

Fig. 370

Click **OK**.

Now you will define the key dimensional parameters that will control the size of this part and later will be associated with the global parameters introduced in the assembly file.

We have assumed that in part files you will enter the parameter names controlling the parts dimensions in lower case letters. In this part file, you will create the following parameters: **width** and **depth**.

 3. Define new user parameters. On the **Manage** tab, in the **Parameters** panel, click the **Parameters** icon. In the **Parameters** window, click the **Add Numeric** button, like in Fig. 371a.

 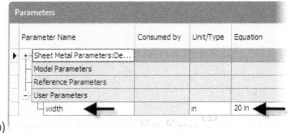

Fig. 371

Enter the parameter name: **width** and the value **20 in**, like in Fig. 371b. Similarly, enter the parameter: **depth**. All entered parameters and their values show Fig. 372a.

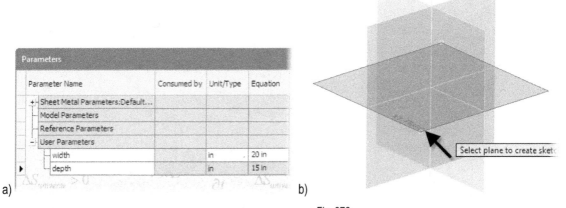

Fig. 372

Click **Done**. Now, you can use these parameters in building your 3D model of the part.

4.   Create a sketch for the first sheet metal face. On the **Sheet Metal** tab, in the **Sketch** panel, click **Start 2D Sketch**. Pick the **XY Plane** like in Fig. 372b. Using the **ViewCube**, set the view to the sketching plane like in Fig. 373.

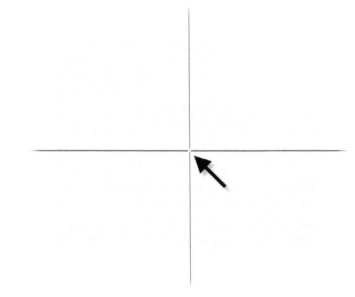

Fig. 373

5.   Draw a rectangle from the center point, with size **20 x 15 in**. When entering dimensions, you will enter parameter names instead of numeric values. On the **Sketch** tab in the **Create** panel, click the **Rectangle Two Point Center** icon. As the center point of the rectangle, select the intersection point of the X and Z axes, indicated by an arrow in Fig. 373.

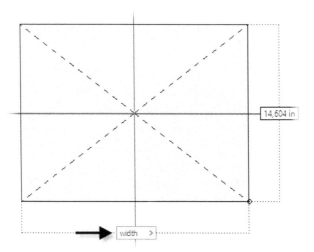

Fig. 374

In the first dimension field of the rectangle, enter the **width**, like in Fig. 374, and press **TAB** to move to the next field. In the second dimension field, type **depth**, like in Fig. 375a.

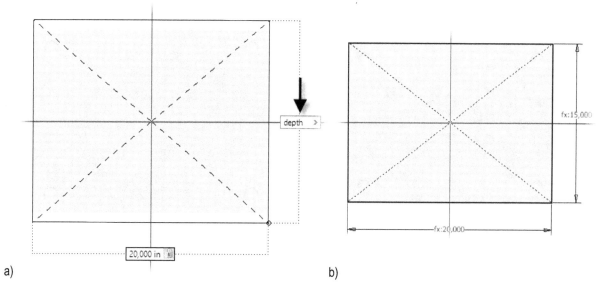

a)

b)

Fig. 375

Press **ENTER** to confirm dimensions of the rectangle. A correctly dimensioned rectangle is shown in Fig. 375b.

6. Finish sketch.

7. Create a main sheet metal face of the base of the metal case. On the **Sheet Metal** tab, in the **Create** panel, click the **Face** icon. Make sure that the face direction arrow points upwards, like in Fig. 376.

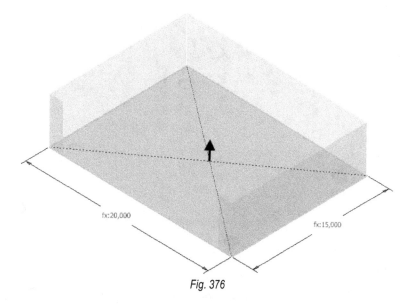

Fig. 376

Click **OK**.

8. Create side and rear walls using the sheet metal design tools. On the **Sheet Metal** tab, in the **Create** panel, click the **Flange** icon. In the **Flange** window, by default, the edge selection tool is active. Pick three bottom edges of the face, indicated in Fig. 377a.

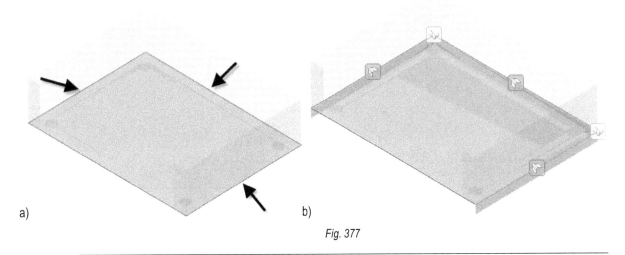

Fig. 377

 If you accidentally mark the wrong edge, you can subtract this edge by pressing SHIFT and pointing it again. You can now change the parameters of bending or corners by clicking on the appropriate symbol in the preview.

The program will preview flanges with the default height, like in Fig. 377b. In this part, you will use a constant value of **2 in** to determine the height of the side and rear flanges. Enter the value **2 in** in the **Distance** field, like in Fig. 378a.

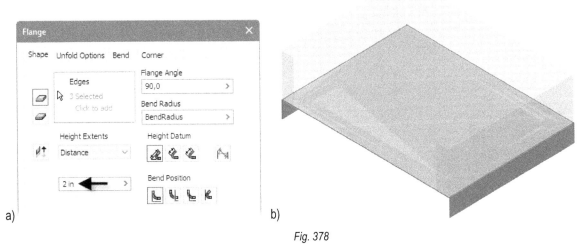

Fig. 378

Click **OK.** Ready part is now like in Fig. 378b.

The cover of the sheet metal case is almost ready. Now, you will assign material and description to this part.

 19. Assign additional iProperties data to the part, and select material. In the browser, right-click on **_100-02:1** and select **iProperties** from the menu, like in Fig. 379a

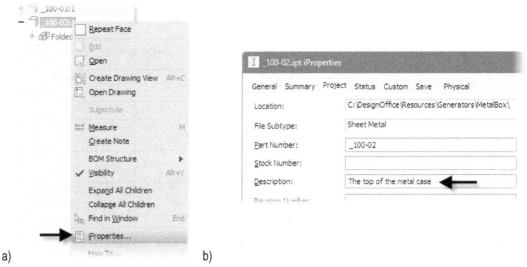

a)   b)

Fig. 379

Go to the **Project** tab and enter the name of the part in the **Description** field, like in Fig. 379b. Click **Apply**.

Now, go to the tab **Physical** and from **Material** drop-down list select **Steel, Alloy**. The program assigns the material and calculates the physical parameters of the parts that are visible on the **Physical** tab, like in Fig. 380a.

a)   b)

Fig. 380

Click **Apply** and **Close**. You can assume, that the part is finished for the time being.

Now you can make a flat pattern of the folded model of this new part. The folded model of the part is saved inside of the part file. After creating a flat pattern, all changes made to the folded model will be transferred to a flat pattern.

 20. Create a flat pattern. On the **Sheet Metal** tab, in the **Flat Pattern** panel, click the **Create Flat Pattern** icon. The program opens a part file in edit mode in the new window and displays the flat pattern, like in Fig. 380b.

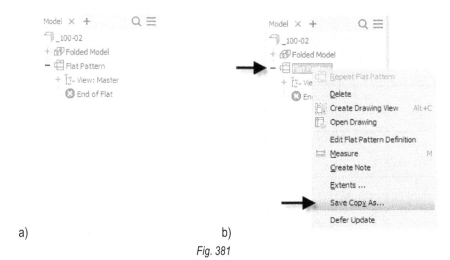

a)   b)

Fig. 381

In the browser, in the structure of the part, the new item **Flat Pattern** will appear, like in Fig. 381a. Double-clicking this item displays the part unfolds. Double-clicking **Folded Model** displays the model in the folded mode.

Flat pattern is also a 3D model. You can save flat pattern as a DXF file for CAM machining, by right-click the **Flat Pattern** and next click **Save Copy As**, as shown in Fig. 381b. Then you can select the file type, folder, and other options depending on the file type chosen.

21. Close the flat pattern. In the **Sheet Metal** tab, in a **Folded Part** pane, click **Go to Folded Part** icon. The program switches to the folded model environment of the part file. Click **F6** to see a whole part, if needed.

22. Close the **_100-02.ipt** file. In **File** menu click **Close** icon or click **X** in the upper right corner of the screen. Click **Yes** in the message window to save the file of the part. You are back in the assembly modeling environment.

Now, put the cover in the right place using the assembly constraints. Before doing so, you must remove the **Flush** constraint that was created when the initial construction plane was selected to determine the location of the first sketch.

23. Remove the **Flush:1** constraint. In the browser, right-click the **Flush:1** link and select **Delete** like in Fig. 382a.

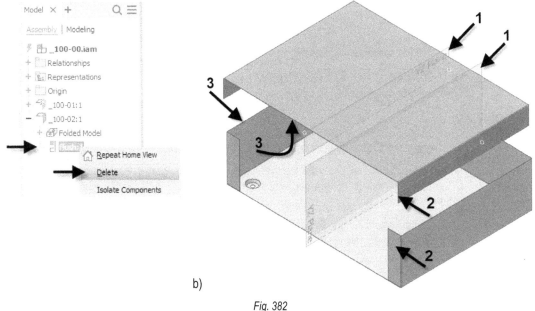

a)   b)

Fig. 382

Now you can freely move part **_100-02** in space. You will use three mate constraints to fix the position of this part. You will use the YZ symmetry planes marked with the number 1 on Fig. 382b, align the edge of the part with the short flanges of parts **_100-01** (marked by 2) and move the surface from the edge of the wall to a distance of **0.25 in** (marked by 3).

24. Set the position of the cover using assembly constraints. On the **Assemble** tab, in the **Relationships** pane, click the **Constrain** icon. In the **Place Constraint** dialog box, the **Mate** constraint type is enabled by default with **Mate** solution. In the browser pick to constraint the YZ origin planes of the components: **_100-01: 1** and **_100-02: 1**, like in Fig. 383a.

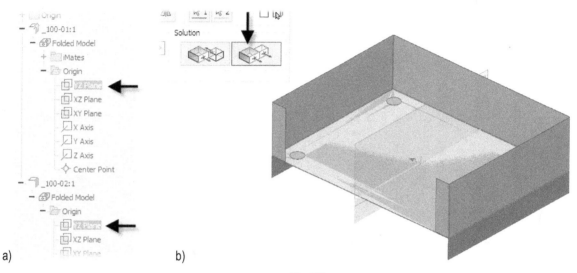

a)   b)

Fig. 383

Switch the solution type to **Flush** so that the program sets both parts like in Fig. 383b. Click **Apply**.

Now, pick the edge of the cover and short flange, indicated in Fig. 384a. Set the **Mate** constraint and the **Flush** solution. Click **Apply**.

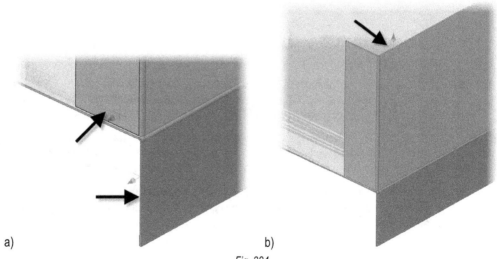

a)   b)

Fig. 384

Switch the solution to Mate and pick an upper edge, indicated in Fig. 384b and the pick the bottom of the cover indicated in Fig. 385a.

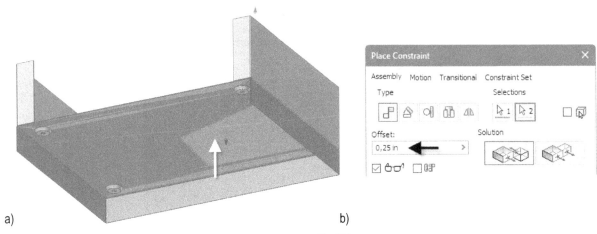

a)   b)

Fig. 385

In the **Offset** field, enter **0.25**, like in Fig. 385b. Click **OK**. Properly constrained model is shown in Fig. 386a.

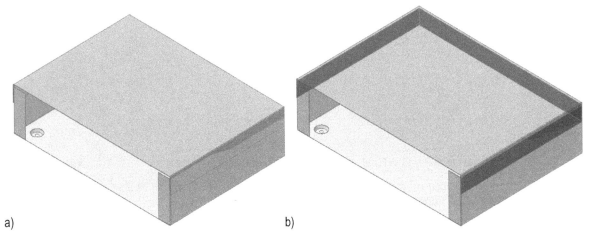

a)   b)

Fig. 386

In both parts, the same values of dimensions have been used, which in turn will cause the parts to collide. You can easily see where collisions occur in the model using the collision analysis tool.

25. Check the collisions in the model. On the **Inspect** tab, in the **Interference** panel, click the **Analyze Interference** icon. Pick both parts and click **OK** in the **Interference Analysis** dialog box. The program will distinguish in red the areas of the collision, like in Fig. 386b. Click **OK** after viewing the collision areas.

To eliminate these collisions, reduce the width and depth of the **_100-01.ipt** part by equal to the sheet metal thickness of the second component. You can assume that the sheet metal thicknesses of both parts will always be equal, so you can correct the dimensions of part **_100-01.ipt** by the value of its own sheet thickness.

26. Correct the dimensions of part **_100-01**. Double-click the model of this part on the screen or in the browser to enter the edit mode. In the browser, expand the contents of the **Folded Model** folder, right-click **Face1** and select **Show Dimension** from the menu, like in Fig. 387a.

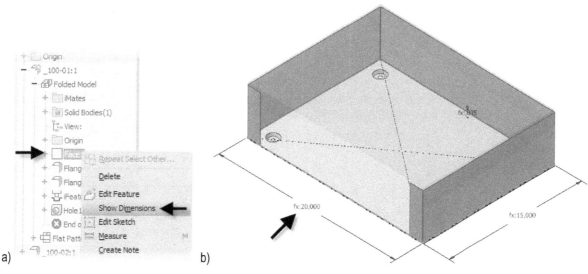

Fig. 387

The program will display dimensions like in Fig. 387b. Double-click on the dimension **fx: 20,000**, indicated in Fig. 387b. In the **Edit Dimension** edit field, enter **–2 * Thickness**, like in Fig. 388a and confirm.

Fig. 388

Now, double-click on the dimension **fx: 15,000**. In the **Edit Dimension** edit field, enter **–Thickness**, like in Fig. 388b and confirm.

27. Finish editing this part, which will automatically update its dimensions. Right-click and choose **Finish Edit** from the menu.

28. Check the collisions again in the model. On the **Inspect** tab, in the **Interference** panel, click the **Analyze Interference** icon. Pick both parts and click **OK** in the **Interference Analysis** dialog box. Now the program should display a message like in Fig. 389.

Fig. 389

Click **OK**.

29. Save the assembly file, but don't close the file if you plan to continue in next exercise.

End of exercise.

In this exercise, you will create the front plate of the metal case. As before, the new part will also be created in the context of an assembly. The ready front plate is shown in Fig. 390.

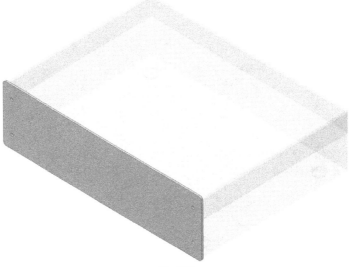

Fig. 390

In the previous exercise, the new part was set in the working position after it was created. In this exercise, before creating the first sketch of the new part, you will determine the position of its initial coordinate system relative to the geometry of the other parts. To determine the position of the initial coordinate system, you will use an additional construction plane placed in the symmetry of the assembly.

Continue to work in the **_100-00.iam** file. If this file has been closed, open it.

1. Create a construction plane symmetrically between the two faces at the main assembly level. On the **Assemble** tab, in the **Work Features** panel, click the **Work Plane** icon. Pick the face of the cover, indicated in Fig. 391a, and then turn the model over and pick face of the base, indicated in Fig. 391b.

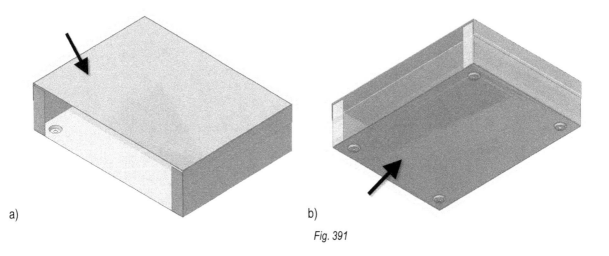

a)   b)

Fig. 391

The ready construction plane is shown in Fig. 392a.

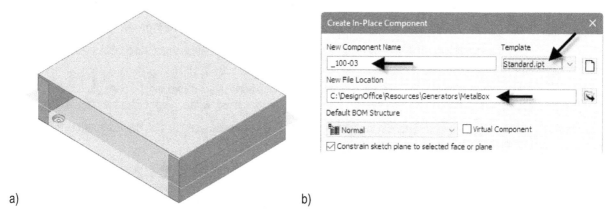

a)   b)

Fig. 392

 2. Create a new part in the context of the assembly. On the **Assemble** tab, in the **Component** panel, click the **Create** icon. In the **Create In-Place Component** dialog box, enter the file name of the new part **_100-03**, and as a template select the standard template for part modeling, like in Fig. 392b. Make sure that the new part will be placed in the folder **...: \ DesignOffice \ Resources \ Generators \ MetalBox**.

3. Click **OK**. The program is waiting for an indication of the plane to place the new component on. Pick the construction plane you just created. The program will place the XY plane of the new part on the construction plane.

For now, you will finish editing this part and set its coordinate system precisely in the expected location, which will facilitate further modeling of parts.

4. Finish editing of this part. Right-click and select **Finish Edit** from the menu.

 5. Determine the position of the coordinate system of the new part. On the **Assemble** tab, in the **Relationships** panel, click the **Constrain** icon. In the **Place Constraint** dialog box, the **Mate** constraint type is enabled by default with solution **Mate.** In the browser, pick to constraint the origin **YZ Plane** of the _100-03 component and the origin **YZ Plane** of the assembly, like in Fig. 393a.

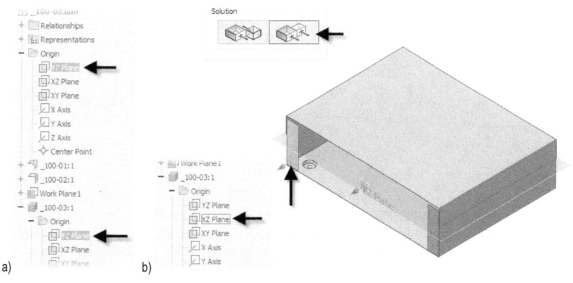

a)   b)

Fig. 393

Click **Apply**.

Now, pick in the browser the origin **XZ Plane** of the **_100-03** component and the flat face of the short flange indicated in Fig. 393b. Set the **Mate / Flush** constraint. Click **OK**.

6. Turn on **_100-03** component editing mode again. Double-click **_100-03:1** in the browser.

    You will start building a new part by defining the key dimensional parameters that will control the size of this part and later will be associated with the global parameters of the assembly file.

    We assume that in parts files we will write the names of the parameters controlling the parts dimensions in lower case letters. In this part file, you will create the following parameters: **width**, **height**, and **handle_size**.

7. Define new user parameters. On the **Manage** tab, in the **Parameters** panel, click the **Parameters** icon. In the **Parameters** window, click the **Add Numeric** button, like in Fig. 394a.

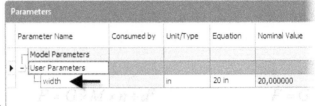

a)   b)

Fig. 394

Enter the parameter name: **width** and the value **20 in**, like in Fig. 394b. Similarly, enter the parameters: **height** and **handle_size**. All entered parameters and their values show Fig. 395a.

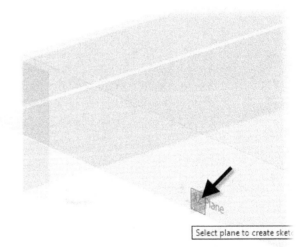

a)   b)

Fig. 395

Click **Done**. Now, you can use these parameters in building your 3D model of the part.

8. Create a sketch of the front plate. On the **Sheet Metal** tab, in the **Sketch** panel, click **Start 2D Sketch**. Pick the **XZ Plane** like in Fig. 395b. Using the **ViewCube**, set the view to the sketching plane like in Fig. 396.

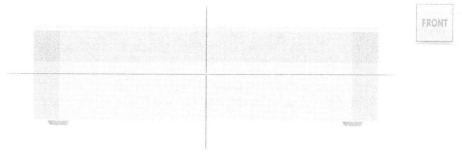

Fig. 396

9. Draw the **Rectangle Two Point Center**, from the center point of the sketch. Enter equations in the appropriate edit fields: **width+0,25 in** and **height+0,535 in**, like in Fig. 397.

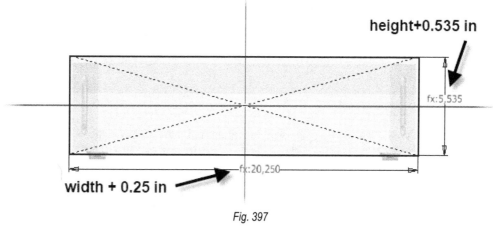

height+0.535 in

width + 0.25 in

Fig. 397

10. Finish sketch.

11. Create a plate using an extrude feature. On the **3D Model** tab, in the **Create** panel, click the **Extrude** icon. In the **Distance A** field, enter a value of **0.15 in**, like in Fig. 398a.

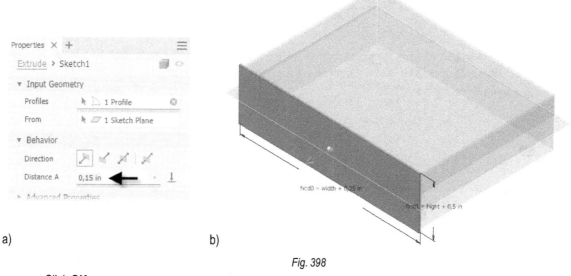

a)   b)

Fig. 398

Click **OK**.

Now you will create holes to mount the handles. The holes will be arranged on a construction sketch whose dimensions will be associated with the parameters controlling the dimensions of the front panel.

12. Create a sketch on the front wall. On the **Sheet Metal** tab, in the **Sketch** panel, click **Start 2D Sketch**. Pick the front face of the plate.

13. Draw the **Rectangle Two Point Center**, from the center point of the sketch. Enter equations in the appropriate edit fields: **width-1,5 in** and **handle_size**, like in Fig. 399.

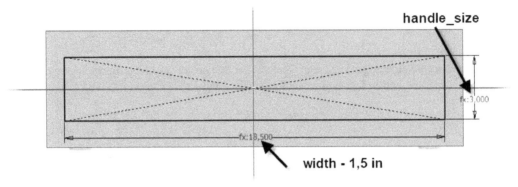

Fig. 399

14. Finish sketch.

15. Insert holes in the corners of the sketched rectangle. On the **3D Model** tab, in the **Modify** panel, click the **Hole** icon. The program displays the Hole properties panel and waits for the location of the holes. Select all four corners of the rectangle, one by one, like in Fig. 400.

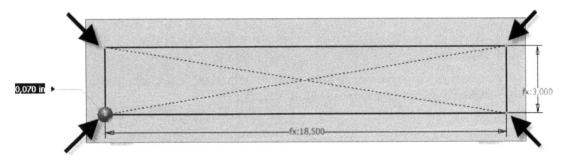

Fig. 400

In the indicated places, the program displays the preview of the hole with the size of the last created hole. In the **Hole** properties panel, set the parameters of the holes, like in Fig. 401a.

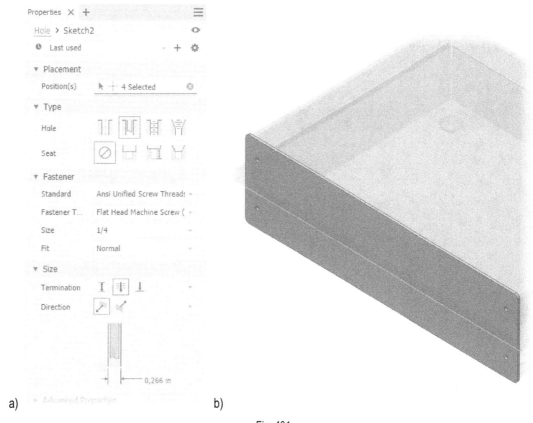

a)   b)

Fig. 401

Click **OK**. The finished holes show Fig. 401b (isometric view).

16. Create rounded corners of the plate with a radius of **0.25 in**, like in Fig. 402a.

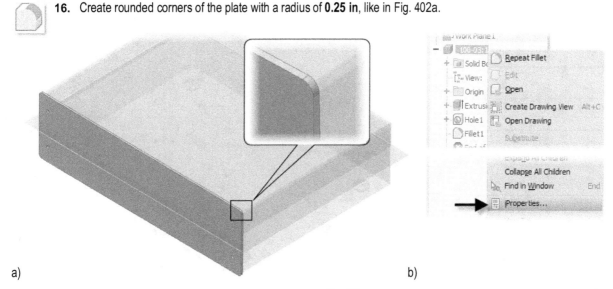

a)   b)

Fig. 402

The front plate is almost ready. Now, you will assign material and description to this part.

17. Assign additional iProperties data to the part, and select material. In the browser, right-click on **_100-03:1** and select **iProperties** from the menu, like in Fig. 402b. Go to the **Project** tab and enter the name of the part in the **Description** field, like in Fig. 403a. The **Part Number** has been completed in the first part save, at the beginning of this exercise. Click **Apply**.

a)   b)

Fig. 403

Now, go to the tab **Physical** and from **Material** drop-down list select **Aluminum 6061**. The program assigns the material and calculates the physical parameters of the parts that are visible on the **Physical** tab, as in Fig. 403b.

Click **Apply** and **Close**. You can assume, that the part is finished for the time being.

18. Finish edits. Right-click and select **Finish Edit** in the menu. Turn off the visibility of the **Work Plane1**. For now, our metal case looks like in Fig. 404.

Fig. 404

19. Save the assembly file, but don't close the file if you plan to continue in next exercise.

End of exercise.

Exercise 26
Inserting handles and footers. Dimensions correction

In this exercise, you will create holes in the flanges of the bottom part of the box, coaxial with the holes in the front panel, which will be used to attach the handles. Then you will insert the handles and footers to the assembly. Finally, you will adjust the dimensions of the bottom part and front plate so that the height of the box is equal to the value of the **HEIGHT** parameter. This will be the last work related to modeling. The finished model of the metal case will look like in Fig. 405.

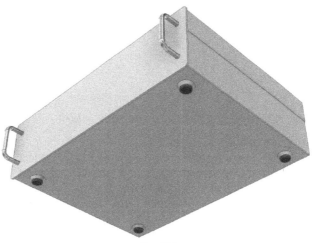

Fig. 405

You continue working on the model saved in the previous exercise.

1. Enter the edit mode of the bottom part – double-click part **_100-01: 1** in the browser or on the graphics screen.

    In this example, a sketch for holes will be created on the construction plane instead of on the model face. Placing the hole's sketch in this way will make it to easier get a symmetrical position of the holes. The construction plane will be offseted from the origin plane to a distance of **depth / 2**.

 2. Create a construction plane for the hole's sketch. On the **Sheet Metal** tab, in the **Work Features** panel, click icon **Offset form Plane**, from **Plane** pull–down menu.

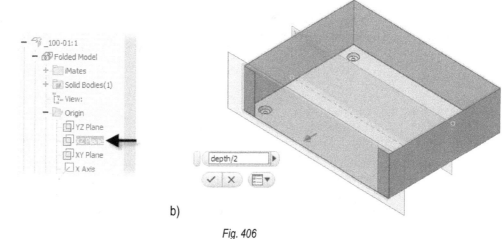

a)   b)

Fig. 406

As reference plane, click the start plane **XZ Plane**, indicated in Fig. 406a, then pull the construction plane towards the front plate and enter **depth / 2** in the distance edit field, like in Fig. 406b. Click **OK**.

3. Create a sketch for the holes. On the **Sheet Metal** tab, in the **Sketch** panel, click **Start 2D Sketch**. Pick the new construction plane, indicated on Fig. 407a.

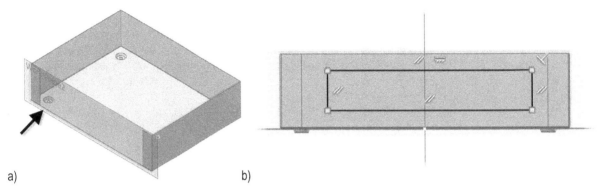

a)   b)

Fig. 407

4. Draw a rectangle, like in Fig. 407b, for now without dimensions.

The location of the holes will be built on the same sketch as in the front panel. In order to ensure that the holes in the bottom part of the case are always coaxial with the holes in the front panel, it is necessary to precisely set the sketch of the holes relative to the front panel. For this purpose, you will project the edge of the front panel to the active sketch. As the reference edge, it is best to select such edges in the front panel, which will always be available regardless of the model version. In this example, the reference edge will be the vertical edge of the front panel.

5. Create a projection of the front panel edge. On the **Sketch** tab, in the **Create** panel, click the **Project Geometry** icon and select the flank edge indicated in Fig. 408a to be projected. To finish, right-click and select **OK**.

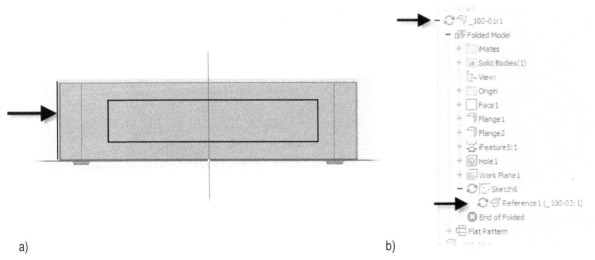

a)   b)

Fig. 408

In the browser, the projected edge will be placed in the node of the new sketch, with the designation of the component from which it was projected. In addition, the sketch and the whole part will receive the attribute of **Adaptive**, like in Fig. 408b. Adaptivity is a software function that will adjust the position of the projected edges to the new position of the edge of the reference component when the dimensions of the front panel change.

6. Determine the position of the new rectangle relative to the available geometry. On the **Sketch** tab in the **Constrain** panel, click the **Vertical Constraint** icon and pick the center of the horizontal edge of the rectangle indicated by 1 in Fig. 409a, and then pick the center point of the sketch, indicated by 2.

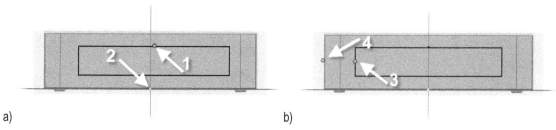

a)   b)

Fig. 409

Then, click the **Horizontal Constraint** icon and pick the center point of the vertical edge of the rectangle indicated by 3 in Fig. 409b, and then pick the center point of the projected vertical edge of the front panel, indicated by 4.

7. Dimension the rectangle. In place of the dimension values, enter parameters like in Fig. 410.

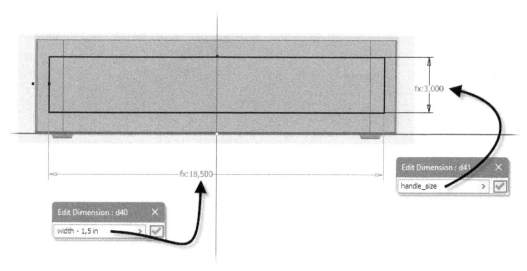

Fig. 410

Finish sketch.

8. Insert holes in the corners of the sketched rectangle. On the **Sheet Metal** tab, in the **Modify** panel, click the **Hole** icon. The program displays the **Hole** properties panel and is waiting for the location of holes. Pick all four corners of the rectangle, like in Fig. 411.

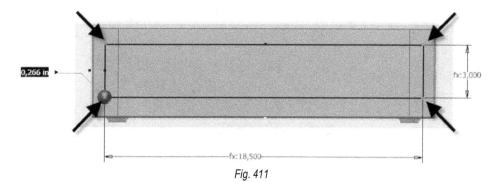

Fig. 411

In the selected corners, the program displays the preview of the size of the hole with the size of the last created hole. In the **Hole** properties panel, set the hole parameters like in Fig. 412a. Then, select the **Termination** option **To**, indicated by the arrow.

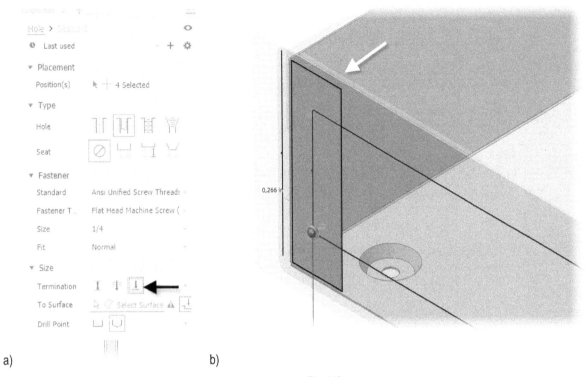

a)   b)

Fig. 412

Click the arrow to the left of the **Select Surface** text and pick the inside face of the short flange, indicated by an arrow in Fig. 412b. Click **OK**. Finished holes are presented in Fig. 413a. The visibility of the working plane has been turned off.

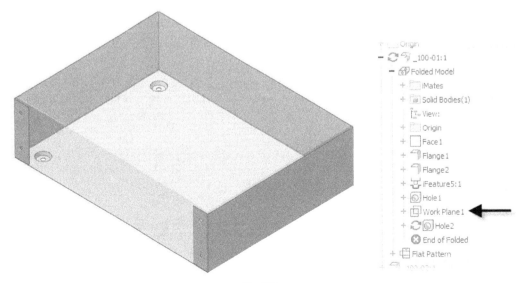

Fig. 413

9.   Finish edit. Right-click and select **Finish Edit**.

Now you will insert handles prepared in *Exercise 20. Library component as iPart. Handle.* And then you will mount them in the holes of the front panel with the **Insert** constraints.

10. Insert two **3-inch** handles. On the **Assemble** tab, in the **Component** panel, click **Place**. In the **Place Component** dialog box, go to the **Accessories** library folder, then **Handles** and select the **Handle type C.ipt** file, like in Fig. 414a.

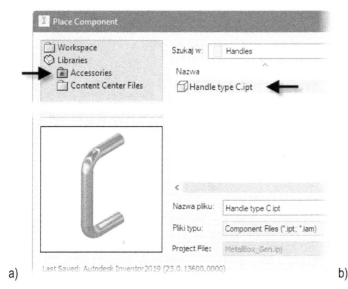

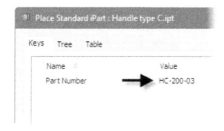

a)   b)

Fig. 414

Click **Open**.

In the **Place Standard iPart: Handle type C.ipt** dialog box, make sure that a 3-inch handle named **HC-200-03** is selected, like in Fig. 414b. Insert two handles like in Fig. 415a. To finish, right-click and select **OK**.

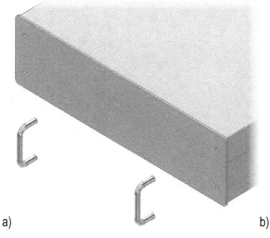

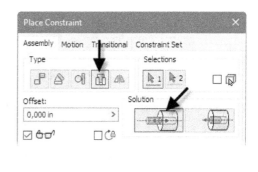

a)   b)

Fig. 415

11. Using the assembly constraints, mount the handles with the holes in the front panel. On the **Assemble** tab in the **Relationships** panel, click the **Constrain** icon. Set the type of constraint to **Insert**, with solution **Opposed**, like in Fig. 415b.

Pick the edge of the hole in the front panel and then pick the circular edge of the handle, like in Fig. 416a. Click **Apply**. The program will set the handle like in Fig. 416b. Next, pick the circular edge of the second end of the holder, like in Fig. 416b and the edge of the second hole in the front panel, like in Fig. 416c. Click **Apply**.

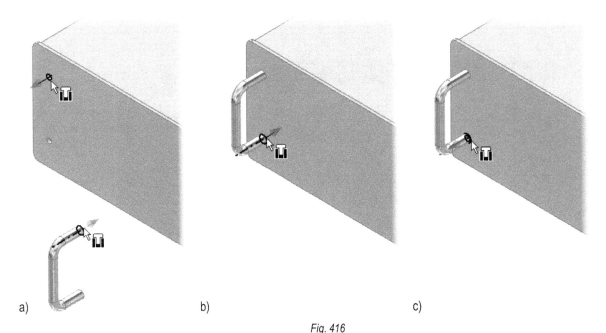

a)   b)   c)

Fig. 416

Set the position of the second holder in a similar way. Correctly inserted handles are shown in Fig. 417a.

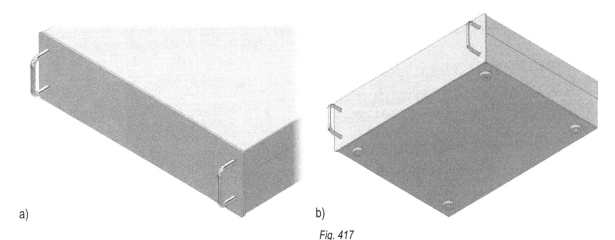

a)   b)

Fig. 417

Now you will insert the footers. The footer model, which was created in *Exercise 19. Library component as a single part. Footer* is equipped with iMate constraint. Similar iMate constrain were also defined in the component **_100-01.ipt** – the bottom part of the case. For fast insertion of footers, you will use these iMates.

12. Set the model view on the screen like in Fig. 417b.

13. Insert footers. On the **Assemble** tab, in the **Component** panel, click **Place** icon. In the **Place Component** dialog box, go to the **Accessories** library folder, then **Footers** and select the **F-035.ipt** file, like in Fig. 418a.

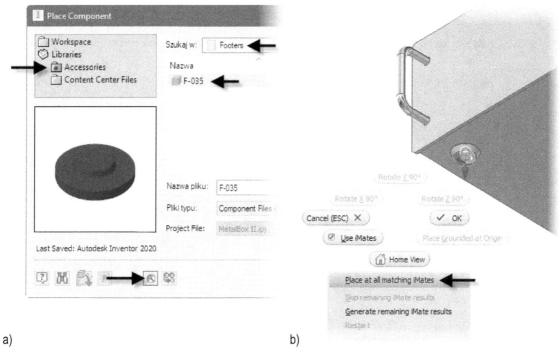

a)   b)

Fig. 418

Make sure the **Interactively place with iMates** button is on, at the bottom of the **Place Components** dialog box. Click **Open**.

The program places the footer in the first compatible iMate constraint. Right-click and select **Place at all matching iMates** in the menu, like in Fig. 418b. All footers will be inserted in all holes in the legs of the bottom component, like in Fig. 419.

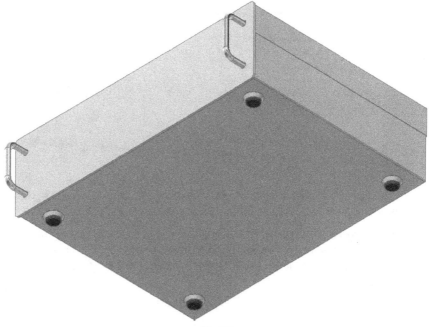

Fig. 419

After inserting the footers, you can do the final adjustment of the height of the bottom component of the metal box and the height of the front plate, so that the total height of the box is equal to the **HEIGHT** parameter, and the height of the front panel is in the right proportion to the box height. You will start by measuring the current height of the box.

14. Measure the height of the box body. On the **Inspect** tab, in the **Measure** panel, click the **Measure** icon.

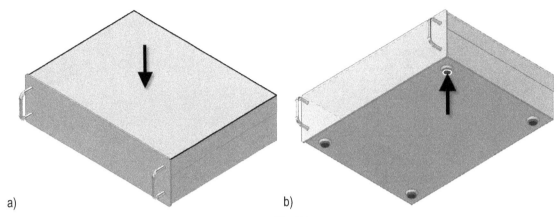

a)   b)

Fig. 420

In order to check the total height, pick the top face, indicated in Fig. 420a, and then rotate the model and pick the footer plane indicated in Fig. 420b. The program will display the measured distance on the model and on the **Measure** tab, like in Fig. 421a.

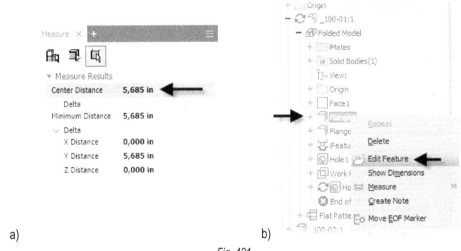

a)   b)

Fig. 421

The **HEIGHT** parameter value is **5 in**, while the measured distance is **5.685 in**. This means that you must do a dimension correction of **0.685 in**. Close the **Measure** panel.

15. Make a correction of the height of the bottom component. Double-click the **_100-01:1** component in the browser or in the graphics screen to enter edit mode. Expand the contents of the **Folded Model** folder, right-click **Flange1** and select **Edit Feature**, like in Fig. 421b. In the **Distance** field enter **– 0.685 in**, like in Fig. 422a.

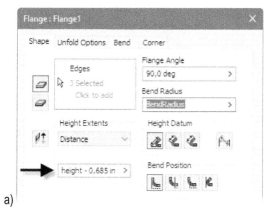 

a) b)

Fig. 422

Click **OK**.

16. Return to the assembly level - right-click and select **Finish Edit**. The program will update the model.

17. Measure the box height again. On the **Inspect** tab, in the **Measure** panel, click **Measure** icon and pick the same planes as in point 14. Now the measured value of the total box height should be like in Fig. 422b. Close the **Measure** panel.

18. Make a correction of the height of the front panel. Double-click the **_100-03:1** component in the browser or on the graphics screen to enter the edit mode. Right-click on **Extrusion1**, select **Edit Sketch**, like in Fig. 423a.

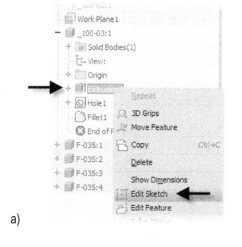 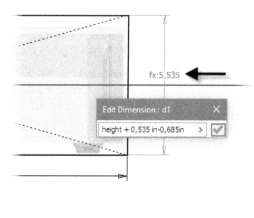

a) b)

Fig. 423

Double-click the dimension indicated in Fig. 423b and add the **–0,685** in the dimension edit field. Confirm the dimension, finish the sketch.

19. Return to the assembly level - right-click and select **Finish Edit**. The program will update the model.

This was the last step in the modeling of the metal case. In the next exercise, you will create an iLogic rule that will allow you to build different variants of this metal case.

20. Save the assembly file, but don't close the file if you plan to continue in next exercise.

End of exercise.

Exercise 27
Creating an iLogic rule controlling the versions

In this exercise, you will create simple iLogic rules that allow you to generate different dimensional variants of the metal cases, with or without handles. The approach presented here shows a simple way of programming basic dependencies that allow generating variants of assemblies. You do not need any programming experience to create these rules. Fig. 424 shows examples of versions of metal cases generated using the iLogic rule that will be created in this exercise and a piece of an iLogic rule.

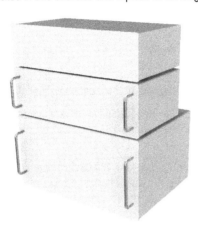

Fig. 424

You continue working on the model saved in the previous exercise. You will start by displaying the iLogic tab in the browser, which will facilitate access to iLogic rules.

1. Turn on the iLogic tab in the browser. Click the **plus** sign in the browser's header and select **iLogic** in the menu, like in Fig. 425a. The program will add an iLogic tab, like in Fig. 425b.

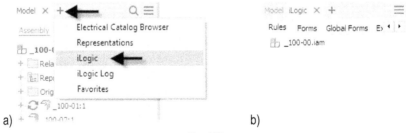

a)   b)

Fig. 425

2. Start creating a rule that controls the versions of the metal case. In the browser, on the **Rules** tab, right-click and select **Add Rule**, like in Fig. 426a.

a)   b)

Fig. 426

In the **Rule Name** dialog box, enter the name of the new rule: **BoxConfig**, like in Fig. 426b and click **OK**. The program displays the iLogic rules editor. In the rule's editor, you can highlight three main areas like in Fig. 427.

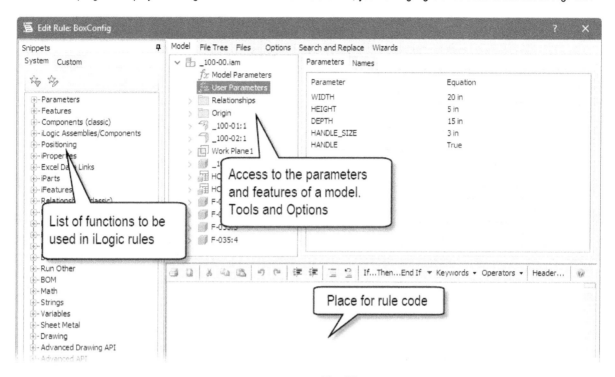

Fig. 427

You will start by associating the parameters defined in the main assembly file with the appropriate parameters in the individual part files.

On the **Model** tab, when you pick the **User Parameters** entry, the parameters defined in the selected file are displayed in the **Parameters** tab to the right. Parameters defined in the main assembly file, written in uppercase letters, are visible in Fig. 427. In this model, in any part files, the same parameter names are written in lowercase, like in Fig. 428a.

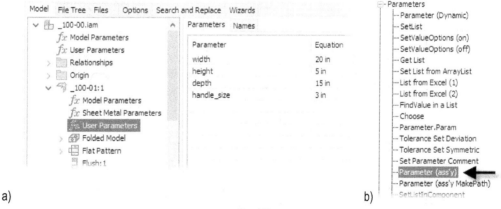

a)   b)

Fig. 428

You will now create a link between user parameters in the assembly file and user parameters in the part files. Changing the parameter value in the assembly file should be passed to the appropriate part files. For this purpose, you will use the **Parameter (ass'y)** function, indicated in Fig. 428b.

Each rule row can be entered manually or you can use the state capture option, which avoids typing errors. In this example, you will use the option of capturing status where it is possible.

3.   Assign parameter values from the assembly file to the appropriate parameters in the individual part files. Start with the bottom panel of the metal case. For the **_100-01: 1** component, expand the list of user parameters and double-click the **width** parameter, indicated in Fig. 429a.

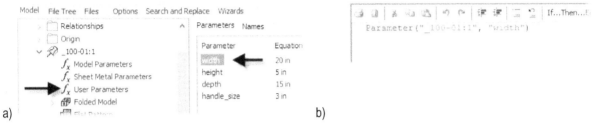

a)   b)

Fig. 429

A line of code will be entered into the rule area, like in Fig. 429b. Make sure the cursor is positioned at the end of this line, enter the **=** sign, and then expand the list of user parameters at the main assembly level and double-click the **WIDTH** parameter, indicated in Fig. 430a.

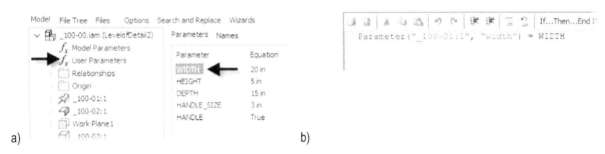

a)   b)

Fig. 430

The **WIDTH** parameter should be placed after the equal sign, like in Fig. 430b.

Proceed similarly, enter the lines that assign parameters for the remaining parts of the assembly. The ready set of functions presents Fig. 431a.

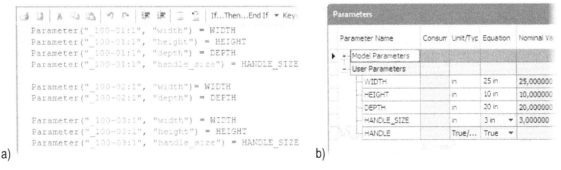

a)   b)

Fig. 431

Check how the rule works with just entered functions. Click **Save & Run**. The program checks for errors and runs the rule - performs the assignment of parameters declared in the rule.

4.   Change the dimensions of the metal case. On the **Assemble** tab, in the **Manage** panel, click the **Parameters** icon. In the **Parameters** dialog box, make sure the **Immediate Update** option is selected, and then set the new values of parameters: **WIDTH**, **HEIGHT**, and **DEPTH**, like in Fig. 431b. The model before and after changing these three parameters is shown in Fig. 432.

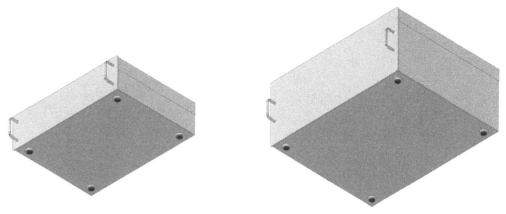

Fig. 432

Restore the previous parameter values in the **Parameters** dialog box and click **Done**.

Now you will add functions that will be responsible for the selection of the handles, depending on the size selected in the **Parameters** window. The handles are an iParts and there are special functions for handling iParts.

5.   Enter the rule edition mode and add options controlling the size of the handles. Double-click the **BoxConfig** rule in the browser in the iLogic panel. The program opens the rule editor dialog box again.

You will now apply a conditional function which – depending on the value of the **HANDLE_SIZE** parameter – select the appropriate iPart handle.

6.   Add functions. Position the cursor below existing rows and click **If ... Then ... End If**, indicated in Fig. 433a.

Fig. 433

The program will insert a conditional function, like in Fig. 433b. In place of **My_Expression**, enter **HANDLE_SIZE = 3**, like in Fig. 434a.

Fig. 434

Position the cursor in the line below, on the function list, expand the **iParts** tree and double-click the **ChangeRow** function, indicated in Fig. 434b. The program will insert a function with two arguments, like in Fig. 435a.

```
If HANDLE_SIZE = 3 Then
iPart.ChangeRow("iComponentName:1", "RowMemberName")

a) End If
```

```
If HANDLE_SIZE = 3 Then
iPart.ChangeRow("Handle type C:1", "HC-200-03")

b) End If
```

Fig. 435

In place of the text strings of arguments, enter the component name and version name, like in Fig. 435b. Add a row for the second handle, like in Fig. 436.

```
If HANDLE_SIZE = 3 Then
iPart.ChangeRow("Handle type C:1", "HC-200-03")
iPart.ChangeRow("Handle type C:2", "HC-200-03")
End If
```

Fig. 436

In a similar way, enter functions for other handle sizes, like in Fig. 437a.

```
If HANDLE_SIZE = 3 Then
iPart.ChangeRow("Handle type C:1", "HC-200-03")
iPart.ChangeRow("Handle type C:2", "HC-200-03")
End If

If HANDLE_SIZE = 4 Then
iPart.ChangeRow("Handle type C:1", "HC-200-04")
iPart.ChangeRow("Handle type C:2", "HC-200-04")
End If

If HANDLE_SIZE = 5 Then
iPart.ChangeRow("Handle type C:1", "HC-200-05")
iPart.ChangeRow("Handle type C:2", "HC-200-05")
End If

If HANDLE_SIZE = 6 Then
iPart.ChangeRow("Handle type C:1", "HC-200-06")
iPart.ChangeRow("Handle type C:2", "HC-200-06")
End If
```
a)

b)

Parameter Name	Consum	Unit/Typ	Equation	Nominal Valu
+ Model Parameters				
− User Parameters				
WIDTH		in	20 in	20,000000
► HEIGHT		in	10 in	10,000000
DEPTH		in	15 in	15,000000
HANDLE_SIZE		in	3 in ▼	3,000000
HANDLE		True/...	True ▼	

Fig. 437

Check how the rule works with just entered functions. Click **Save & Run**. The program checks for errors and runs the rule - performs the assignment of parameters declared in the rule.

7. Check new functions are working. On the **Assemble** tab, in the **Manage** panel, click the **Parameters** icon. In the **Parameters** dialog box, make sure the **Immediate Update** option is selected and set the **HEIGHT** parameter to **10 in**, like in Fig. 437b. Now you can choose different **HANDLE_SIZE** values from the list. In Fig. 438a, different handles are shown in the side view.

a)

b)

Fig. 438

In the wireframe view style, you can check if the holes are correctly spaced after changing the size of the handles. In Fig. 438b there are shown examples of two versions of the cases with handles, in the wireframe view.

Close the **Parameters** dialog box.

Now you will add functions that will be responsible for enabling or disabling of the handles. In addition, turning on or off the handles also means the necessity to turn on and off the constraints and holes.

8. Enter the rule edition mode and add functions to control the presence of the handles. Double-click the **BoxConfig** rule in the iLogic panel of the browser. The program re-opens the rules editor dialog box.

The handle will be placed if the **HANDLE** parameter is set to **True**, otherwise, the handle will not be placed. To achieve this goal, you will use a conditional function which – depending on the value of the **HANDLE** parameter – will adequately switch handles, constraints, and holes on or off.

9. Add conditional functions. Position the cursor below existing rows and **click If ... Then ... End If**, indicated in Fig. 439a.

a)
```
End If

If HANDLE_SIZE = 6 Then
iPart.ChangeRow("Handle type C:1", "HC-200-06")
iPart.ChangeRow("Handle type C:2", "HC-200-06")
End If
```

b)
```
If My_Expression Then

End If
```

Fig. 439

The program will insert a conditional function, like in Fig. 439b. Place the cursor in an empty row, indicated in Fig. 439b, and then insert the **Else** operator, by clicking on the menu, like in Fig. 440a.

a)
```
End If


If My_Expression Then
|
End If
```
| If...Then...End If |
| ElseIf...Then |
| Else |

b)
```
If My_Expression Then

Else

End If
```

Fig. 440

The program will insert the **Else** operator and add empty rows, like in Fig. 440b.

In place of **My_Expression**, enter **HANDLE = "True"**, like in Fig. 441a.

a)
```
If HANDLE = "True" Then

Else

End If
```

b)
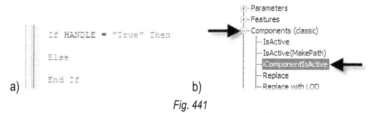
- Parameters
- Features
- Components (classic)
  - IsActive
  - IsActive(MakePath)
  - iComponentIsActive
  - Replace
  - Replace with LOD

Fig. 441

Position the cursor in the line below **If**, then in the list of functions, expand the **Components** tree and double-click the **iComponentIsActive** function, pointed in Fig. 441b. The program will insert a function with one argument, like in Fig. 442a.

a)
```
If HANDLE = "True" Then
Component.iComponentIsActive("iPartA:1")
Else

End If
```

b)
```
If HANDLE = "True" Then
Component.iComponentIsActive("Handle type C:1") = True

Else

End If
```

Fig. 442

Complete the function like in Fig. 442b. Insert and complete the function for the second handle, like in Fig. 443a.

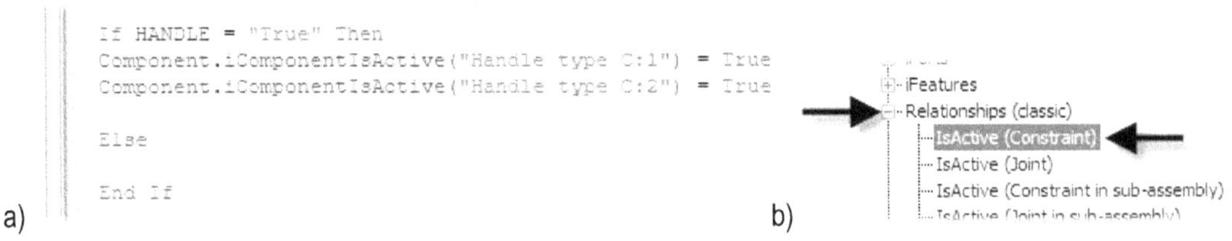

```
If HANDLE = "True" Then
Component.iComponentIsActive("Handle type C:1") = True
Component.iComponentIsActive("Handle type C:2") = True

Else

End If
```

a)

b)

- iFeatures
- Relationships (classic)
  - IsActive (Constraint)
  - IsActive (Joint)
  - IsActive (Constraint in sub-assembly)
  - IsActive (Joint in sub-assembly)

Fig. 443

The next step: controlling of the constraints. Position the cursor below the last line entered, then in the list of functions expand the **Relationships** tree and double-click the **IsActive** function, indicated in Fig. 443b. The program will insert a function with one argument, like in Fig. 444a.

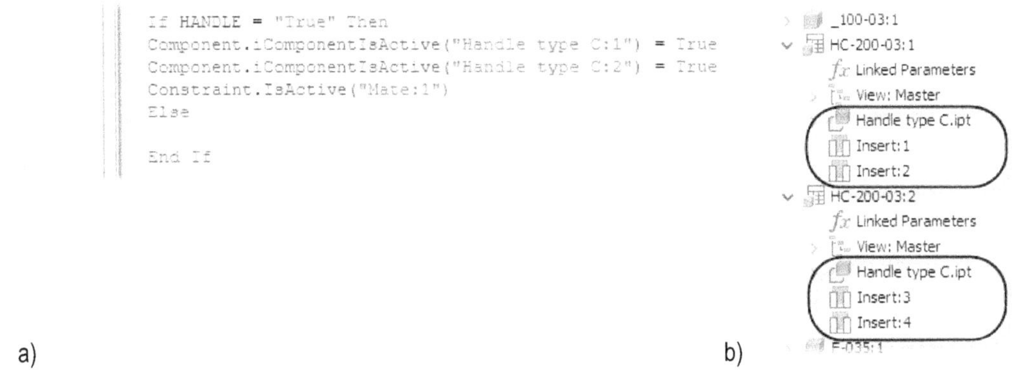

```
If HANDLE = "True" Then
Component.iComponentIsActive("Handle type C:1") = True
Component.iComponentIsActive("Handle type C:2") = True
Constraint.IsActive("Mate:1")
Else

End If
```

a)

b)

- _100-03:1
- HC-200-03:1
  - fx Linked Parameters
  - View: Master
  - Handle type C.ipt
  - Insert:1
  - Insert:2
- HC-200-03:2
  - fx Linked Parameters
  - View: Master
  - Handle type C.ipt
  - Insert:3
  - Insert:4
- F-035:1

Fig. 444

Complete the function by entering the constraints names of the handle. In this model, there are four constraints of handles. The names of constraints are visible in expanding the content of the given version of the iPart handle, in the upper part of the **Edit Rule** window, like in Fig. 444b. Insert the names of the constraints marked in Fig. 444b from your model – in your model, the constraint number may differ from the numbers in the illustration.

Put in three more lines of the same function. The finished functions controlling the constraints of both handles are shown in Fig. 445a.

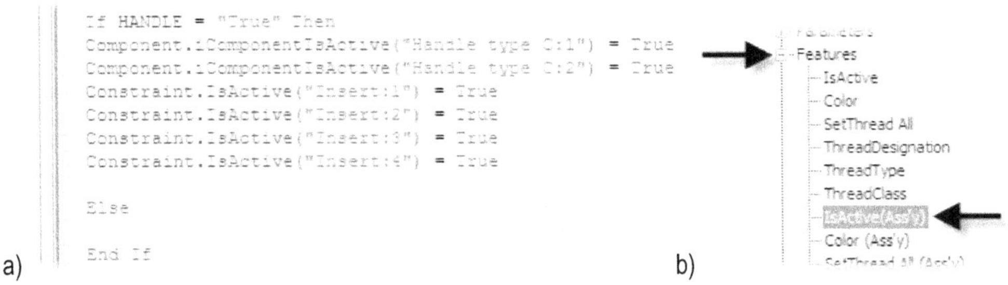

```
If HANDLE = "True" Then
Component.iComponentIsActive("Handle type C:1") = True
Component.iComponentIsActive("Handle type C:2") = True
Constraint.IsActive("Insert:1") = True
Constraint.IsActive("Insert:2") = True
Constraint.IsActive("Insert:3") = True
Constraint.IsActive("Insert:4") = True

Else

End If
```

a)

b)

- Features
  - IsActive
  - Color
  - SetThread All
  - ThreadDesignation
  - ThreadType
  - ThreadClass
  - IsActive(Ass'y)
  - Color (Ass'y)
  - SetThread All (Ass'y)

Fig. 445

There are holes associated with the handles. No handles mean no holes. You will now enter functions that are responsible for controlling the holes.

Position the cursor below the last line entered, on the list of functions expand the **Features** tree and double-click the functions of **IsActive (Ass'y),** indicated in Fig. 445b. The program will insert a function with two arguments, like in Fig. 446a.

```
If HANDLE = "True" Then
   Component.iComponentIsActive("Handle type C:1") = True
   Component.iComponentIsActive("Handle type C:2") = True
   Constraint.IsActive("Insert:1") = True
   Constraint.IsActive("Insert:2") = True
   Constraint.IsActive("Insert:3") = True
   Constraint.IsActive("Insert:4") = True
   Feature.IsActive("Part1:1", "featurename")
Else

End If
```

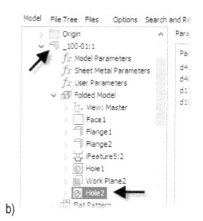

a)   b)

Fig. 446

The holes associated with the handles are located in two parts: **_100-01** and **_100-03**. You can easily check the hole's name in the tree of the component. In this example, the holes in the **_100-01** component, which are associated with the handles, have the **Hole2** designation, like in Fig. 446b, while in the **_100-03** component they have the **Hole1** designation, like in Fig. 447a.

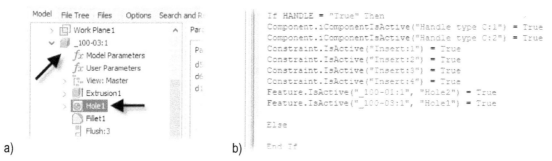

a)   b)

Fig. 447

Insert one more line of this function and complete with the arguments for the holes of both parts, like in Fig. 447b.

The conditional function **HANDLE = "True"** corresponds to the situation in which the handles are inserted. After the operator **Else**, you will place a set of functions responsible for the situation when the handles are not present.

Copy the previously entered function set and change the value **True** to **False**, like in Fig. 448a.

```
If HANDLE = "True" Then
   Component.iComponentIsActive("Handle type C:1") = True
   Component.iComponentIsActive("Handle type C:2") = True
   Constraint.IsActive("Insert:1") = True
   Constraint.IsActive("Insert:2") = True
   Constraint.IsActive("Insert:3") = True
   Constraint.IsActive("Insert:4") = True
   Feature.IsActive("_100-01:1", "Hole2") = True
   Feature.IsActive("_100-03:1", "Hole1") = True

Else
   Component.iComponentIsActive("Handle type C:1") = False
   Component.iComponentIsActive("Handle type C:2") = False
   Constraint.IsActive("Insert:1") = False
   Constraint.IsActive("Insert:2") = False
   Constraint.IsActive("Insert:3") = False
   Constraint.IsActive("Insert:4") = False
   Feature.IsActive("_100-01:1", "Hole2") = False
   Feature.IsActive("_100-03:1", "Hole1") = False
End If
```

Parameter Name	Consumed I	Unit/Typ	Equation	Nominal Value
+ Model Parameters				
− User Parameters				
WIDTH		in	20 in	20,000000
HEIGHT		in	10 in	10,000000
DEPTH		in	15 in	15,000000
HANDLE_SIZE		in	3 in ▼	3,000000
HANDLE		True/...	False ▼	

Add Numeric ▼   Update   Purge Unused

Link   ☑ Immediate Update

a)   b)

Fig. 448

Check how the rule works after entering a new set of functions. Click **Save & Run**. The program checks for errors and runs the rule - performs the assignment of parameters declared in the rule.

10. Check new functions. On the **Assemble** tab, in the **Manage** panel, click the **Parameters** icon. In the **Parameters** dialog box, make sure the **Immediate Update** option is selected, and then set the **False** value for **HANDLE**, like in Fig. 448b. The program will create a version of the metal case without handles and holes, like in Fig. 449.

Fig. 449

11. Return the value to **True** for the **HANDLE** parameter and close the **Parameters** dialog box after a model update.

You already know how this simple mechanism for assigning parameter values works. Now you will extend the iLogic rule with functions that will control whether the given dimensions have exceeded the admissible values.

You can assume that the box cannot be lower than 5 inches and higher than 10 inches. In addition, you enter a limitation of the size of the handles so that you cannot insert a handle larger than the height of the box. The function will warn you that the permissible value has been exceeded and will automatically set the permissible parameter limit.

The first condition you create will apply to the height. You can assume that if a box height value less than 5 in was entered, a message will be displayed and the height will be set to 5 in by default. Similarly, if a height value more than 10 in was entered, a message will be displayed and the height value will be set to 10 in. To achieve this goal, you will use conditional functions and a function that displays a message box.

12. Add conditional functions. Position the cursor in front of the first rule row and click the **If ... Then ... End If**, a button pointed in Fig. 450a. The program will insert a conditional function, like in Fig. 450b.

Fig. 450

In place of **My_Expression**, enter **HEIGHT <5**, like in Fig. 451a.

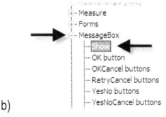

Fig. 451

For this condition, use the function that displays the message box. Position the cursor in the line below, on the function list, expand the **MessageBox** tree and double click the **Show** function, indicated in Fig. 451b. The program will insert a function with two arguments, like in Fig. 452.

```
If HEIGHT < 5 Then
MessageBox.Show("Message", "Title")

End If


Parameter("_100-01:1", "width") = WIDTH
Parameter("_100-01:1", "height") = HEIGH
Parameter("_100-01:1", "depth") = DEPTH
```

Fig. 452

In place of the **Message** and **Title** arguments, enter texts like in Fig. 453. The **Message** argument displays the warning message, while the **Title** argument is the name of the message box.

```
If HEIGHT < 5 Then
MessageBox.Show("The height of the box can not be less than 5 in. We set 5 in.", "Height issue")

End If
```

Fig. 453

Insert a function that sets the limit value of height, in the row below the function displaying the message window, like in Fig. 454.

```
If HEIGHT < 5 Then
MessageBox.Show("The height of the box can not be less than 5 in. We set 5 in.", "Height issue")
HEIGHT = 5
End If
```

Fig. 454

Click **Save & Run**. Now you can check how the function works.

13. Check the function controlling the exceeding of the box height range. On the **Assemble** tab, in the **Manage** panel, click the **Parameters** icon. In the **Parameters** window, make sure the **Immediate Update** option is selected, and set the **HEIGHT** parameter to **3 in**, like in Fig. 455.

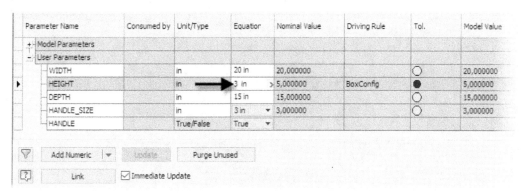

Parameter Name	Consumed by	Unit/Type	Equation	Nominal Value	Driving Rule	Tol.	Model Value
+– Model Parameters							
– User Parameters							
WIDTH		in	20 in	20,000000		○	20,000000
HEIGHT		in	3 in >	5,000000	BoxConfig	●	5,000000
DEPTH		in	15 in	15,000000		○	15,000000
HANDLE_SIZE		in	3 in ▼	3,000000		○	3,000000
HANDLE		True/False	True ▼				

▽ Add Numeric ▼   Update   Purge Unused

[?] Link   ☑ Immediate Update

Fig. 455

Confirm the entered value by moving to another cell with the **TAB** key or by pressing **ENTER**. The program will display a message box as in Fig. 456.

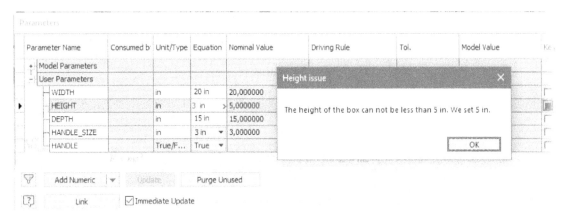

Fig. 456

Click **OK**. Note that in the value of the **HEIGHT** parameter was set to **5 in**, like in Fig. 457.

Parameter Name	Consumed by	Unit/Type	Equation	Nominal Value	Driving Rule
+ Model Parameters					
– User Parameters					
WIDTH		in	20 in	20,000000	
HEIGHT		in	5 in	5,000000	BoxConfig
DEPTH		in	15 in	15,000000	
HANDLE_SIZE		in	3 in ▼	3,000000	
HANDLE		True/False	True ▼		

Fig. 457

At the same time, an entry appeared in the **Driving Rule** column informing about the name of the rule that controls this parameter. Click **Done**.

14. Complete the rule with functions controlling exceeding the range of height and size of the handles. Start the rules editor, insert functions and fill in the function's arguments, like in Fig. 458.

```
If HEIGHT < 5 Then
MessageBox.Show("The height of the box can not be less than 5 in. We set 5 in.", "Height issue
HEIGHT = 5
End If

If HEIGHT > 10 Then
MessageBox.Show("The height of the box can not be more than 10 in. We set 10 in.", "Height issue
HEIGHT = 10
End If

If HANDLE_SIZE > (HEIGHT-1.5) Then
MessageBox.Show("To big handle. We set 3 in.", "Handle size issue")
HANDLE_SIZE = 3
End If

Parameter(" 100-01:1", "width") = WIDTH
```

Fig. 458

Click **Save & Run**. Now you can check how the function works.

fx **15.** Check the function controlling the exceeding of the box height range. In the **Parameters** window, set the parameter **HEIGHT** to **12 in** and press **TAB**. The program will display a message like in Fig. 459.

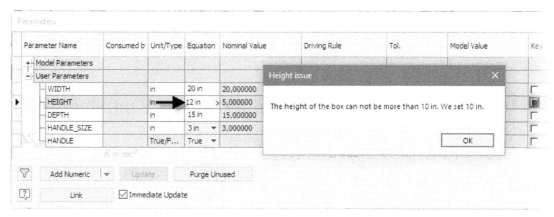

Fig. 459

Click **OK**. The height of the metal case will be set at **10 in**.

Now set the handle size to **6 in**, like in Fig. 460a. The program will create a **10 in** case with a **6 in** handles, like in Fig. 460b.

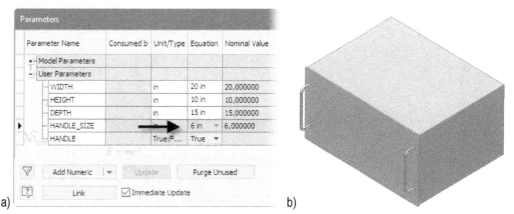

a) b)

Fig. 460

Now change the box height to **5 in** and press **TAB**, which will display a message like in Fig. 461.

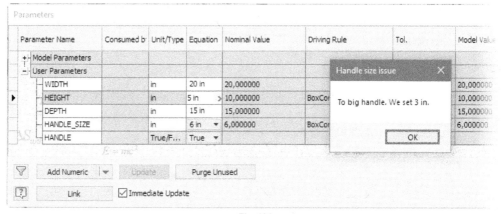

Fig. 461

Click **OK**. The size of the handle has been set to **3 in**. Click **Done**.

You can assume that the parametric model of the metal case is controlled as expected. In the next exercise, you will create a form for controlling parameters from the level of a convenient dialog.

16. Save the assembly file, but don't close the file if you plan to continue in next exercise. End of exercise

Exercise 28
Creating a Form for parameters control

In the previous exercise, the parametera control was carried out from the **Parameters** dialog box. The Inventor also offers the option of creating a special parameter control form, which will contain only selected parameters and other relevant information. You will create here the form shown in Fig. 462a.

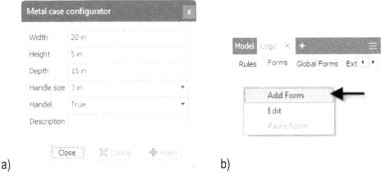

a)   b)

Fig. 462

In addition to the parameters controlling the dimensions, it will be possible to add a description of the metal case version here.

You continue working on the model saved in the previous exercise.

1. Create a form controlling the parameters of the model. In the browser, go to the **Forms** tab, right-click and choose **Add Form** in the menu, like in Fig. 462b. The program displays the form editor window and an empty form named **Form1**, like in Fig. 463.

Fig. 463

Put the parameters of the metal case on the form. Grab the **WIDTH** parameter and drag it to the form edit field, like in Fig. 464a.

a)   b)

Fig. 464

This will add a field controlling the **WIDTH** parameter to the form dialog box, like in Fig. 464b. Similarly, drag the remaining parameters to get the appearance of the form shown in Fig. 465.

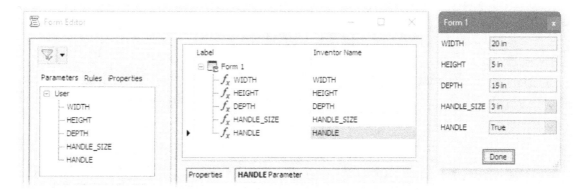

Fig. 465

Change the parameter names displayed in the form, like in Fig. 466.

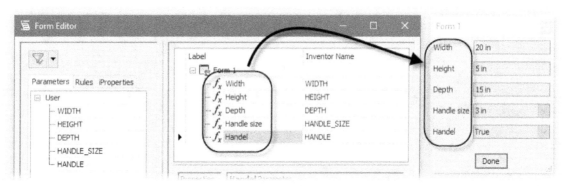

Fig. 466

Add iProperties. Go to the **iProperties** tab, grab and drag the **Description** property to the form like in Fig. 467.

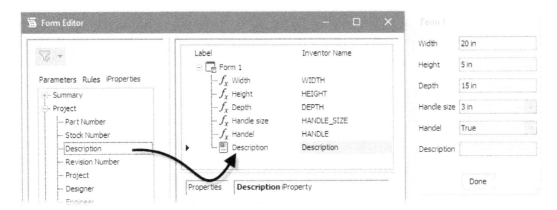

Fig. 467

Change the properties of the form window - title and buttons set. Pick the icon on the left side of **Form1**, like in Fig. 468a, which will display the form's properties at the bottom of the editor, like in Fig. 468b.

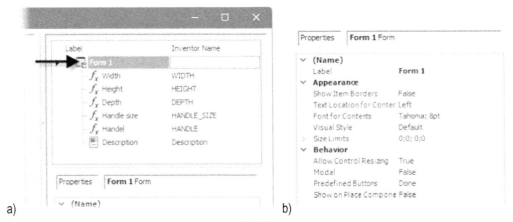

Fig. 468

Now enter the new form name in the **Label** field: **Metal case configurator**, like in Fig. 469a.

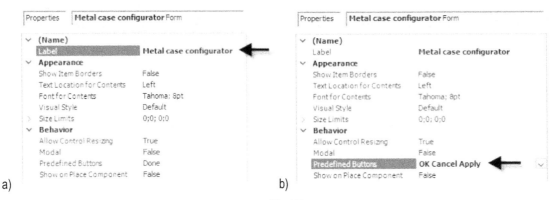

Fig. 469

From the **Predefined Buttons** list, select the **OK Cancel Apply** button set, like in Fig. 469b.

You can assume that the form is ready. Click **OK** in the form editor dialog box. In the browser, a new button **Metal case configurator** appeared, like in Fig. 470a, which is used to open the form in order to obtain another variant of the metal case.

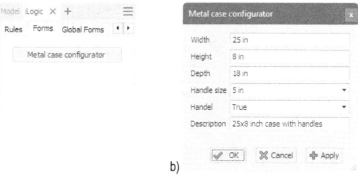

a)   b)

Fig. 470

2. Check how the form works. In the browser, click the **Metal case configuration** button and enter the dimensional parameters and description like in Fig. 470b. Click **Apply**. The model should be rebuilt to a version like in Fig. 471a. Click **Close**.

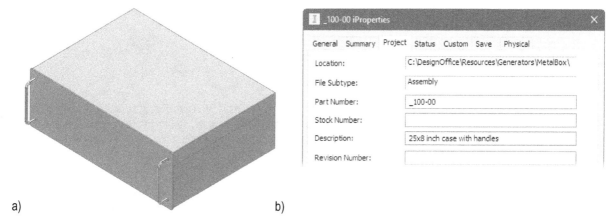

a)   b)

Fig. 471

Check the iProperties. On the **Project** tab, in the **Description** field, a description should appear like in Fig. 471b.

3. Restore the previous dimension values in the form and clear the **Description** field.

---

*Using the iLogic function, you can parameterize the filling of the **Description** field. Try to make a rule myself, when you will gain more experience in iLogic programming.*

You can assume that the model is ready. The last operation before the completion of work with the 3D model is to review, complete and organize the bill of materials database, which will result in the correct list of parts in the assembly drawing and export BOM file if needed.

4. Open the BOM dialog box. On the **Assemble** tab in the **Manage** panel, click the **Bill of Materials** icon. The program will display the **Bill of Materials** dialog box with the **Model Data** card filled, like in Fig. 472.

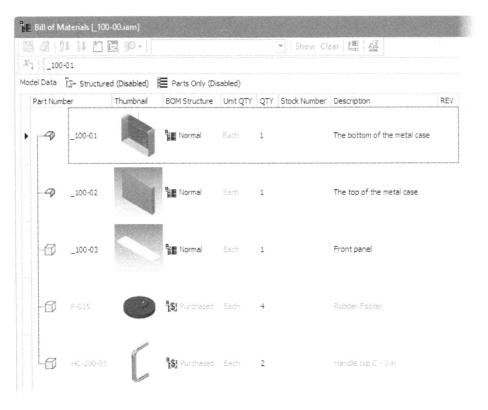

Fig. 472

On **Model Date** card, there are listed all components of the assembly. You can fill in missing information or correct existing data here. The content of the **Structured** or **Parts Only** card is used to create the parts list and export BOM data to other software, like ERP. The **Structured** card presents a component BOM view which includes subassemblies and parts of the main level, while the **Parts Only** card shows parts of all levels. In this example, no subassemblies have been created, which means that the contents of both cards are identical. In the next steps, you will use the content of the **Structured** card.

5. Enable the **Structured** card. Switch to the **Structured** tab, then right-click and select **Enable BOM View**, like in Fig. 473.

Fig. 473

The card's content view shows Fig. 474.

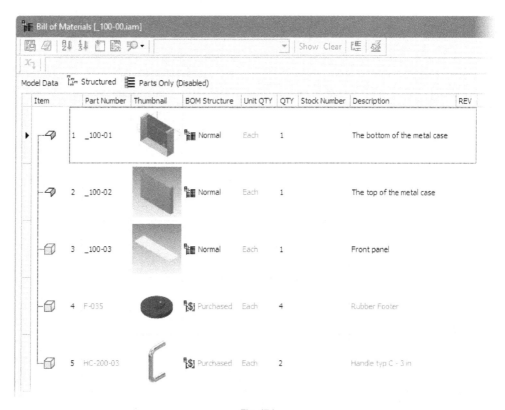

Fig. 474

The **Item** column appears in this view. Make sure the component numbering is correct. If necessary, you can manually move the whole row of the component to place it in the correct position and then renumber the components by clicking the **Renumber Items** icon.

Click **Done**. Now you can prepare the drawing documentation of this model.

6. Save the assembly file, but don't close the file if you plan to continue in next exercise.

End of exercise

Exercise 29
Creating 2D drawings for the version generator

In this exercise, you will create drawing documentation of the metal case model. It should be crated a main assembly drawing, which includes a parts list and three drawings of the parts. Each drawing should be saved in a file with the same name as the associated 3D model file from which the main view was generated.

All drawings will be based on the template prepared in the exercise *Adjusting the title block in the template file of the* drawing, on page 5.

The drawings are part of the version generator file set. Each version created using the procedure for generating a version will contain a set of correctly named and updated drawings.

1. Create the main assembly drawing of the model, containing views, dimensioning and parts list, shown in Fig. 475. Choose the format **C** of the sheet.

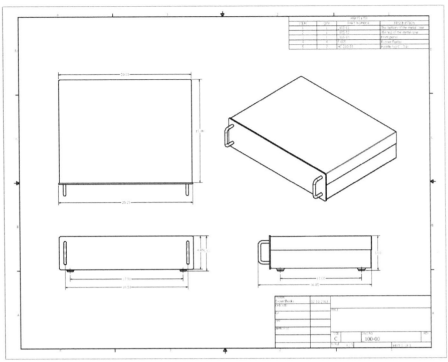

Fig. 475

2. Save the drawing file with the name **_100-00.dwg**.

3. Create drawings for parts: **_100-01.ipt**, **_100-02.ipt** and **_100-03.ipt**. Drawings should include views, dimensioning and annotations. Select any sheet formats. Save each drawing in a separate file with a name such as the part name. Examples of drawings are shown in Fig. 476.

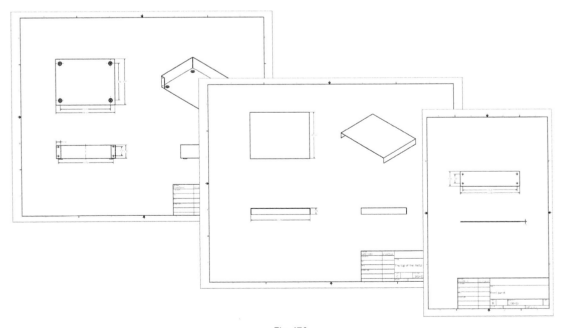

Fig. 476

4. Close all open files. End of exercise.

Exercise 30
Generating of metal cases variants

You can assume that you have to design metal cases for industrial electronic devices. The devices will be stacked on top of each other, so the width of the cases should be the same, while the height and depth will vary, due to the components that will be placed inside. To quickly create the necessary metal cases, you can use the version generator, which will create the appropriate set of 3D models and related drawing documentation for each version of a metal case.

In this exercise, you will see how you can generate a variant of the model of the metal case from the set of files prepared in the previous exercises of this chapter. You will create a set of two metal cases with different heights and depths. The first housing will have handles, while the second will haven't. After the variant has been made, each of the housings can be further modified depending on the needs. Ready-made metal cases prepared for further work are shown in Fig. 477a.

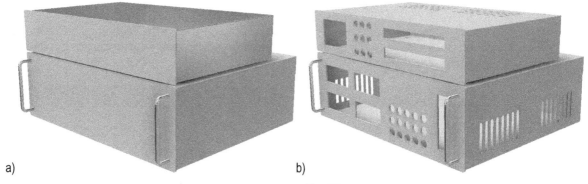

a)   b)

Fig. 477

In Fig. 477b, you can see an example of modifications introduced in the generated versions of the metal cases.

The process of generating variants is simple and consists of the following stages:

- Creating a version in the original generator assembly file. File saves.
- Create copies of files with new names and in a new location.
- Editing files to obtain the final shape of the model.
- Updating and completing the drawing documentation of version.

You can assume that the general designation of the designed device is **MB25**. As the first variant, you will create a metal case with dimensions (W x D x H) equal to **25 x 20 x 8 inch**. Dimension settings and additional options will be made in the original generator file.

 1. Determine the dimensions and options of the variant. Open the **_100-00.iam** assembly file. Display the form dialog box and enter dimensions like in Fig. 478a. Add a description of the model: *Case of main control console MB25.*

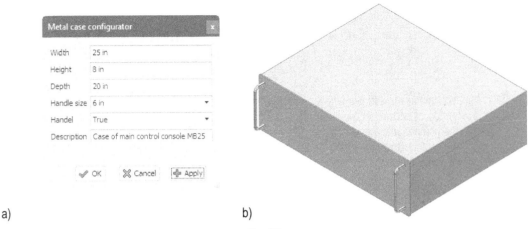

a)   b)

Fig. 478

Click **Apply**. The model presented in Fig. 478b will be created. Click **Close**.

2. Save the assembly file and close. Make sure that no files are opened.

3. Create a copy of the project with new file names and in the new location. In the **Tools** panel, on the **iLogic** tab, click the **iLogic Design Copy** icon. In the **iLogic Design Copy** dialog box, select all drawing files for copying, indicated in Fig. 479.

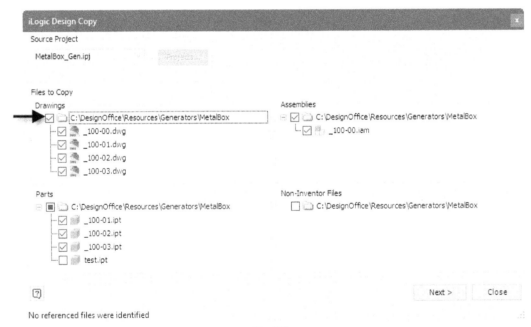

Fig. 479

The program will automatically select all related files to be copied - the main assembly file and part files. Click **Next**.

In the **iLogic Design Copy Settings** dialog box set the copy destination folder and file name prefix. Click the **Browse** button in the **Destination** area and create the **MB25** folder in the **Designs** subfolder, like in Fig. 480a, which will be the folder of the new device with the general designation **MB25**.

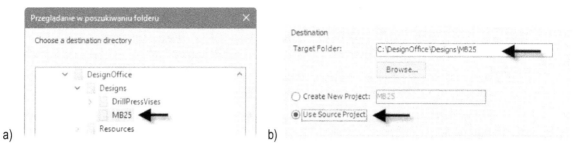

Fig. 480

The new folder should be entered in the **Target Folder** field, like in Fig. 480b. Make sure the **Use Source Project** option is selected.

In the **New File Prefix** field, enter the **MB25_H8H** identifier like in Fig. 481a. Make sure the **Update Part Number** option is checked. You can assume that the **H8H** designation means the Height **8** inch and Handles. In the upper part of the window, the names and location of files are updated on an ongoing basis, like in Fig. 481b.

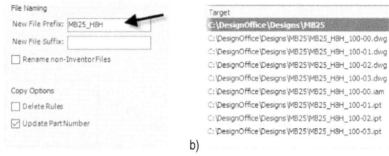

Fig. 481

The correct final option settings for creating a copy are like in Fig. 482.

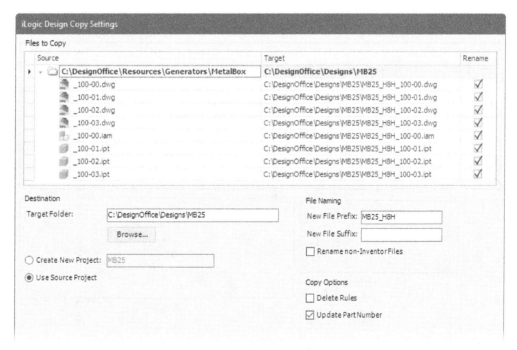

Fig. 482

Click **Start**.

After copying, click **Close** in the **Design Copy Progress** window. By default, the folder where the files were copied is opened to check if everything went well. Close the **Windows Explorer** with the destination folder.

Now you will generate the second variant - the case with dimensions (W x D x H) equal to **25 x 15 x 5** inch without handles. The name of this model is: *Case of decoder console MB25*, and a name designation is **MB25_H5**.

 4. Determine the dimensions and options of the new variant. Open the **_100-00.iam** assembly file. Display the form dialog box, enter dimensions, turn off handles and add a description of the model: *Case of decoder console MB25*, like in Fig. 483a.

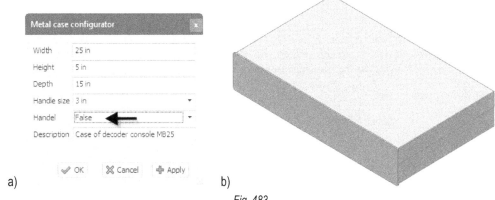

a)   b)

Fig. 483

Click **Apply**. The model presented in Fig. 483b will be created. Click **Close**.

 5. Save the assembly file. After clicking the **Save** icon, the **Save Level of Detail Representation Changes** window is displayed, because disabling the handles means changing the representation of the detail level. Enter the name of the detail level representation, like in Fig. 484a.

a)   b)

Fig. 484

Click **Yes**. Click **OK** in the **Save** dialog box.

After saving the assembly file in the new representation of the level of details, in the browser, the name of the current representation is placed in brackets next to the name of the assembly. The list of available representations is visible after expanding the contents of the **Representations** folder > **Level of Detail**. A new representation of the level of detail is created if any components are suppressed. Browser content related to the level of detail is indicated in Fig. 484b.

6. Close all files.

7. Create a copy of the project with new file names and in the new location. In the **Tools** panel, on the **iLogic** tab, click the **iLogic Design Copy** icon. Like with the previous version, in the **iLogic Design Copy** dialog box, select all drawing files for copying, indicated in Fig. 485.

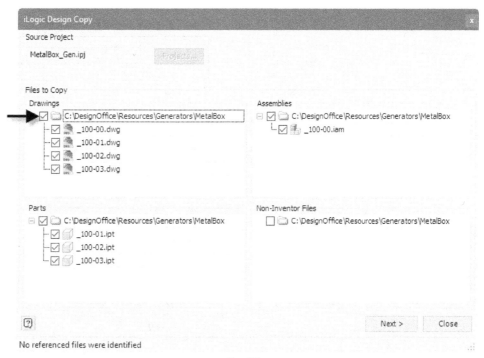

Fig. 485

The program will automatically select all related files to be copied - the main assembly file and part files. Click **Next**.

In the **iLogic Design Copy Settings** dialog box set the copy destination folder and file name prefix. Click the **Browse** button in the **Destination** area and select the **MB25** folder in the **Designs** subfolder, like in Fig. 486a, which will be the folder of the new device with the general designation **MB25**.

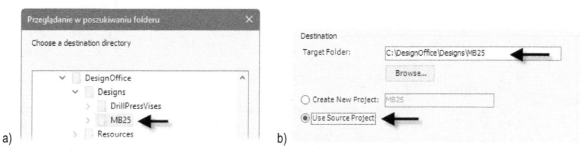

Fig. 486

The selected folder should be entered in the **Target Folder** field, like in Fig. 486b. Make sure the **Use Source Project** option is selected.

In the **New File Prefix** field, enter the **MB25_H5** identifier like in Fig. 487a. Make sure the **Update Part Number** option is checked. You can assume that the **H5** designation means the **Height 5** inch, no handles. In the upper part of the window, the names and location of files are updated on an ongoing basis, like in Fig. 487b.

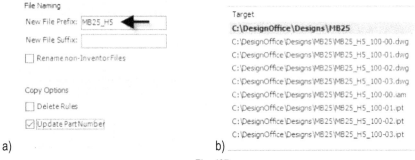

a)   b)

Fig. 487

The correct final option settings for creating a copy are like in Fig. 488.

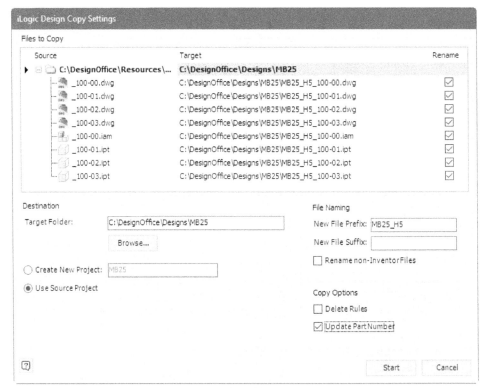

Fig. 488

Click **Start**.

After copying, click **Close** in the **Design Copy Progress** window. By default, the folder where the files were copied is opened to check if everything went well. Close the **Windows Explorer** with the destination folder.

In this way, two sets of files were prepared for two different versions of the metal cases. You will now insert both generated versions into a new empty assembly file and modify their contents according to the needs of each device's design. You will start by changing the current project file.

8. Change the current project file from the version generator project file to the global working project file for all designs. On the **Get Started** tab, in the **Launch** pane, click **Projects**. Double-click the **MyDesigns** project file, indicated in Fig. 489.

Fig. 489

Click **Done**.

9. Start a new assembly file. Click the **Assembly** icon in the **My Home** window or click the **New** icon> **Standard.iam**.

10. Insert the model of the first assembly. On the **Assemble** tab, in the **Components** panel, click **Place**. In the **Place Component** window, go to the **MB25** folder and select the **MB25_H8H_100-00.iam** file indicated in Fig. 490a.

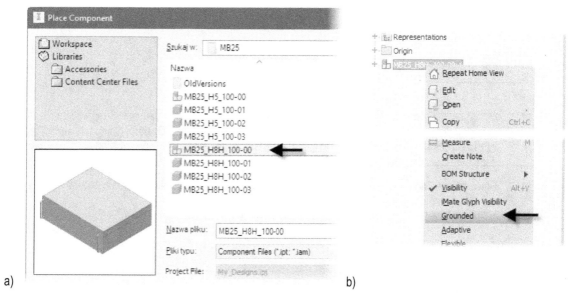

Fig. 490

Click **Open**. Insert one copy of this version. To finish press **ESC**.

11. Locate the model using assembly constraints or lock its position using the **Grounded** option, like in Fig. 490b.

12. Insert the model of the second assembly. Click the **Place** icon again. In the **Place Component** window, go to the **MB25** folder and select the **MB25_H5_100-00.iam** file, indicated in Fig. 491a.

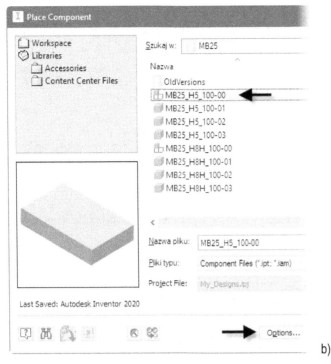

a)   b)

Fig. 491

Since you put a non-handles version, you can immediately incorporate the correct representation of the level of detail. Click the **Options** button indicated in Fig. 491a. In the **File Open Options** dialog box, select representation **With no handles** indicated in Fig. 491b, and click **OK**. In the **Place Component** window, click **Open**. Insert one copy of this version. To end press **ESC**.

13. Place the second case in the right position. Using the assembly constraints, place a second model on the top of the first model like in Fig. 492a.

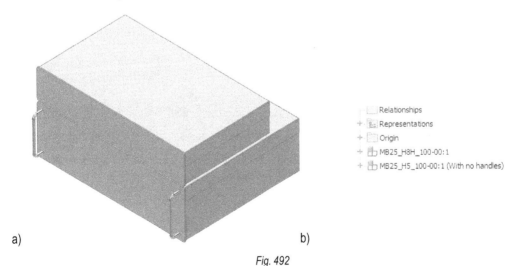

a)   b)

Fig. 492

You have two subassemblies now. The names of both subassemblies are visible in the browser, like in Fig. 492b. Both components, created with the use of a version generator, are ready for further work and should now be adapted to the requirements of the current design. You can now enter the edit mode of each subassembly and adjust their parts to the project requirements. An example view of cases after modifications is shown in Fig. 493.

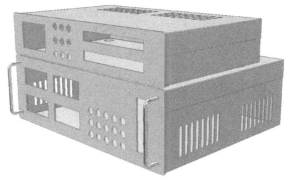

Fig. 493

 14. The project **MB25** is finished. Save main assembly file with the name **MB25_100-00.iam**. Create the main assembly drawing with required dimensions, annotations, and parts list.

Each assembly has a set of related drawings. Changes made to the model will be automatically reflected in the associated drawing documentation. It is enough now to review each drawing, fill in the missing elements and organize them - there is no need to create drawings from scratch.

The assembly drawings of both versions of the metal cases after modifications are shown in Fig. 494. It is worth to note that drawing titles and parts lists contain appropriate names and numbers of components.

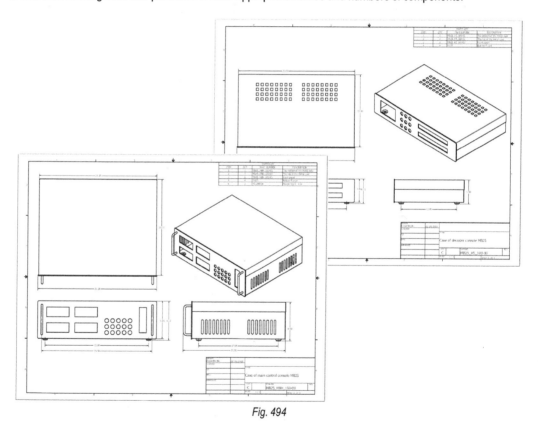

Fig. 494

 *In the base view of the subassembly without handles, the level of detail must be activated: **With no handles**. For this purpose, right-click on the base view, select **Edit View**, and then in the **Level of Detail** list select **With no handles**.*

The drawing of each part has also been modified accordingly. Review the parts drawings for both versions of metal boxes if you have made modifications to individual parts to add missing dimensions and annotations.

End of exercise.

Summary of Example No 3

If you correctly followed all the exercises contained in this chapter, you can:

- Model simple sheet metal parts using basic tools and create flat patterns.
- Control dimensions and features of the part in part files using simple iLogic functions.
- Define global parameters in the main assembly file and transfer their values to related part files using the iLogic function.
- Control the use of iParts in an assembly using the iLogic function.
- Control such features like holes and assembly constraints across all parts using the iLogic function.
- Create a dialog box to conveniently control the parameters and options of the variant.
- Design a generator of versions of the product containing associated drawing documentation.
- Generate many versions of a simple subassembly using the variant generator, which contain correctly named 3D models and related drawing.

You've learned the fundamental principles of parametric design using iLogic in the Autodesk Inventor 2021 software and fundamentals of creating parametric version generators. Now, you have an open road to developing automation in designing your products, using the iLogic functionality. Good luck!